The art
of thinking
in a digital
world

The art
of thinking
in a digital
world

BE LOGICAL
BE CREATIVE
BE CRITICAL

Luc de Brabandere

with

Lina Benmehrez & Jonas Leyder

PETER LANG
Oxford - Berlin - Bruxelles - Chennai - Lausanne - New York

Bibliographic information published by the Deutsche Nationalbibliothek.
The German National Library lists this publication in the German National Bibliography;
detailed bibliographic data is available on the Internet at http://dnb.d-nb.de.

A catalogue record for this book is available from the British Library.

Library of Congress Control Number: 2024921232

Edited and translated by Felicity Still.

Cover image: *Selfie de l'Homme*, copyright Jean-Claude Salemi.
Additional work on the cover by Dominique Paquet.
Additional back cover illustration by Rodolphe Duprey.
Additional back cover illustration AI-generated with a prompt to draw a portrait of Luc de Brabandere in the style of Magritte.
Cover design by Peter Lang Group AG

ISBN 978-1-80374-442-1 (print)
ISBN 978-1-80374-479-7 (ePDF)
ISBN 978-1-80374-480-3 (ePub)

DOI 10.3726/b21758

This book is dedicated to my grandchildren:
Lou, Marilou, Violette, Maroussia, Arthur, Lila and Charlie
– you are the future and the future is yours.

Contents

Figures

Preface

When Luc first approached me about the concept of this book, I was immediately on board. A book that connects the dots between Luc's ideas and contributions and that links them to digital transformation is essential! Luc's pursuit of new insights has always inspired me as a colleague, first as a fellow partner at BCG and now as a professor at IMD. Always as a friend. There is simply nobody like Luc anywhere. Over the years, I have been guided by his ability to view the world through multiple lenses, helping to frame ideas in new boxes. In my opinion, Luc challenges – and adds to – conventional wisdom. Luc's approach to digital thinking is about adapting to significant changes and anticipating the 'what ifs' of our future.

Consider Luc's idea that 'to change is to change twice'. This concept profoundly resonates with me as it helps frame the climate challenge. Firstly, there is the awakening to our environmental challenges, which happens relatively swiftly. This is about awareness. Once we understand something differently, there is no going back. That's the 'Eureka!' moment. Secondly, there's the gradual evolution in how we address the climate challenges, a process that unfolds over a longer time. This is about action. Global awareness of the climate crisis has surged over the past years, while the change will take many decades. In my teaching, I often use the 'change twice' principle to illustrate how to close the gap between knowing and doing.

As the saying goes: 'nothing is as practical as a good theory.' Luc's work is a testament to the practical value of sound theory. In a world where technology often outpaces our understanding of its implications, this book illustrates how a solid intellectual foundation is beneficial and essential. I deeply respect Luc's ability to synthesize complex philosophical ideas in order to apply them to personal and business decisions. This method forms the backbone of his book, offering a wealth of frameworks that are both intellectually rigorous and practically useful. Luc's work addresses the core challenges of the digital era, providing profound and accessible insights. He bridges the gap between complex theories and everyday applications, showing how abstract concepts can yield tangible results. His ability to simplify intricate ideas without losing their essence is a testament to the depth of his understanding and clarity of thought.

For example, Luc has been vital in helping me frame 'future-back' approaches here at IMD. Instead of incremental, step-by-step planning, we can project ourselves into a future ambition and then ask: 'How did we get there?' This helps us to avoid becoming narrow-minded and trapped by the current when we need courage to create the future.

I now want to highlight two aspects of Luc's work that are omnipresent throughout the book. Firstly, the use of cartoons and illustrations. We all know that a good picture is worth a thousand words. Luc helps us to convey those thousand words through simple images. When I left BCG, my most valued parting gift was a cartoon from Luc that illustrated the importance of balancing exploring for the future with exploiting current capabilities and products in the present. It was framed as a graveyard showing companies that had focused too much on one or the other. Priceless! The second element is humour. We don't learn as well by just being serious. We need to see the fun and the surprising.

I would say that using images and humour are two elements that make Luc a great storytelling teacher. Luc's unique perspective is particularly evident in his discussion of digital transformation. We must go beyond the buzzwords and hype. We need a nuanced perspective to consider the opportunities and challenges of the digital age. By reframing the digital world, Luc provides fresh insights that inspire readers to think differently and embrace change with confidence and curiosity, empowering them to navigate the digital landscape more effectively.

As I reflect on Luc's work, I admire his learning mindset. His ability to continuously reframe and adapt is a source of inspiration, reminding us of the importance of staying curious and open-minded. Luc's approach to digital thinking is not just about surviving in a digital world but about thriving in it.

I am grateful for this opportunity to share my appreciation for Luc's enormous contribution. His insights and perspectives are invaluable, offering anyone seeking to navigate the complexities of digital transformation multiple lenses and perspectives to do so. This book is a testament to Luc's dedication to learning and passion for helping others confidently embrace the future.

As you embark on this journey through Luc's exploration of digital thinking, I urge you not to simply read, but to actively engage on the principles that he outlines and to apply them in your own context. Remember, change is not a destination but a journey, and with the right mindset and tools, we can all become better navigators of the digital landscape.

With profound appreciation,
Knut Haanaes, Professor, Lundin Sustainability Chair at IMD

Looking backwards

Be logical. Be creative. Be critical. Every time I read the subtitle of this book, my entire professional life flashes before my eyes, because these are the three forms of thought that have been by my side throughout it all.

- As an engineer in applied mathematics, freshly graduated from the university in Leuven, I started my career as a programmer in a bank. In 1985, I published my first book, *Les Infoducs*,[1] in which I imagined the advent of the internet.
- Just before I turned 40 I wanted to transform my passion for creativity into a profession and so became a consultant. By the time I was 40 I had a better idea of who I was: a philosopher! But as Nietzsche said, now I had to become who I was, so I went back to university, at University of Louvain, to study philosophy.
- Today, I want to help leaders, teachers, students and ... my grandchildren to think critically in a world that has become digital.

You could say, tongue in cheek, that mathematics is a game with rules but no real objective, and that philosophy is a game with an objective but no real rules. To make a long story short, I stepped from one to the other!

Danish philosopher Søren Kierkegaard once said: 'Life can only be understood backwards; but it must be lived forwards'.[2] This is something that I have been feeling intensely in recent years. The common thread throughout my work has been the intention to transmit. As an engineer, it was knowledge that I wanted to pass on. As there is no established science of creativity, when I was a consultant I wanted to transmit my passion and energy. Today I am a philosopher and I want to share my values and my experience.

Looking back, I realize how privileged I have been.

I was lucky enough to be born in Belgium in 1948 in a supportive family.

I was lucky enough to study mathematics in my twenties and philosophy in my forties, both felt like the right timing (doing the opposite would be hard to imagine!).

---

1. This could be translated as *The Infoducts*, by analogy with aqueducts. All translations are our own unless otherwise specified.
   Luc de Brabandere and Anne Mikolajczak, *Les Infoducs: Un Nouveau Mot, Un Nouveau Monde: L'informatique Au Macroscope: Essai* (Paris: Duculot, 1985).
2. Søren Kierkegaard, *Journalen* (Copenhagen: Søren Kierkegaard Research Center, 1997). Danish short form of quote by Julia Watkins, translation by Palle Jorgensen.

I was lucky enough to study computer science ... without computers! At university, we would queue to drop off our punch cards and then enjoy access, for just a few minutes, to a single computer that ran mostly at night. Without easily available machines, the course was focused more on theory than on practice. In other words, we were forced to compute less, and think more!

I'm lucky to have written this book after the public discovered ChatGPT.

And last but not least, I have been lucky to work and study for fifty years with inspiring people.

They have made my life so interesting; I would like to thank all of them for this.

This is priceless.

Luc de Brabandere – Hoves, Belgium, Summer 2024

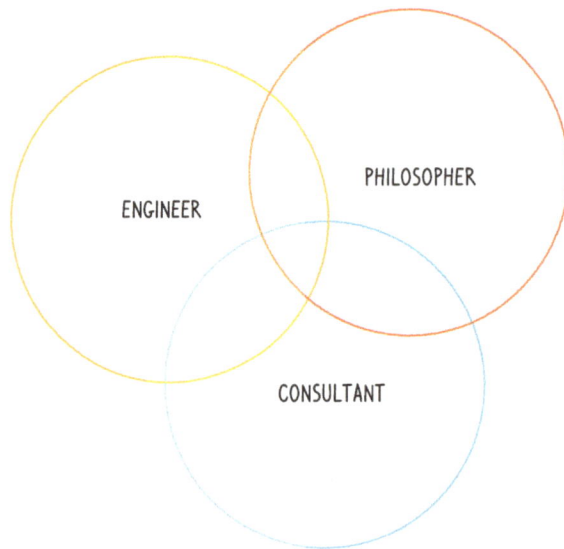

ENGINEER

PHILOSOPHER

CONSULTANT

Acknowledgements

The idea for this book that you're holding came to me during a conversation with Sarah Springman in October 2019. Back then, she was Dean of ETH Zurich and wanted to draw the attention of future engineers to the importance of critical thinking. With her colleagues Christoph Niedermann and Judith Zimmermann, Sarah invited me to Davos in January 2020 to present my ideas at the ETH Pavilion. The structure that I'd chosen for my presentation, *Be Logical, Be Creative, Be Critical*, was received well and ETH decided to sponsor the book that I was getting ready to self-publish under the same title.

But the deadlines were very short …

So I put together a team that turned out be exceptional: Lina Benmehrez and Thomas Doutrepont who I'd been lucky to have as students, as well as Martin Saive, Louise Neys, Eve Wasmuth, Dominique Paquet, Tonu, Charline Couppez and Arnaud Duquesne. At the Boston Consulting Group (BCG), Ryoji Kimura, Antoine Gourevitch and Alan Iny were also very supportive.

And all our efforts paid off: *Be Logical, Be Creative, Be Critical* was shipped on time to Zurich at the end of 2020.

But that was just the first half of this adventure!

In February 2022, at the London Book Fair, a meeting between Lina Benmehrez and Lucy Melville would be decisive. Arnaud Béglé, CEO of Peter Lang, and Lucy Melville, who would later become Group Publishing Director, offered us a publishing deal. At Peter Lang still, Ashita Shah and Shruthi Maniyodath have been of great help all along the way. I've always had one foot in the academic world and one foot in the corporate world so I couldn't have wished for a better fit: an academic publisher who wants to branch out to the corporate world.

And from there things gained momentum.

At the BCG, support for my work was confirmed by James Tucker and Boryana Hintermair from the CFS Practice, which I belong to, Nikolaus Lang for the BCG Henderson Institute which he manages, and again Antoine Gourevitch, within the framework of his research on Deep Tech.

Knut Haanaes, who was a BCG Partner when I was and is now doing me the honour of prefacing this book, then invited me to IMD Lausanne to give a presentation to his MBA students. He introduced me to Delia Fischer, Chief Communications Officer, and Sarah Toms, Chief Learning Innovation Officer, and then IMD was onboard with this book which is also my university course.

At Cartoonbase, the team gained more members with Jonas Leyder, Rodolphe Duprey, Fernanda Carcamo, Anne Mikolajczak and Felicity Still. Vince and Jérôme Viguet hopped on. By doing so, Cartoonbase, alongside the BCG, IMD and Peter Lang, became the fourth corner of this magic square.

A special thanks goes to Rodolphe Duprey and Dominique Paquet for the excellent care and talent they put into this book's illustrations, to Louise Neys for creating the original visual identity, and to Jean-Claude Salemi for letting us use the wonderful artwork which serves as a basis for the cover of this book.

And of course, throughout all of this, my family and friends have been an ever-present source of support, inspiration and encouragement.

I am incredibly grateful to all of these people. *The Art of Thinking in a Digital World* isn't my book. It's our book.

Thinking is no longer what it used to be …

The very shape of the Egyptian pyramids shows that, already in ancient times, people tended to work less and less.

For me, it all started back in the summer of 2008, when Facebook was only four years old. Two influential US magazines both dedicated their front covers to the same issue: how our thinking is being influenced by technology.

The cover of *The Atlantic* asked 'Is Google making us Stoopid?', whilst *Wired* magazine claimed 'The end of Science' on its cover.

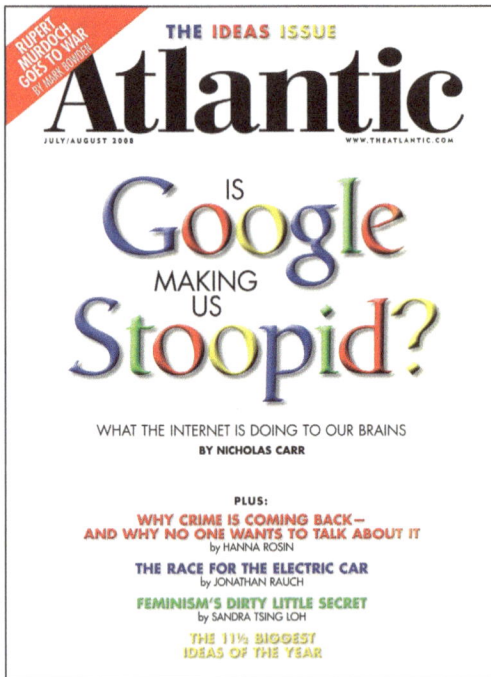

Figure 1. *Cover of The Atlantic, July/August 2008*

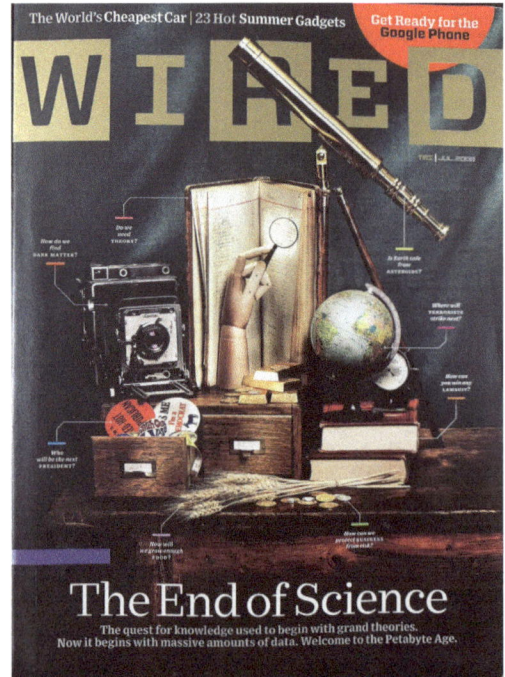

Figure 2. *Cover of Wired, July 2008*

- According to Nicholas Carr in *The Atlantic*, Google's rich information database has changed our way of thinking by removing our capacity to do in-depth research and to focus, whilst also affecting our cognition and weakening our ability to think critically. Google treats information as a commodity and the company's founders believe that the ultimate search engine will be smarter than people. This suggests that intelligence is the result of a mechanical process, that is, a series of steps that can be isolated, measured and optimized.
- According to Chris Anderson, then editor-in-chief of *Wired*, 'the data deluge renders the scientific method obsolete'.[1] Correlations are enough and models are no longer useful. This revolutionary notion has sparked the interest of some philosophers. Could we really work without concepts and

---

1.   Chris Anderson, 'The End of Theory: The Data Deluge Makes the Scientific Method Obsolete', *Wired*, June 2008, <https://www.wired.com/2008/06/pb-theory/> [accessed 24 May 2024].

theories? Is Plato and Aristotle's legacy suddenly under threat? And could this mean the imminent disappearance of the consulting business?

What these two highly provocative magazine covers did was to ignite a very useful discussion that is still ongoing to this day. Was it a coincidence that a single topic was brought up with two different insights at the same time? There's no way of knowing for sure, but it was definitely a hot topic at the time. For several years now, people have been increasingly concerned about the impact of technology on how we imagine, conceptualize, write, experiment, experience and communicate, how we take care of ourselves. And as far as we are concerned, the advent of technology also affects the way we learn, teach, build strategies and run businesses.

Sixteen years after these two seminal articles were published, the topic is more critical than ever. We all think differently in a digital world. New threats also mean new opportunities. That's why we want to convince business leaders to make a second effort in trying to understand how the brain works. A second effort? Absolutely.

The first effort was made successfully thirty years ago. And many people have incorporated cognitive science into their thinking processes over the last three decades. Thanks to bestsellers such as Kahneman's *Thinking, Fast and Slow*,[2] Thaler and Sunstein's *Nudge*,[3] Goleman's *Emotional Intelligence*[4] or Taleb's *The Black Swan*,[5] notions about the limits of rationality have been widely disseminated throughout the business community. But all four belong mostly to the pre-digital era.

The time has now come for business leaders, teachers and responsible citizens to take a second leap of faith: with the rise of the internet, social media and AI, the context has changed so much that cognitive science is definitely entering a new paradigm.

This book is an invitation. If we design the future as a simple addition to the ideas and tools available to us today, we are setting ourselves up for disappointment. New technology will only hold significant meaning if it is accompanied by new mental models. We have to learn how to properly use the internet to prevent it from using us. We must comprehend the limits of artificial intelligence to make the most of what it has to offer. Thinking is an art, not a science, and we must rediscover it, recalling its inescapable rules while also benefiting from its degrees of freedom.

In this book we'll be inviting you to not only look backwards but also to look forwards. We'll be travelling back in time to Ancient Greece and observing how the first philosophers suggested modelling

2.   Daniel Kahneman, *Thinking, Fast and Slow*, 1st edn (New York: Farrar, Straus and Giroux, 2011).
3.   Richard H. Thaler and Cass R. Sunstein, *Nudge: Improving Decisions about Health, Wealth, and Happiness* (New Haven, CT: Yale University Press, 2008).
4.   Daniel Goleman, *Emotional Intelligence* (New York: Bantam Books, 1995).
5.   Nassim Nicholas Taleb, *The Black Swan: The Impact of the Highly Improbable* (London: Allen Lane, 2007).

thought, but we'll also be looking to the future by imagining how this digital wave could fundamentally transform the relationship that we have with the tools at our disposal.

In the first chapter, I'll explain how a painting of a wooden pipe by René Magritte set fire to my imagination and became the inspiration for this book. Magritte claimed he was not a painter who thought, but a thinker who communicated through painting … He would have been a leading influencer in today's world.

Chapter 2 catapults us into the heart of the matter. Thought is presented as a game with some rules which cannot be ignored. The brain should be perceived as an engine with two strokes whose differences, strengths and weaknesses must be understood.

What do we mean by 'digital transformation'? How is today's world different to the world pre-internet? Chapter 3 will provide a method to answer these questions.

The art of thinking is intrinsically linked with the art of talking. Ideas and words maintain a complicated relationship because thought and language interact permanently. In Chapter 4 we will look at how rigorous reasoning begins with the choice of adequate vocabulary.

When we add numbers together, we're thinking. When we have a nightmare, we're also thinking! Between the two lie many other forms of thought that all coexist. It is therefore useful to bring order amongst them and to regroup them into three modes, that constitute the subtitle of this book, 'Be Logical, Be Creative, Be Critical'. Chapter 5 broadly introduces these three forms of thought, sketching their first relevant interactions.

Chapters 6, 7 and 8 offer in-depth insight into these three different domains:

- Logic is a systematic study of the form of arguments, investigating the general principle of valid reasoning. It is the science that studies the conditions for the correct use of the words 'then' and 'therefore'.
- Creativity is the ability of an individual to change their own perception of things.[6] We too often confuse creativity and innovation. The latter is the process that allows an organization to change reality. Innovating is acting, it is not thinking.
- Thinking in a critical manner means trusting with caution, it means regulating our trust according to the reliability of the source, the strength of the argument presented, the communication channel and our ability to judge. Successful critical thinking determines whether or not we have good reasons to believe or to do what people are attempting to persuade us to.

I am a philosopher. My work isn't about *what* to think about any given topic but more about *how* to think about it. My job isn't about providing food or even recipes. It's about provoking hunger, sparking the desire to continue, to search, to clarify and to never stop thinking. This will be explained at the end of this book.

---

6. This definition is influenced by the Palo Alto school, and more largely by the field of systems thinking. This distinction is explained in-depth in *The Forgotten Half of Change* (Chicago, 2005).

Chapter 1 – From Belgium with love

You will never strike oil by drilling through a map of Texas!

1.1. The Magritte effect

I live within biking distance of Lessines, a small Belgian town that you have probably never heard of. But if the Belgian surrealist artist René Magritte and his famous 'Ceci n'est pas une pipe' painting[1] ring any bells, it might interest you to know that he was born in Lessines.

Ceci n'est pas une pipe. In case your French is a bit rusty: 'This is not a pipe'. This doesn't make much sense at first glance since there is, in fact, a pipe in the middle of the painting. But it can't be smoked because ... well it isn't a pipe. Now it makes more sense. What at first sight might have seemed odd is suddenly more obvious. Magritte was right as this isn't actually a pipe: it's a drawing of a pipe, a picture of a pipe, a sketch of a pipe, a simplification of a pipe, a whatever-you-want of a pipe. But definitely not a pipe!

So how did such an obvious statement become such a famous sentence? When we say '2 + 2 doesn't equal 5', it's true but useless. Where does the difference lie? It lies in the number of mistakes we make. Generally we are able to recognize when we add numbers incorrectly, but we tend not to realize that we confuse a pipe and an image of a pipe.

Making this mistake is probably the most important glitch of the human brain. Too often we tend to forget that the market segmentation is not the market, that the company's organization is not the company, that the business model is not the business. More generally, we forget that accounting is not financial flows, that Maslow's pyramid is not the needs of the client, and that our brain is not the sum of its left part and of its right part.

We should use *Ceci n'est pas une pipe* as a reminder of this, since our minds can only hold simplifications of everything. It should appear as a blinking message: 'CAUTION: always remember that the

---

1.   René Magritte, *La Trahison des Images [The Treachery of Images]*, 1929, Los Angeles County Museum of Art.

models we use when thinking are elementary mental constructions, they don't actually exist in the real world'.

But Magritte's painting is just one example in a long list of similar warnings. Many philosophers, artists and even humorists, before him and after him, have delivered the same message but packaged it slightly differently.

Spinoza once said   *'The concept of a dog doesn't bark!'*

Russell claimed   *'Equations do not explode!'*

Other authors used other metaphors:

The map is not the territory![2]
The menu is not the meal!
Nobody ever died in the crash of a flight simulator!

Despite multiple reminders, repeating the message again and again seems to be pointless. If you ask someone whether they are familiar with the Google logo, they will reply 'of course' and think that you're asking a really odd question. But if you then ask that same person to name the colour of each of the six letters, they probably won't be able to answer. Why is that? Because they don't actually know what the Google logo looks like, they can only recognize it. And that is not the same thing. Once again, Magritte and his warning have been forgotten. What is being envisioned is a blurry simplification which is enough to recognize the logo, but it's not the same thing as the logo.

---

2.   Alfred Korzybski, *Science and Sanity: An Introduction to Non-Aristotelian Systems and General Semantics* (Lakeville, CT, 1933).

1.2. In a fight between you and the world ...

For many years now, I have been adamant that Magritte is the perfect introduction to the art of thinking, for two reasons:

1. He pinpoints where it's happening: most of the time, thought unfolds between the outside world and ourselves. The thought process is located between the reality of the world (the pipes) and all of the simplifications made in our mind (the pictures of pipes).
2. As thinkers, our greatest threat is confusing what we have within us with what lies in front of us.

Thanks to Magritte, we now have a better idea of what could be called the 'thought playing field'. Experience has proven just how fertile this metaphor can be, so we shall pursue it. All games have rules, with some playing the game better than others ... and the same applies to thought.

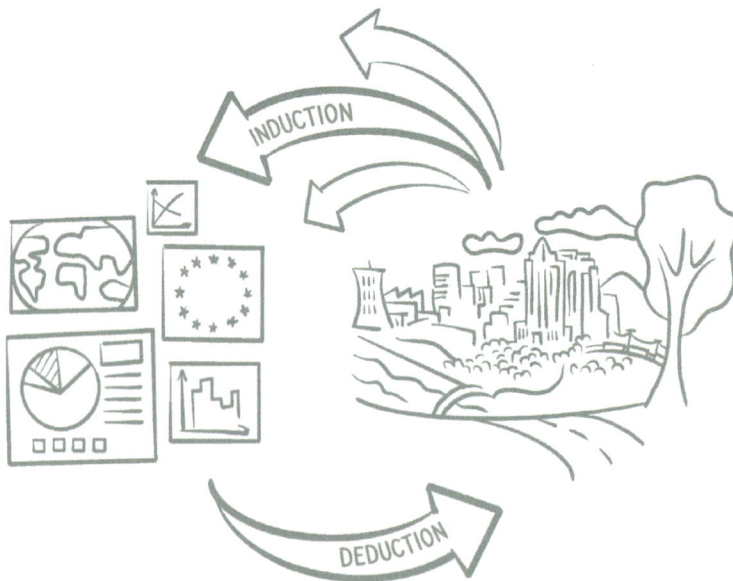

In the case of thought, the game is very challenging and whilst no one will ever think perfectly or understand exactly how it works, there is room for improvement within all of us. Before searching for more detail, for better tactics or strategies, let's start with two important clarifications that immediately follow Magritte's insight.

- The brain is a two-stroke engine and thought happens in two movements: the first goes from right to left on the model above, from the world to us. It simplifies what we see and builds stereotypes, paradigms, maps, scenarios, patterns and frameworks. The second movement is from left to right on the model, from us to the world, and puts those simplifications to work. If you believe that 'students' might be a profitable segment for your market, a lot of things can be done to grab their attention. But don't forget that other segmentations are possible and, moreover, that the concept of a student will never graduate ...

– While moving from left to right can be a rigorous process managed through logic and mathematics, the back and forth movement of thinking will always involve some uncertainty, risk or a leap of faith. The process with which we simplify what is in front of us cannot be 100 per cent rigorous. There is no theory or exact science of thought. It is and will always remain an art form, for better or for worse.

Thought comes down to simplifying what is in front of us and making use of those simplifications. There are two processes involved and they are completely different: the first one is called *induction* and the second one *deduction*.

Where is the best place to start? Kafka once said: 'In the fight between you and the world, back the world'.[3] Let's take his strong advice by starting on the right!

This model appears to be symmetrical with two kinds of reasoning, but it isn't, and it would be a mistake to treat deduction and induction as belonging to the same category. The difference is that deduction is nothing more than a science of 'what follows on from what?', whilst induction is a theory of reasoning. Logical proof is an abstract and codified structure of propositions, whilst reasoning is an active process.

The full name of deductive thinking is 'hypothetico-deductive thinking'. A thought starts with hypotheses and ends in a conclusion. A perfect deduction is possible.

But as you are aware, this particular playing field slopes to the right. We will often favour deduction over induction because it's easier. When deducing, not only is it downhill but we've also got a tail wind behind us.

Inductive thinking, on the other hand, demands that an effort be made. We're therefore uncomfortable with it. It requires us to let go, since perfect induction is impossible, partly because it would take an infinite amount of time.

Magritte was decisive when choosing the model that would accompany us throughout this book. But he wasn't alone. Other thinkers have steered and confirmed our choices.

Let's start with those who have modelled thought into two modes: *spirit of finesse* and *spirit of geometry* according to Blaise Pascal, *right brain* and *left brain* according to Roger Sperry, *lateral thinking* and *vertical thinking* according to Edward de Bono, etc. On a more distant note, we can't leave out the possibility that the model of yin and yang has also influenced us in ways we don't understand precisely.

---

3. 'Im Kampf zwischen dir und der Welt sekundiere der Welt.' Franz Kafka, *Die Zürauer Aphorismen*, 1931.

1.3. On the shoulders of influencers

We haven't come up with anything new here. To paraphrase Newton, our project is built on the shoulders of giant thinkers: we didn't get here on our own. There is no point without a point of view. Every model has a modeller, and every modeller has … influencers. A great number of philosophers, writers and psychologists have mentored us and will continue to mentor us, guiding us through our work. Let's summarize.

In the beginning was Heraclitus. He declared that you can't step in the same workshop twice, and reminded us that the participants contribute to the success of the work session just as much as the facilitator does.

Francis Bacon once said 'Nature to be commanded must be obeyed'.[4] Just as a surfer complies with the laws of the waves in order to ride them to a destination, or a balloonist obeys the forces of the wind to fly to the spot they want to reach, great thinkers start by understanding, then focus on remembering and respecting the brain's manual in order to command it.

Games have rules which have to be respected in order to be played. But there is no rule for choosing which game to play! We simply pick a model out of the many options available. Our goal is to push the model we chose to its limit. Thomas More said 'Tradition is not to preserve the ashes but to pass on the flame'. This quote often comes to mind when I walk into an auditorium or seminar room. No matter how old or experienced my students are, I always feel the urge to pass on to them what I have been fortunate enough to learn.

Bertrand Russell's work on the refoundation of logic is what shaped the analytic, rationalistic and detached tradition which dominated Anglo-American philosophy in the twentieth century. His formal logic of relations, derived from his flair for contradictions and paradoxes, sent Aristotle's syllogism back to the 'Museum of Beautiful and Useless Ideas'.

I once graduated from university in 'applied mathematics', but this area doesn't actually exist. There are only applied mathematicians. The same can be said for 'applied philosophy', where only applied philosophers exist. Russell was definitely one of them and our goal is to be as useful as he has. And last but not least, Russell was an optimist with a cracking sense of humour!

By inviting us to proceed only with 'clear and distinct' ideas, René Descartes has in fact helped us to construct this model and the concepts it contains. He believes that: 'we must use all the resources of intelligence, imagination, senses, and memory, to see an intuition that is distinct from simple propositions'.[5] This is also what led us to choose mainly simplifications and visualizations as tools

---

4.   *'Natura enim non nisi parendo vincitur'.* Francis Bacon, *Novum Organum Scientiarum*, ed. by James Spedding, Robert Leslie Ellis, and Douglas Denon Heath, trans. by James Spedding and unknown (London, 1858).
5.   René Descartes, *Regulae Ad Directionem Ingenii*, 1701. We translate here from the French text established in René Descartes, 'Règles Pour La Direction de l'esprit', in *Oeuvres de Descartes*, trans. by Victor Cousin, Levrault (Paris, 1826).

to achieve our goal. However, we must not rely purely on reasoning, nor overestimate the power of observation and experience.

Albert Camus once said, 'To misname an object is to add to the misfortune of the world'.[6] We think his insight is important, and apply it more broadly by questioning the language and the names we use.

Regarding the model's form, an old tradition is to use a dualistic view, which can be traced back in Western philosophy at least as far as Plato. The term *dualism* generally refers to the idea that there are two fundamental categories of things or principles within a particular field. Plato's famous theory of Forms established a difference between the sensible world of pure substances and the intelligible world of Forms.

It's common knowledge that Plato's student Aristotle disagreed with his famous teacher! According to Aristotle, Plato's theory of Forms was paralysing and prevented anyone from acting. After abandoning Plato's ambition of an absolute, he introduced the concept of category. And this turned out to be the greatest invention of all time, by making it possible to move from theory to practice. Classifying and organizing what lies 'in front of us' was Aristotle's project.

Baruch Spinoza's philosophy is the fuel we needed to make the model run and to do things right. The human mind constructs fictive ideas that it believes to be images of reality. Spinoza's main task was to criticize these abstractions. He once said: 'We don't like things because they are beautiful, things become beautiful because we like them'. There is no right or wrong, but there are good and bad things, to the extent that they increase or decrease our power of action.

Immanuel Kant famously said: 'Experience without theory is blind, but theory without experience is mere intellectual play'. In other words, thought is a constant to and fro on the playing field because 'you can't see the pipe as it is, you see it as you are'.

Amongst the most recent of our influencers, Daniel Kahneman (who passed away during the writing of this book) incorporated the need to build bridges between disciplines. A psychologist and specialist in cognitive bias, he won a Nobel Prize for ... Economics in 2002![7] With his 'fast and slow'[8] system (another dualistic view), he has helped us to understand that our model went through several cognitive biases over the course of its conception. If we are aware of these cognitive biases, then we have already made good progress, since a human being cannot think without them. By keeping them in mind, we can change the model over time to maintain its usefulness. Here are some more biases that we are conscious of:

– We were born in the Western world. Although tricky to define and understand, it structures our way of seeing things. The way in which we perceive the world will therefore differ from that of someone in another part of the world, and our simplifications are based on this perception. Most of the examples, concepts and personalities we mention come from the Western world.

---

6. 'Mal nommer un objet, c'est ajouter au malheur de ce monde.' Albert Camus, 'Sur une philosophie de l'expression', *Poésie* 44 (1944). The title of this article translates to *On a philosophy of expression*.
7. The Nobel Memorial Prize in Economic Sciences, which we will, as most do, happily refer to as the Nobel Prize for Economics.
8. See Kahneman (2011) cited above.

- English is not our mother tongue. We will see in Chapter 4 that a language is a representation of the world, and that two people who don't speak the same language can't think in the same way.
- We are talking from a philosophical point of view. A sociologist, neurologist, lawyer, cognitive scientist, etc. will use different concepts and dimensions to achieve the same goal. A psychologist, for example, might highlight the emotional dimension.
- I work in the corporate world. I have written this book for those who work in business and for those who will work in the sector in years to come. By focusing on graphic design, by selecting the best diagrams and by explaining the most difficult concepts in the simplest terms, my aim is to be as useful to them as possible.

This book takes a philosophical approach, aimed at being rigorous, even when we are not using numbers.

We have so far introduced our main model as a first simplification and explained how we were influenced when building it. It can be seen as a first attempt to present an executive summary of our influences and their different ways of thinking, and to organize them in a single frame. This comes with a warning: *this is not thought!*

1.4. Visual storytelling

Canadian philosopher Marshall McLuhan was the first intellectual to look into the societal consequences of the mediasphere. In his book *The Gutenberg Galaxy*,[9] published in 1962 – so well before computer networks would be connected with analogue networks – he imagined the emergence of a 'global village' and spoke of 'real time'.

Ultraconservative and unsympathetic but highly visionary, he already claimed that: 'Money [is] the poor man's credit card'.[10] This is all the more impressive given that, in his day, technology was still analogue. The visionary hadn't imagined that someday, on the other end of the phone, there would be not a person but a computer. And almost as if he'd wanted to argue his point until the very end, the media prophet died just a few weeks after John Lennon was assassinated by a man who had been driven mad by television, and a few weeks before Ronald Reagan introduced Hollywood to the White House.

McLuhan said: 'the medium is the message',[11] and we can agree with him on this point. A book that intends to clarify needs to be clear! We have chosen the Venn diagram as our main visualization tool and, before we use it, it is useful to recall its principles with a simple example.

Picture this: in front of you are a fishing rod, a cookie, a fish tank, a mo'ai, an emerald, a panda, a concrete beam and an alabaster egg cup. At first glance, these eight objects may look like somewhat of a motley crew, with no obvious links between them. But let's take a closer look!

A mind that wanders is a mind that classifies, that looks for categories. Faced with chaos, it can't resist the temptation of looking for order. Come to think of it, amongst these eight items, some are fragile, like the piece of shortbread, whilst others aren't, like the concrete beam. But both are mundane objects, whilst the panda and the alabaster egg cup aren't. But the latter two, that share a common scarcity, can be differentiated by their weight. *Et cetera, et cetera...*

A quick glance at the eight elements (and as we'll see later on, the number eight is obviously not chosen at random) reveals three dimensions: weight, fragility and rarity. And these three dimensions can be combined two by two. Both the light and heavy elements can be sturdy or fragile, rare or banal. This means that there are eight possible combinations. This thought experiment might seem like trying to solve a Rubik's Cube, but it's easier to understand with a diagram. A small illustration, in this case, is worth a thousand words.

Let's organize our thoughts around three circles, set out as shown in the diagram below. A first observation is a happy one: there are eight well-defined areas (if you take into account the area outside of the three circles, as you can't deny that it's part of the diagram).

9.   Marshall McLuhan, *The Gutenberg Galaxy: The Making of Typographic Man* (Toronto, 1962).

10.   Marshall McLuhan, *Understanding Media: The Extensions of Man* (London, 1964).

11.   See McLuhan (1964) cited above.

Let us now assign one of the three dimensions to each circle. The top left circle will contain the light objects. Everything outside of this circle is therefore heavy. We'll then repeat the process with the other two circles.

And there you have it, our eight initial objects have each found their place in the diagram! The mo'ai is part of the rare objects and is thus in the upper right circle. Being also both sturdy and heavy, it stands outside of the other two circles. The concrete beam, on the other hand, is neither rare, nor light, nor fragile, and so it sits outside of all three circles.

Our initial set of objects was reminiscent of a pile of nonsense. But now that we're looking at them through the three circles, the heterogeneous mass has become structured. You could say that the flea market has become a clerk's tidily ordered office. And yet the objects are the same!

There is therefore strength in a good diagram, an added value in an appropriate figure. Logicians themselves recognize this. The first to do so seems to have been Leonhard Euler, who might have arrived at that conviction during one of his walks over the bridges of Königsberg. But it was a British mathematician, John Venn, who popularized Euler's approach, with what is known today as the 'Venn diagram'.[12]

These circles are both a lens and a kaleidoscope. They diffract confusion like a prism breaks down light. The result is a rainbow of categories.

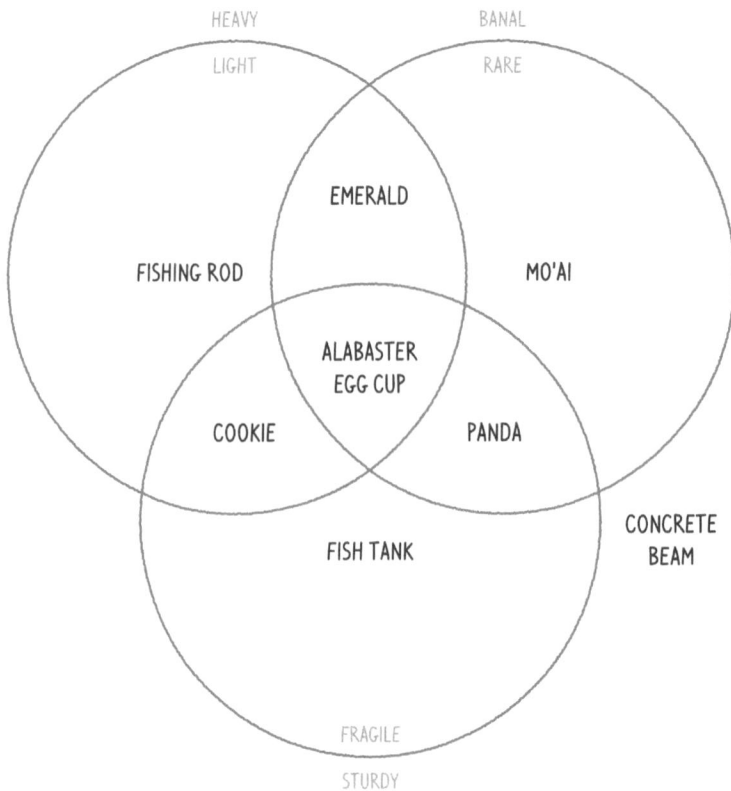

12. J. Venn, 'On the Diagrammatic and Mechanical Representation of Propositions and Reasonings', *The London, Edinburgh, and Dublin Philosophical Magazine and Journal of Science*, 10/59 (1880), 1–18.

Chapter 2 – Thinking is a game

The difference between adults and children is the size of their toys.

2.1. What is a model?

What do market segmentation, a balance sheet and a strategic vision all have in common? Their first shared characteristic is glaringly obvious: all three concepts are part of everyday business language.

What do the law of supply and demand, gross national product and Kondratiev waves have in common? Their first shared element is also pretty obvious: these three concepts often pop up in the field of economics.

But just as a train can hide another train, a correct answer can hide another. A more formal view tells us that all six concepts share something: they are the direct result of a deliberate simplification of things.

In order to organize clients into categories, a large proportion of their specificities needs to be overlooked. The assets and liabilities of a company at any given time are only a picture of its cash flow, already lagging behind, and a CEO planning the dream future of their company can only do so with words. Supply and demand suggest crossing two curbs that are only approximations. GNP evolution is solely a summary account of a country's overall health, and Kondratiev merely represented theoretical frequencies observed in economic evolution.

These six examples show how useful it is to reduce the complexity that surrounds us. It allows us to grasp our environment, to talk about it and sometimes to alter it. This process aimed at simplifying things is called *modelization*.

Most of the time, we think using elementary mental structures called models. The examples above, taken from the business world, are models which help to deal with diversity, complexity and evolution. But managers should keep Magritte in mind, because the models they are using are not the reality they're faced with!

The word 'model' is trivialized, sanitized. It's the next-door neighbour of 'thingy' and 'whatshisname' in the insipid neighbourhood of meaningless words. This word is nevertheless rich and can be interpreted in four very different ways.

– At first, the model was the object to imitate. Of course, words must here be understood in a broad sense, since the sculptor sees the 'object' as the subject, and 'imitating' or recreating a three-dimensional object won't suit a painter looking to represent a picture in two dimensions. But the model remains the thing that we copy, that we reproduce with a certain form of desire. It even quickly feels ideal. The American model has made us dream, the fashion industry and its supermodels still do ...
– From something to imitate, the model then becomes a type, a category. Car manufacturers offer basic models and luxury models. They sometimes even tell customers to wait for the launch of a new, more adventurous model! We can't be adventurous when imitating, and the word 'model' takes on a completely different meaning. It's used to classify, to organize.

- With the development of applied mathematics, the mathematical 'model' made its grand entrance into the world of science. The primary objective of researchers was to simulate being able to understand, to improve and sometimes to make forecasts. Meteorological phenomena or nuclear reactions have been schematized by equations.
- The word 'model' has recently taken on even more meaning. You'll often hear talking about mental models, business models, … and of LLMs (large language models)! Models can be found in all disciplines, they're used to communicate better, teach better, think better, manage better, and even care and heal better.

The purpose of a model is not to portray reality. No model can pretend to be 'true'. The most relevant aspect is its usefulness. A model is a fiction even if it can drive science forward. Its goal is to stylize reality, to make the important traits more prominent. The clearer the pursued objective, the more likely it is that the model will be effective.

A model is more of a caricature than an actual portrait, more of a diagram than a drawing. A modelization deliberately simplifies but sometimes unconsciously forgets. It should *a priori* neglect what is *a posteriori* negligible, obtaining a maximum of similarities in a minimum of traits. It stems from a long series of decisions, is never accomplished, and is always slightly frustrating. We can't create a model without making choices. Which dimensions should be prioritized? Which elements should be put on the back burner? There are dozens and dozens of different modelisations of human behaviour. Many books on management are built around a model that the author believed to be more useful than the others available, convinced that their model should henceforth serve as a model. Let's not forget Abraham Maslow's warning: if the only tool you have is a hammer, it is tempting to treat everything as a nail.[1]

At the beginning of a modelization, there is always a process of renunciation, that of obtaining a unified image of reality. Then there are concessions to be made. Accepting not to have all necessary information, using what is available without knowing its origin, admitting that what is important isn't always quantifiable, taking clearly unrealistic hypotheses such as a consumer's rationality or market transparency. All too often, when we label something as simple, it would be more appropriate to call it simplified.

Two situations are possible. Sometimes you find yourself in direct contact with reality. When watching a football match from the stands, or when facing a candidate that you're thinking of hiring for example. You cannot escape simplifications. Peremptory judgements on the players or the referee will ensue, and only one or two remarks will be made about the candidate. But at least you experienced the situation directly.

This situation is actually quite rare. The same match broadcast on TV will go through a specific selection of images decided by the crew, and the commentator's remarks will direct our thoughts. The same goes for the candidate. If interviewed over the phone or online, we'll miss some of the body language used, and our opinion of them won't be the same as if we'd met them in person.

---

1. 'I suppose it is tempting, if the only tool you have is a hammer, to treat everything as if it were a nail'. Abraham H. Maslow, *Psychology of Science* (New York, 1966).

What lies ahead in our professional life? Very rarely do we come into direct contact with the facts we use. We essentially have before us reports, newspaper articles, number charts, meeting notes, statistics, quotations, future-oriented scenarios. In other words, when we think, we mostly simplify other people's simplifications!

To make a long story short, a model is a goal-oriented mental construction in which reality is simplified in order to be apprehended in a useful way.

2.2. Two modes of thinking

When a parent says: 'I'm thinking about my kids', that's true. When a bank manager says 'I'm thinking about my customers', that isn't true in the same way. And we're not second guessing their good faith here. It's simply not the same because it's not possible. How can someone think of hundreds of thousands, possibly millions of different people at once? It's not possible to think about customers the same way you think about your kids. But the majority of managers does. So, what and how is a boss thinking when making this statement? Two cases are possible:

– They could be thinking of certain individuals in particular, reflecting on a specific comment made by a customer. The manager is thinking of a friend or parent who is a customer, recalling criticism overheard by accident in an office or store and they are acting in good faith.
– They could be thinking about individuals in general and assembling the customers into categories: seniors, SMEs, young mothers, night shift workers, etc. With each segment that the manager wrongly considers to be homogeneous, dominating characteristics are being attributed. They are producing an archetype, an average abstract profile which is supposed to represent the whole category.

Retirees, students, the unmarried, commuters, or even sportsmen are suddenly transformed into a silhouette with a blurred face, portrayed as an ambassador to their equivalent, arithmetic average of that category and standard profile all at once, that each category member can sneak into. But these conceptual ghosts don't exist.

As we discussed in the first chapter, 'a consultant', 'an expat' or even 'a lawyer' don't exist – they don't have an identity card, we cannot shake their hand or name the last film they saw. And when a manager is thinking about the use of a particular profile, they must be careful because *this is not a customer*.

Thinking can unfold in two different ways. The one on top in the landscape model we've seen in Chapter 1 is called 'induction'. It creates general hypotheses through the use of a handful of specific elements. The other is called 'deduction'. It leads to necessary conclusions through premises accepted as they are. From now on, we will call this model 'the I/D model'.

We simplify things through induction, and we use these simplifications when deducing. We model reality through an inductive process, and deduction allows us to use these models.

To summarize, we can establish that when we are thinking, either we are simplifying things or we are using simplifications. Visually, on the I/D model, we are either on the arrow above, or the arrow below.

A quick glance at the diagram might make it seem like these two movements are symmetrical. This is hardly the case: almost everything differentiates the two phases of thought. Let's start by analysing this second phase.

What is deducing?

With deduction, thinking starts with a concept, a hypothesis – remember, deduction is also called the hypothetico-deductive process – and transcends reality by following the rules of logic, sometimes using algorithms.

A deduction can be seen as perfect and if we start over, we'll get the same result. But deduction's weakness is often its starting point. From shaky or false hypotheses, we can indeed deduce anything. A correct deduction isn't enough to confirm the conclusion is true. At best, it shows that it's true that we can conclude.

It's easy to make a mistake when deducing; a human being isn't a machine and can be influenced by the way the question was asked. Let's illustrate this with an example. If you ask someone how many pairs of objects can be made from a group of ten identical objects, they will estimate the answer pretty quickly. If you ask them how many groups of eight objects are possible, they might feel like there are less, which is obviously wrong because each group of two will have a corresponding group of eight … A mistake is therefore being made when deducing, but the mistake isn't debatable.[2] We will come back to this in Chapter 6.

What is inducing?

When we deduce, we're manipulating concepts that need to be defined. But before we conceive and we deduce, we first need to perceive and induce. A mathematical analogy creates the following image:

- Perception would be arithmetic. I'm adding up my observations. I see a, then I see b, then c, etc.
- Conception evokes algebra. The concept would be an x, a variable that could be worth a, b or c, but also become something else later.

Let's imagine that a concept is a drawer in which things can be put. These things are different if we take all of their aspects into consideration, but they are also logically linked because of some partial similarities.

The content of the drawer and the filing system will vary from one person to another according to the degree of their knowledge, their goals or their culture for example. If many drawers are mostly universal, for example the concepts of 'horse' or 'computer' mean roughly the same thing for everyone, part of the chest of drawers still remains flexible and can be adapted by someone depending on their thoughts.

We need to be careful. If there is a newspaper and a box of matches on a table, and you ask someone how many objects are on said table, they'll probably answer 'two'. But every single page of the newspaper is an object, as is every match in the box.

The real challenge related to thought obviously lies in this induction phase, where concepts are formed, strategies elaborated and models built. Thought stems from observations, to achieve hypotheses

---

2.   The correct answer is 45.

which we can't be 100 per cent sure of. We prove a theory by illustrating it, but as the proverb goes, the proof of the pudding is in the eating. A perfect induction is impossible because amongst other things, it would take an infinite amount of time. There are no available algorithms, at most heuristics, 'ways of finding', the reliability of which cannot be total.

An induction means letting go, shortcutting, it's a sort of challenge, because it's not rational to be 100 per cent rational. If someone insisted on studying all possible vacation possibilities, they would never go on vacation.

The prison and the comfort zone

To illustrate the main difference between these two phases of thought, I'll ask you to finish this short sentence:

– 'An example of a car is … '

Very quickly, you'll say 'a Fiat', 'a BMW', 'a Tesla' …

I'll now ask you to finish the following sentence:

– 'A car is an example of … '

Again, you'll quickly reply that it's a vehicle or a means of transport. But you could just as well have said that it's an example of something you enjoy drawing, an example of a threat to the environment, an example of something that gives you more freedom, an example of social status marker, of something the human genius created or even an example of … a word with three letters.

The first type of sentence is easy to finish because it requires little thought. You start with the image you have of a car and an answer is instantly deduced. If you replied 'camembert', you'd be told that this isn't correct. In deductive mode, once definitions are agreed upon, mistakes aren't contestable, unless in bad faith.

The second type of sentence puts us in a different position. It forces us to start from the world facing us. It invites us to induce a concept or a category.

A first answer of a 'beaten track' nature comes to mind rather quickly. A car is indeed an example of a means of transport, and this first idea is often the mark of a previous correct deduction. But we're less sure we're right, and for good reason. It's not possible to be 100 per cent right! The other answers are also acceptable, no matter how subjective. A strange sense of freedom, sometimes similar to vertigo, overwhelms us. Each different point of view will finish the sentence in a different way. A pre-school headmaster might say that the car is an example of danger, a tax inspector might say that the car is an example of a source of tax income, etc.

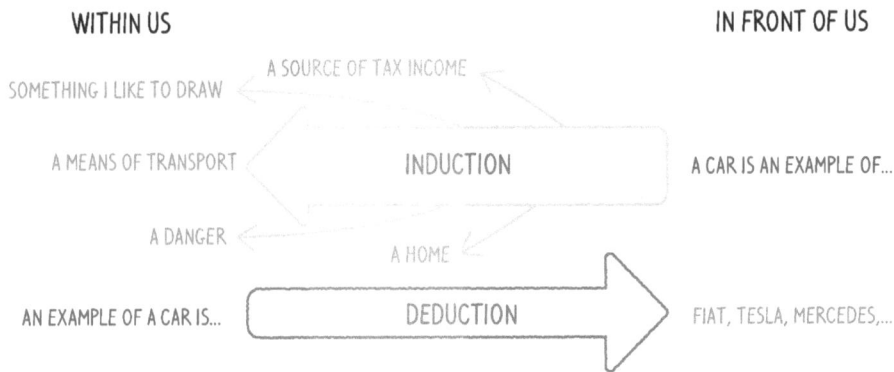

WITHIN US   IN FRONT OF US

A SOURCE OF TAX INCOME

SOMETHING I LIKE TO DRAW

A MEANS OF TRANSPORT   INDUCTION   A CAR IS AN EXAMPLE OF...

A DANGER

A HOME

AN EXAMPLE OF A CAR IS...   DEDUCTION   FIAT, TESLA, MERCEDES,...

Put yourself in the shoes of a teenager, a homeless person, a hospital manager, a historian, a writer, a blind person, or a programmer. How would they finish the sentence 'The car is an example of ... '? There are as many answers as there are humans on Earth, and this is symbolized by the arrows on the drawing above.

Induction goes from individuals to the universal. It builds scientific theories. Deduction goes from the universal to the individual. It refutes scientific theories. Deduction analyses over time with the help of existing models. Induction synthesizes at a given time, it visualizes in space and suggests new models.

It's now clear that our I/D model of thought isn't symmetrical. Deduction is a form of simple reasoning. Its starting point is taken as is, without taking into account all the difficulties that hampered its development. A deduction is concluded with logic, necessarily from a few concepts. If I have an idea of what a 'budget' and a 'balance' are, I can form an opinion on the 'balanced budget' suggested to me for next year.

The starting point of induction, on the other hand, is the group of observations that I can make and that will be influenced by concepts within me. Inductive reasoning starts with an infinite number of premises and cannot be purely logical. Deduction starts from concepts, while induction is conceptualization itself in action.

When we deduce, we're in jail, restricted by hard rules. But when we induce, we're only restricted by our tendency to stay in our comfort zone.

It's no surprise that the *problem of induction* is considered to be a significant problem in philosophy. It's the challenge associated with its generalization, its transition from observed to non-observed. It hides behind several questions, such as:

- Just because something has always been the case, will it always be the case?
- Can statistics lead to certainties?
- Can habits of experience govern the laws of nature?
- When can I go from 'really a lot' to 'all'?

The problem with induction isn't as much its method as its legitimacy, since induction isn't logically valid. I can induce a false conclusion from true premises.

But even more fundamentally, as David Hume pointed out in the eighteenth century,[3] induction relies on ... induction! The simple fact of wanting to make observations presupposes that it's worth observing, that there are regularities, principles to discover and ... that useful models exist. Claiming that knowledge originates in the senses is a starting point that doesn't come from the senses. Argumentation is therefore circular.

One thing is for sure, induction explorers won't stop searching anytime soon!

About ambiguity

What is being evoked here has a name: ambiguity. Ambiguity is the frequent situation where what lies in front of us can be interpreted in different ways. Ambiguity isn't an exception, it's almost a rule. And we'll see in Chapter 7 that it's even good news, as it lies at the heart of the creative process.

The acronym VUCA therefore doesn't make much sense because even though we may be faced with complexity, uncertainty and volatility, the same can't be said for ambiguity. This is because a situation, an image, or a word can't be ambiguous. They are what they are. They may give us a feeling of unease but that is entirely on us.

The illustration below on the left could, for example, be interpreted as a labyrinth under construction, or ... as the uppercase letter H. But, depending on your interpretation, you'll either expect or be very surprised by the picture on the right.

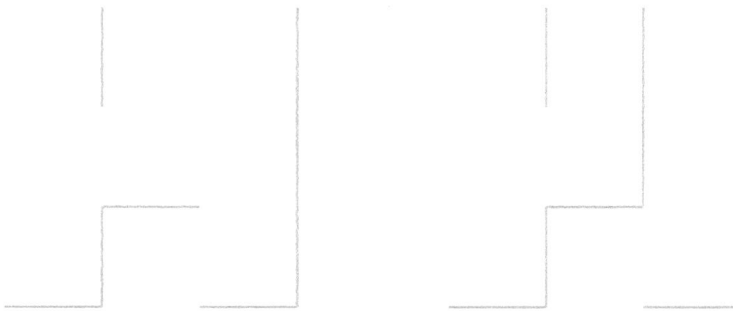

About uncertainty

How will worldwide meat consumption evolve in the coming years? You don't know, and neither do I, because the question is too vast. For many years now, there has been an ever-increasing number of vegetarians and the impact of cattle farming on the climate is a hot topic.

The formulation of the question about the future of meat is simple enough, but it's a terribly difficult question to tackle. It is nonetheless possible to make hypotheses and to construct a thought process,

3.   David Hume, 'An Enquiry Concerning Human Understanding', in *Essays and Treatises on Several Subjects* (London, 1777).

to make a diagram with the different alternatives: 'if ..., then ... ' projections are possible because 'the question is in the air'. In this first type of uncertainty, the question is precise and the framework is defined. In other words, we know what we don't know, and we are therefore deducing.

But this isn't always the case. For example, no one had ever really wondered whether Volkswagen was organizing large-scale cheating to avoid anti-pollution rules. And yet, when it came to light that indeed they were, the shock was even greater because we didn't know that we didn't know.

This type of event – when you have the answer before the question – is often referred to as a 'black swan', in homage to seventeenth-century Dutch explorers who were convinced that all swans were white, and were stunned to suddenly see a black one on a trip to Australia. The possibility of black swans had never been envisioned seriously by Europeans, and so the black swan became the symbol of this second type of uncertainty. Today, the black swan is a very unlikely event that has a significant impact.

Black swans are at the heart of the scenario method. During the brainstorming sessions, one or several black swans are presented to the participants who are then asked to induce and to find explanations for their appearance.

In *Thinking in new boxes*,[4] published in 2013, we featured a workshop where we'd asked for an explanation as to why air traffic would drop by 80 per cent ... in 2020! And that's exactly what happened!

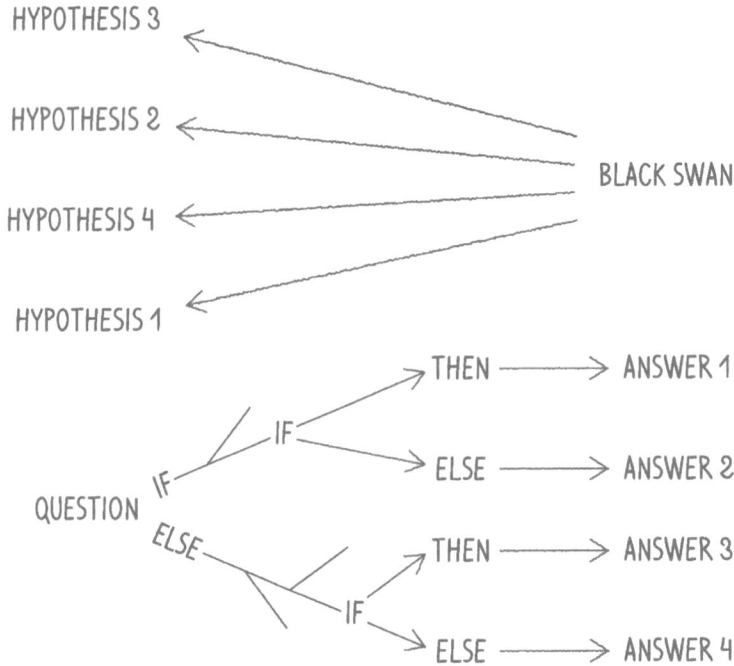

---

4.   Luc de Brabandere and Alan Iny, *Thinking in New Boxes: A New Paradigm for Business Creativity* (New York, 2013).

2.3. Two modes of changing

Now that we've compared both movements of thought and highlighted the essence of what separates them, let's concentrate on another fundamental difference between the left and right sides of the playing field. If we observe the evolution of things over time, it is obvious that it unfolds differently on either side.

On the right, nothing is set in stone. A town, a singer, a company are not the same on Wednesday as they were on Tuesday, and they'll change again the following day. Everything we're faced with is constantly changing, in a continuous and necessary manner.

However, this often doesn't change anything within us. For a majority of topics, the simplifications we use today are the same that we used yesterday, last week, last month, even last year.

These don't change very much, but when they do, it's always a shock. It's no surprise, since going from a simplification to another cannot happen without disruption. Change in us is not very frequent and it's discontinuous.

We will return at length to this vital difference when we talk about creativity and cognitive bias.

WITHIN US

IN FRONT OF US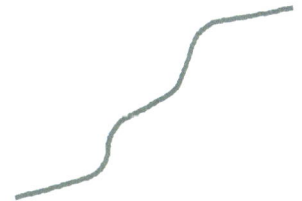

Obeying the laws of change

Let's summarize a few important points regarding change.

1. *It's impossible not to change*

The first law of change dates back to Heraclitus. It isn't possible to step in the same river twice. Change is inevitable.

2. *Part of change isn't written in advance*

Change is inevitable but there are usually two ways of facing it. Either you position yourself as the driver of what is happening and seize the opportunity to steer it in the direction you want it to go. Or you suffer through events and become a passenger of change, sometimes even a victim of it. So basically, you have to choose between a *Eureka* approach and a *Caramba* approach!

3. *There is nothing more difficult than changing the order of things*[5]

This sentence, which seems so contemporary, is in fact just slightly paraphrased from a book published … 500 years ago! Once the Heraclitean imperative had been put forward, it was indeed Machiavelli who reminded us how difficult it is to comply with. In his treatise entitled *The Prince*, written in the sixteenth century and commissioned by his boss Lorenzo de' Medici, he insists on the unavoidable resistance that would be caused by attempting to modify things. Such a book would today be called 'A white paper on innovation'. The message would be the same, only the language would change.

4. *There are two types of change*

We can change things, and we can change our way of seeing things. One is possible without the other and the other is possible without the one. Installing wind turbines everywhere won't necessarily come with a sense of energy shortage and, *a contrario*, we can recognize climate change as a major challenge without changing our consumption habits.

Changing reality takes time. It requires a continuous movement performed by a group of people. The digital transformation has been happening for several years and is still happening today. On the other hand, perception is individual, since a group doesn't have perception, and so changing your own perception needs to be done by everyone individually. And while changing reality can be done very gradually, this second change is necessarily a shock.

5. *You can change your perception, even if reality doesn't change*

The Solar System is exactly the same as it was before the Copernican revolution!

6. *Successful change is necessarily twofold*

- Someone who is always late will start being on time once they change their organization AND what they consider to be timeliness. In other words, they will change if they change the *reality* of their agenda and the *perception* that they have of the importance of better time management. Simply reducing the number of meetings won't be enough if it's not accompanied by a real desire and delight to be on time.
- Merging companies A and B will only be a success if the reality of both these entities changes (a single balance sheet, a single IT system, etc.) AND if the group of people involved share the same strategic vision. In other words, C won't exist if ex-A or ex-B continues to exist!

These two examples prove that 'changing means changing twice', that only a change in perception makes a change in reality irreversible. Real change, the kind that we want to accomplish, is necessarily two-sided.

New technologies only have meaning if they're accompanied by new mental models.

---

5. 'there is nothing more difficult to take in hand, more perilous to conduct, or more uncertain in its success, than to take the lead in the introduction of a new order of things.' Niccolò Macchiavelli, *Il Principe* (1532), as appears in the translation by William Kenaz Marriott, *The Prince* (London, 1908).

The first modern petroleum well was drilled in the middle of the nineteenth century. But for years, the only thing that was done with it was to burn it. It was only at the end of the nineteenth century that the idea of modern combustion engines was developed. The revolution of petrol was to make it explode, not just to use it as an easy substitute for coal.

I introduced and developed these ideas at length in *The Forgotten Half of Change*, published in 2005.[6] This book explores and explains how we must become as good at changing our perceptions as we have become at changing reality. And how true creativity can only be achieved if you are willing to break the rules that have locked you in a set way of thinking, not just doing.

7. *Change isn't possible unless certain things don't change*

A change is only ever partial, and only possible if certain things don't change. A 100 per cent change would mean no change. There is asymmetry here because what is observable evolves and what is permanent is more discreet. It's easy to see that today's Paris isn't the same as the Paris of twenty years ago. But it's less easy to pinpoint what hasn't changed in the city. It's the same for your company or the school you grew up in.

So what's new ? In 1609, Kepler published *Astronomia nova*;[7] in 1620, Bacon published *Novum Organum*;[8] in 1647, Pascal published *New experiments regarding the vacuum*;[9] in 1698, Denis Papin published *Treatise of several new machines*[10] ... There is a long list of geniuses, scholars and innovators of all kinds who have reinvented their field whilst leaving a great deal of their dimensions unaffected.

In his novel *The Leopard*, Italian writer Giuseppe Tomasi di Lampedusa tells the story of a nineteenth-century Sicilian aristocrat who anxiously witnesses the ongoing revolutions. He tells his nephew 'If we want everything to stay as it is, everything must change'.[11]

8. *We can only observe change if we have a fixed point of reference*

If you want to find out the weight of a fast-driving heavy goods vehicle, being in another vehicle on the same highway won't give you the answer. You'd need to be seated on the side of the highway. It's only possible to detect the mechanics and dynamics that are at play from a stable and fixed location. Take a recent IKEA catalogue and remember what it was like seventy years ago ... They're simultaneously the same and different!

9. *If we want to change what is in front of us, we may not change what is within us*

Imagine a company where every Monday morning an email is sent out with the subject line: 'Strategy update'. The company would very quickly come to a grinding halt. If the company is able to change its products and services, it's because the strategy doesn't change. In other words, it's because they stop

6. Cited above.
7. Johannes Kepler, *Astronomia Nova* (Heidelberg, 1609).
8. Francis Bacon, *Novum Organum Scientiarum*, 1620.
9. Blaise Pascal, *Expériences Nouvelles Touchant Le Vide*, 1647.
10. Denis Papin, *Traité de plusieurs nouvelles machines* (Paris, 1698).
11. *'Se vogliamo che tutto rimanga come è, bisogna che tutto cambi'*. Giuseppe Tomasi di Lampedusa, *Il Gattopardo* (Milan, 1958).

thinking that the company can start acting. It's no coincidence that in French we say that we 'stop' a strategy.

10. *Most of the changes in front of us are exponential*

When I was born, there were two and a half billion people on Earth. This number was reached through slow growth over thousands of years, and then more than doubled in less than fifty years. Today that number has reached the eight billion mark. The same goes for climate change. Average global temperatures and extinction rates are going up rapidly; Arctic sea ice is disappearing at an accelerating pace. Everything is happening faster ... There is no time to lose.

2.4. Simplifying and using simplifications

The I/D model introduced in Chapter 1 only contains a dozen words. But that was enough to already suggest a first definition of thinking, and to remind us of some of the particularly important rules of thinking. We now need to dig deeper, to the heart of the matter.

In this detailed version, we'll be taking a closer look at the four sides of the playing field, with all of their diversity and nuances.

- On the right, a series of words used to describe what lies before us.
- On the left, even more words describe the wide variety of simplifications that live within us.
- Above, the induction process appears in all its complex glory. Perception, language, memory, imagination, each of these themes is subject to simplifications that live within us.
- Below, the deductive approach appears as a group of functions and possible methods. They are each, in their own way, aiming for the same goal: to lead to a conclusion.

In order to build this more refined version of the model, we have adopted several other principles. We limited ourselves to around 130 words and avoided including synonyms, only keeping one version of each concept we included.

There are a lot of ways of organizing these groups of words: you could classify them by characteristics or even regroup them into categories. Discovery, invention and creation are, for example, the three inductive processes that could lead to a finding (as we will see in Chapter 7). But this book's objective is to give an overview of the subject, not to try our hand at categorizing in this way, so we elected to present words in alphabetical order.

Depending on one's activity or profession, some of the words in the model will take on more or less significance:

A cartoonist will probably feel more proximity with caricature, form, image or representation for example, whereas a lawyer might spend more time discussing code, system, law and judgement. Both teachers and sociologists will care about culture and explanation, but one will give priority to memory while the other will more readily question representation, etc. The model can be adapted for everyone's use, and its exact content is less important than its structure.

In order to build this I/D model, some choices had to be made.

WITHIN US

ARCHETYPE
ASSOCIATION
ASSUMPTION
AVERAGE
AXIOM
BELIEF
BOX
CANVAS
CARICATURE
CATEGORY
CAUSE
CHART
CLAIM
CODE
CONCEPT
CORRELATION
CRITERIA
CULTURE
DEFINITION
DIMENSION
EXPERTISE
FINDING
FORECAST
FORM
FRAMEWORK

GESTALT
GUESSTIMATING
HABIT
HYPOTHESIS
IDEA
IDENTITY
IDEOLOGY
IMAGE
INSIGHT
JUDGMENT
KNOWLEDGE
LAW
NORM
MAP
MATRIX
MEMORY
METAPHOR
METHOD
METRICS
MINDSET
MODEL
MYTH
OPINION
PARADIGM
PATTERN

PLAN
PREMISE
PRINCIPLE
PROFILE
REPRESENTATION
RULE
RUMOR
SCENARIO
SKETCH
SPECIES
STATEMENT
STEREOTYPE
STRATEGY
STRUCTURE
SYMBOL
SYSTEM
TABOO
TEMPLATE
THEORY
THESIS
TRUTH
VALUE
VISION
ETC.

ABDUCTION   CURIOSITY   INTENTION
ABSTRACTION   DISCOVERY   INVENTION
ANALOGY   DOUBT   LANGUAGE
ASTONISHMENT   EXPERIENCE   OBLIVION
ATTENTION   EXPLORATION   PERCEPTION
BIAS   HEURISTIC   QUESTION
BISOCIATION   IGNORANCE   SYNTHESIS
CREATION   IMAGINATION   *ETC.*
CREATIVITY   INTERPRETATION
CRITIC   INTUITION

INDUCTION

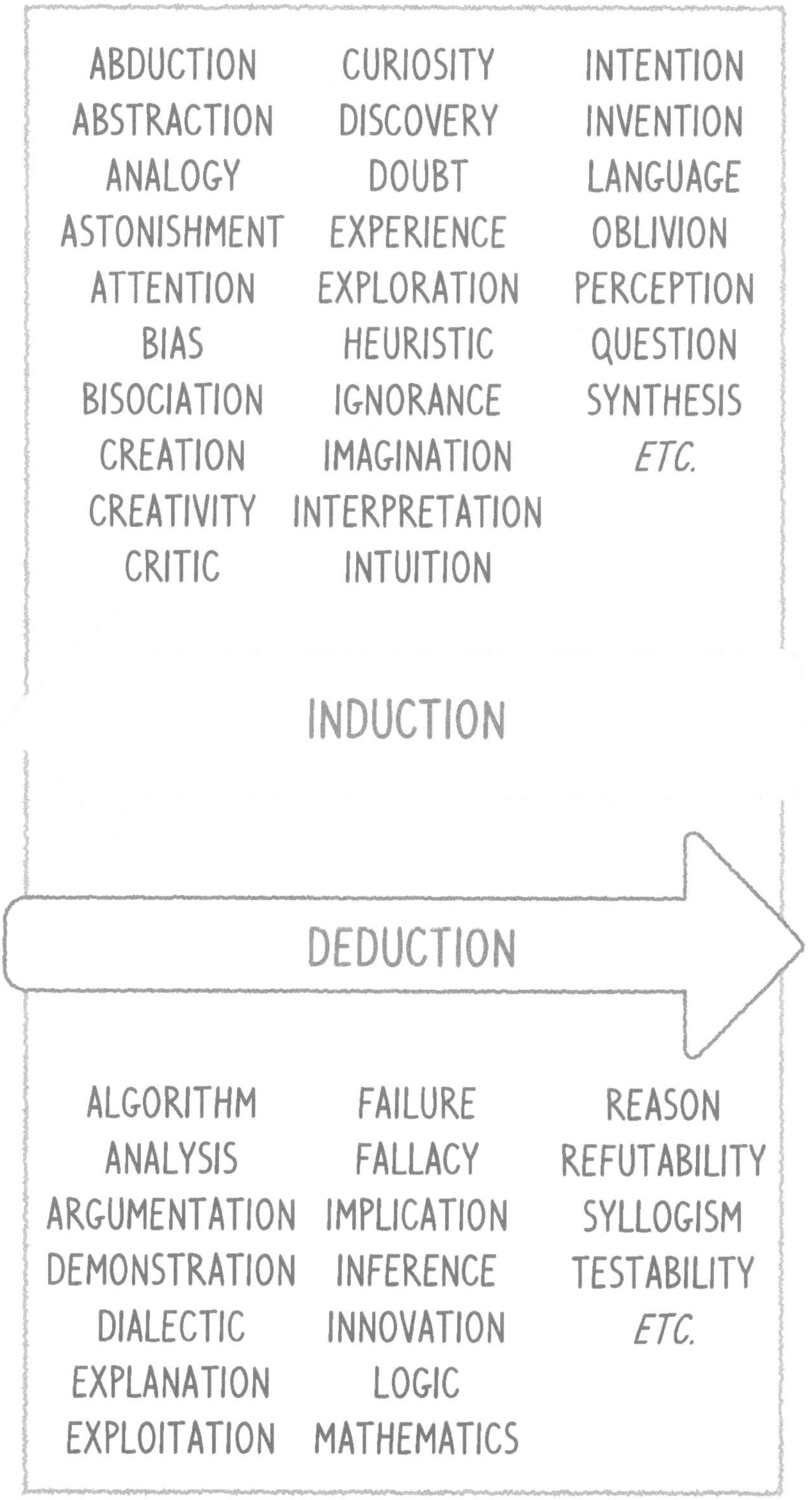

CONTENT
BIG DATA
EFFECT
EVENT
EVIDENCE
EXPERIMENT
FACT
INFORMATION
MEASURE
MEGATRENDS
NUMBER
REALITY
WEAK SIGNALS
ETC.

DEDUCTION

ALGORITHM   FAILURE   REASON
ANALYSIS   FALLACY   REFUTABILITY
ARGUMENTATION   IMPLICATION   SYLLOGISM
DEMONSTRATION   INFERENCE   TESTABILITY
DIALECTIC   INNOVATION   *ETC.*
EXPLANATION   LOGIC
EXPLOITATION   MATHEMATICS

For example, we display each word only once but ...

- Cognitive 'bias' can be found in both induction and deduction ...
- Some words like 'invention', 'analogy' or 'intuition' are used to describe both a process and its outcome.
- The word 'experience', or the word 'argument' could be in four (!) different places!

This forced us to make some pragmatic choices. For example, 'analogy' is placed within the process of induction, since 'metaphor' is more often used to qualify an outcome of this process.

Some more comments about the words in the I/D model:

- English spelling can be tricky, as different rules apply for British and American English. For example, the Brits favour a 'u' after 'o', like in 'rumour' or 'humour'. But the Americans keep it simple, without the 'u'. We have mostly adopted British spelling.
- The meaning of English words can also be different on either side of the Atlantic, and Brits and Americans disagree on what such simple things as 'pants' are. We have once again sided with Team UK in this friendly match.
- Languages are wonderful things, but they're no strangers to the occasional bout of complexity. False friends being a prime example of this: words that either sound almost the same but mean very different things, or that are spelt in nearly the same way but mean different things. These false friends can be found within the same language, or across languages. We have tried to remain aware of them, and invite our readers to do so too.

  - In English for example, though very similar, 'experience' and 'experiment' are not the same thing. An experiment is something which is done to test a hypothesis and to see the results. An experience on the other hand is something that has happened to you.

  - French and English have many false friends, to the great despair of many trans-Channel students! In English, a 'memory' is an image or information that your brain has acquired and stored: it translates to *un souvenir* in French. But a 'souvenir' in English is a physical memento that you bring back from somewhere.

- The words on the model are presented in isolation, without much context or explanation. Many many books, sometimes hundreds, have been written about most of these words! So never hesitate to go off down a rabbit hole for each one and discover what else has been written and debated about each word, they're all fascinating!

Finally, the same rule applies to this I/D model as for all other models. Its main goal isn't to be true, but to be useful. This version of the model will accompany us throughout the rest of the book.

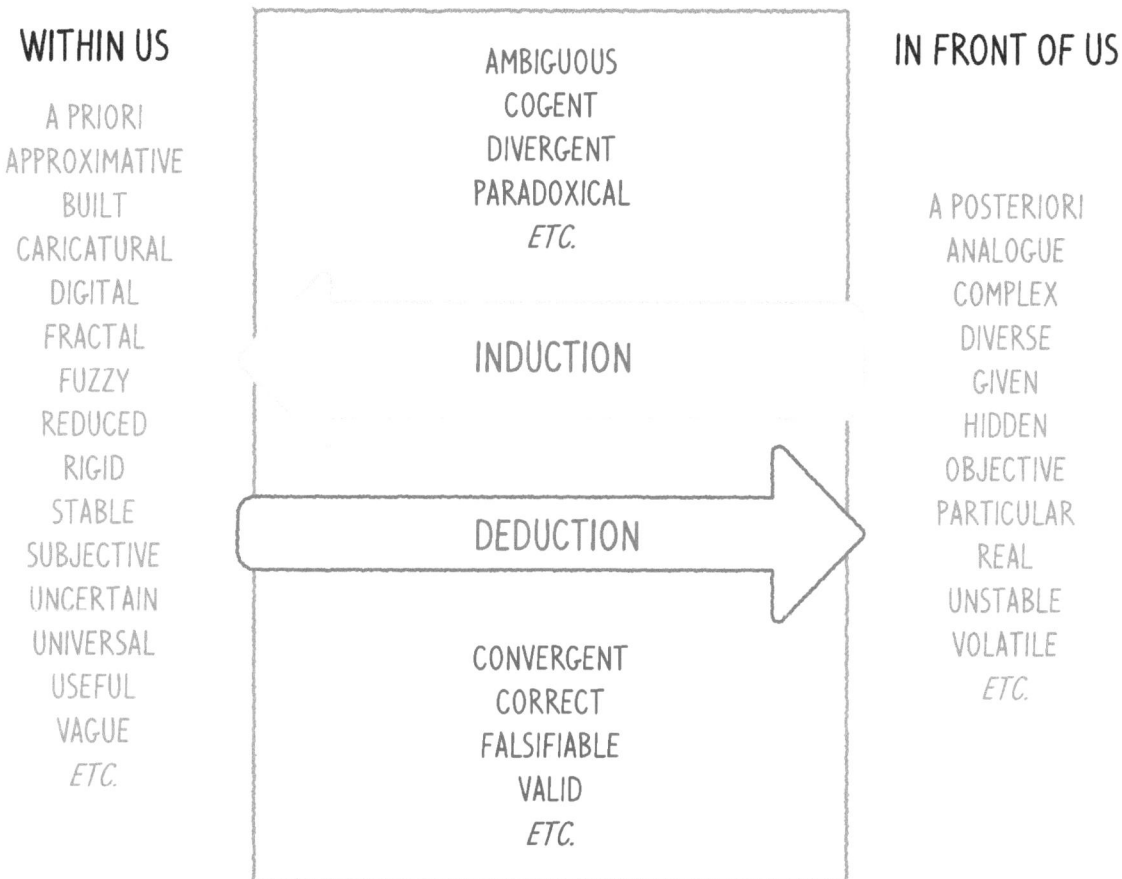

WITHIN US

A PRIORI
APPROXIMATIVE
BUILT
CARICATURAL
DIGITAL
FRACTAL
FUZZY
REDUCED
RIGID
STABLE
SUBJECTIVE
UNCERTAIN
UNIVERSAL
USEFUL
VAGUE
ETC.

AMBIGUOUS
COGENT
DIVERGENT
PARADOXICAL
ETC.

INDUCTION

DEDUCTION

CONVERGENT
CORRECT
FALSIFIABLE
VALID
ETC.

IN FRONT OF US

A POSTERIORI
ANALOGUE
COMPLEX
DIVERSE
GIVEN
HIDDEN
OBJECTIVE
PARTICULAR
REAL
UNSTABLE
VOLATILE
ETC.

Figure 13. *Possible attributes of the model, Dominique Paquet*

Chapter 3 – Digital transformation

The Stone Age did not end because we ran out of stone.

3.1. Matter and information

In order to observe the world's digital shift, let's obey the eighth law of change and choose a fixed point: the link between matter and information. This choice can be justified in two different ways.

First, since the dawn of time, humankind has manipulated and used matter when working: plants, cattle, clay. To do so, they have used information: methods, measures, calculations. To build the pyramids, the Egyptians became masters in carving blocks of granite, which were cut in Aswan and shipped all the way to Cairo on the Nile. But they had also become highly skilled geometricians who could calculate angles in three dimensions.

Second, the link between matter and information being used as a fixed point has long since proved its worth. And it has already seen its fair share of changes as it was formalized ... 2,300 years ago, by Aristotle himself! According to him, a sculptor who is making a statue of a horse 'informs' the marble. Seen in this way, a fossil is a stone that is carrying information about a leaf or a crab which disappeared millions of years ago.

Three major changes emerge thanks to the fixed point we're using.

1. Matter is limited (*despite the opposite being believed for a long time*)

For centuries, in the Western world, matter was for all practical purposes considered to be unlimited: the world was imagined as an infinite reservoir of resources to be exploited. It was unimaginable that there could be finite quantities of water, wood and coal, that we could run out of these things. But today we know that is not true. Even sand has become a rare resource, and environmentalists make their points more clearly than ever before.

2. Information is unlimited (*despite the opposite being believed for a long time*)

For centuries, information was considered to be limited and manageable. Today we know that is not true, no one could possibly conceive of an *Encyclopédie*[1] that would contain all of the knowledge in the world. Even Wikipedia, probably the biggest and most accessible collection of knowledge of our time, cannot claim any kind of exhaustivity.

---

1.   Denis Diderot and Jean Le Rond D'Alembert, *Encyclopédie, ou Dictionnaire raisonné des sciences, des arts et des métiers* (Paris, 1751).

3. Information has replaced matter at the heart of the economic system

The first two changes are no strangers to the headlines, so we won't be pursuing them any further.

The third change, on the other hand, is what concerns us in this book.

At the beginning of the twentieth century, most of the labour force gravitated around matter. A miner would extract it, a lumberjack would chop it, a baker would transform it, a sailor would ship it, an apothecary would sell it. Farmers, bricklayers and boatmen were all physically exhausted at the end of the day.

A century later, two thirds of the workforce revolve around information. A developer codes it, a manager tracks it, a designer conceptualizes it, a consultant explains it, an advertiser spices it up, a journalist makes it accessible. Many IT workers, accountants, professors and civil servants do some kind of physical exercise at the end of the day to relax.

The link between matter and information has shifted to a link between information and matter!

We will develop this further in Chapter 7.

3.2. Old questions and new answers

When tackling a difficult problem, it is important for a philosopher to choose relevant questions to answer. We will consider seven of these questions that all have a common denominator. When matter was being discussed, their answers were fairly simple. But now information has taken a much bigger role, and the answers have become much more complex!

1. Where are things?

In the material world, the question of space wasn't a problem. Where's my guitar? Where's my book? When you're sitting at the opera, where is the music? They're right here. And if they're here, then they can't be anywhere else. But where is the result of the latest Manchester United match? On the stadium screens? On my phone? In the papers? Space has become cyberspace, but there are no tangible distances or surfaces there.

Space was an easy concept. Long since organized in three dimensions, compartmentalized, structured on all sides with boundaries, between public and private space. But now it's all up in the air, agitated, blurred, chaotic even.

Can we even enter cyberspace given that it's everywhere? What is a financial 'place' today? And what does relocating a market mean when its location actually doesn't matter anymore? Won't we all one day become 'office-less'? And the companies that we see everywhere, where actually are they?

2. When are things happening?

In the material world, the question of time was also secondary. There have always been mornings and evenings, springs and autumns. Time passed at a constant speed, identical for all and relatively easy to measure. But is time still a measure of work? Increasingly not, it seems. And what time is it on the internet? As is the case at the North Pole or on the Moon, it is whatever time you want it to be, or whatever time we agree it is.

Just like space, time was also a peaceful concept: the world's great grandfather clock, as Jacques Brel sang, said yes, said no, and chimed in our living rooms.[2]

But now the clock is confused. What should its position be in a society that now functions in real time? And anyway, what was time like before it was real? In accounting terms, a diesel engine used to be written off over time, but how should a search engine be written off today?

Time is no longer the same for everyone. Static for some, dynamic for others. Even the night/day rhythm has been altered. Shops are increasingly open 24/7, the internet has made it into our bed sheets, and even though many self-help books and apps now focus on the importance of rest and

---

2.   Jacques Brel, *Les Vieux* (1963).

sleep, these needs are made to compete with other, supposedly more interesting, technological pastimes.

And let's not forget that *real* time doesn't actually exist. In the same way a football match being broadcast *live*, doesn't actually exist. Depending on the type of transmission they've chosen, your neighbour could be seeing the goals a whole two seconds before you! The images captured on camera go through a whole series of decoders, amplifiers, satellites and coaxial cables before reaching the channel that has paid a premium for the rights, who then sends these images pre-charged, compressed, buffered, remastered, sometimes encrypted, treated. And even at the speed of light, when placing financial orders, it's better to have shorter fibre optics cables than your competitors.

3. Who owns things?

Whose bike is this? Who has bought a chainsaw? Who owns this plot of land? Who is the owner of this diamond? So many banal questions that have kept generations of shopkeepers, lawyers and even policemen going.

But they've all answered these questions with an 'either/or' logic. If it's them, it can't be someone else.

Who owns John Lennon's last song? Who do the results of the election belong to? Who has the formula to calculate π? We've left the 'either/or' logic behind and have moved towards the 'and' logic. He has the recipe for pizza, and so does she! We've left behind a binary logic.

Non-fungible tokens (NFTs) now make it possible to uniquely identify the 'original' owner of anything – usually a digital object – by recording on a blockchain, but they consume an enormous amount of energy. Is the expense really worth it?

4. How can things be classified?

In the material world, there is no choice. A library has to be organized into sections and a supermarket into aisles, otherwise no one would ever find anything. We do however have a choice in the way we do this, as the choice of categories remains subjective and contextual. But classifying supermarket products by alphabetical order wouldn't make much sense, no more than organizing a library by book size. To further the evolution of science, the Linnés and Mendeleevs of this world organized the living species or the chemical elements into categories.

The use of categories allows us to formulate judgement and to build reasonings, to think about the world, and even to improve it. So that's good news! Thank you categories!

But categories have three characteristics which can pose serious problems if ignored:

– They don't exist![3]
– They are rigid and fixed in a world that isn't.
– They are blurry.

---

3.   See Chapter 2.

There is no science of categorization. A category always has an arbitrary, subjective and conventional aspect. It's never true or false, and the only way of appreciating it is to understand its utility. For the supermarket manager, the young fathers category might include as many people as the young mothers category, but it's probably less useful. The same could be said for a category for all left-handed customers, or for those who enjoy genealogy.

Aristotle, to whom we owe the very idea of a category, wasn't really bothered about these manufacturing defects because what he wanted above all was to establish the laws of logic, the science of correct reasoning. And he did this at the cost of two very restrictive hypotheses:

- A category is homogeneous: it isn't possible to be either a little bit of a consultant or a lot of a consultant. Rather, you are a consultant or you're not.
- A category is decidable: you can always tell whether someone is a consultant or not.

And this is obviously not the case: categories are neither homogeneous, nor decidable. It's easy to tell that a taxi is more of a means of transport than a tank or a spacecraft is, and, after all, isn't wine also fruit juice?

The expression 'changing categories' can be understood in two different ways. It can either mean going from one existing category to another or it can mean changing the way of classifying. In the first case, the date of first European expeditions to the Americas went from 'end of the fifteenth century' to 'end of the tenth century' when new evidence was discovered. In the second, biologists decided that pachyderms, for example, were no longer a category they wished to use when they switched to phylogenetic nomenclature.

Both things happened to Pluto in 2006, when the International Astronomical Union clarified the definition of a planet, created the new category of 'dwarf planet', and put Pluto in that new box.

The world is changing under our very eyes, but we keep using categories which were established in the years following the Second World War.

When you type 'philosopher' into Google, before you even press Enter, a dozen suggested categories appear under the search box. Enlightenment philosophers, French philosophers, famous philosophers, etc. A first astonishment comes from the choice of these categories, and the redundancy that ensues: Voltaire would for example land in all three. You could also wonder why, when you typed 'philosopher' singular, you end up with plural suggestions. And you may also wonder why two people typing the word 'philosopher' at the same time won't always get the same results.

But the fourth astonishment is even more significant: why is Google even suggesting categories? We've lost sight of this a little, but ever since Aristotle it seemed to be taken for granted that categorization was necessarily the result of a compromise of which only humans were capable: that of forgetting a large part of the world in order to be able to think about it.

Of course, Google itself doesn't create these categories: they are merely suggested to it by user behaviour, and the results you see are only ever the ones that Google estimates to be the most relevant for you, based on what it knows about you.

But the question is an important one. And is asked in time (why is History chopped into eras?) and in space (where do the suburbs of London end?). Francis Bacon had already stated that knowledge is power.[4] Michel Foucault went a step further: it's the way in which we structure information that is the source of power.

With big data, do we still need categories? Some claim that we don't. At the start of this book we mentioned a thought-provoking article that was published in 2008 in *Wired* magazine. The publication's chief editor, Chris Anderson, was announcing the end of science! According to the author, thanks to the sheer volume of information, the storage capacity and the computing power now available, not only is the use of categories no longer necessary, but all scientific models will also become obsolete! So is it goodbye to sociology, taxonomy, psychology and ontology?

We obviously disagree – you need only to think of all the geniuses who, like Da Vinci, Aristotle or even Einstein, didn't need and didn't use data at all.

5. Why are things happening?

Why was there a major financial crisis in 2008?

Because subprime mortgages were bad bonds? Because buyers didn't have sufficient financial knowledge to understand what they were buying? Because the level of accumulated debt in the world had broken all records? Because the rating agencies didn't do their jobs properly? Because these agencies are private companies? Because bank shareholders wanted a 15 per cent return on equity, forcing managers to take greater and greater risks? Because the authorities agreed to banks putting their toxic products into a separate subsidiary? Because traders started taking bets on the financial health of whole countries? Because the bonuses of these market operators were too high? Or because they were taking cocaine? Because they had been partially replaced by robots? Because flash trading made it possible to automatically carry out operations that no one understood or controlled? Because, because, because, ...
This list of questions could go on and on. But is it really useful? Shouldn't the question actually be about how to build a more robust and fairer financial system?

It may seem anecdotal, but all of this leads us to a hypothesis: in a world that is increasingly digital, shouldn't we be investing less in understanding things that have passed, and more on projects that will lead to a better future? The main question is no longer 'Does A cause B?', it is now 'We have A and we have B, now what?'

As a Chinese BCG partner laughingly told us in a company-wide reunion, the Chinese make fun of Westerners who are still trying to understand which came first between the chicken and the egg. Don't ask the question, 'eat both.'

---

4.   Francis Bacon, *Meditationes Sacrae*, 1597.

The simultaneity of two events can be explained in four different ways.

1. Coincidence

Imagine that, in the news headlines on TV you hear that Samsung is launching a new type of connected watch and that, in Paris, the French football team beat Nigeria the previous evening. You'll consider both these statements for what they are: as two separate news stories that bear no connection. It's often called a simple coincidence, but that's actually a pleonasm, because coincidence itself can't be complicated.

But if the news about the football victory were preceded by another headline along the lines of 'Heavy downpours yesterday evening in the capital', the human mind is built in a way that it will establish a link between the two and risks thinking 'It is true that the players from Sahel aren't used to such heavy rain'. Coincidences aren't easy to accept!

2. Correlation

It's a fact: the countries that produce the most Nobel Prizes are the countries where the amount of chocolate consumed per capita is the highest.[5] There is a correlation, that is, a statistical link. But there is no certainty, nor causal relationship between the two. It's not because more chocolate is sold in a country that there are more great scientific minds in this country.

If a 36-year-old dentist living in Morocco buys a new book about the harmful effects of sour sweets, it is highly likely that a 41-year-old dentist living in Tunisia could also be interested in the same book. This is understandable and an algorithm can make a recommendation based on it. But Chris Anderson goes one step further. He says that even when we don't understand, we can act. If it looks like the owners of a Renault go to the cinema more often on Tuesdays than on Thursdays, you don't need to understand why before you adapt your advertising accordingly. According to Anderson, correlation trumps causality. Marketing can move forward without a coherent model, without a specific segmentation, and even without any mechanistic explanation at all.

Post hoc, ergo propter hoc. Translated literally: 'After this, therefore because of this'. This is a mental shortcut that is taken too often. As French science philosopher Étienne Klein puts it, just because there are frogs after the rain does not mean that it has rained frogs![6]

3. Conjunction

A particular case is a certain correlation: when there is a 100 per cent likelihood that event A will be accompanied by event B, and therefore A implies B. Lightning implies thunder, but this certitude is not always synonymous with causality. Leibniz gave the example of two clocks.[7] As they move together, one could believe that they're following one another and that the movement of one is making the other move. No, this is simply a conjunction, traditionally called implication in logic.

5. Franz H. Messerli, 'Chocolate Consumption, Cognitive Function, and Nobel Laureates', *New England Journal of Medicine*, 367/16 (2012), 1562–4.
6. Étienne Klein, 25 September 2022, <twitter.com/EtienneKlein/status/1573960821629222912> [accessed 29 May 2024].
7. Gottfried Wilhelm Leibniz, 'Second Explanation of the New System', January 1696.

4. Causality

We see that the glass breaks after it has fallen and we think that it has broken because it fell.

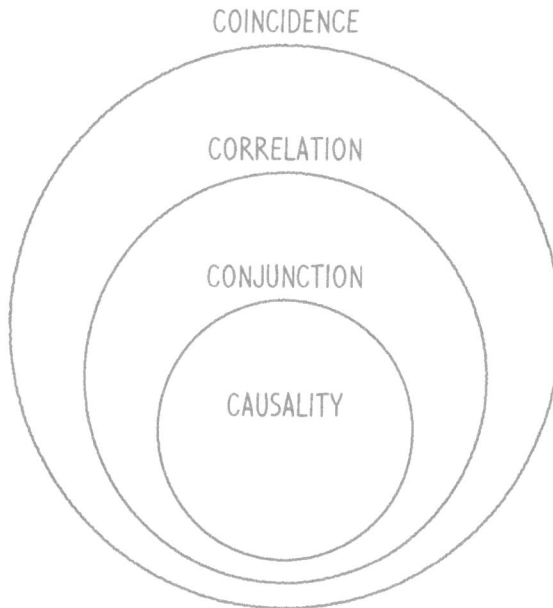

COINCIDENCE

CORRELATION

CONJUNCTION

CAUSALITY

According to Kant, the step from observation to explanation would not be possible without the concept of causality *a priori*. That's because it isn't possible to see a cause in the same way that you see a bright colour or a pointy shape: you'd be going beyond the raw information received by the eyes and ears.

When two events follow each other, it is often true that one causes the other. The cause produces, leads to, conditions, provokes something else. The rooster crows when the sun rises. It's more than a conjunction, sunrise has caused the cacophony of cock-a-doodle-doos.

Come to think of it, why wouldn't it be the other way round? What is stopping us from thinking that the crowing is causing the sunrise? Identifying a cause doesn't mean that it has been understood. The Egyptians built the pyramids, but the pyramids also built the Egyptian people.

Looking for causes is inherent to any scientist, whatever their discipline. Some psychologists,[8] who studied the profound nature of our emotions, even wondered: 'Are we shaking because we're scared or are we scared because we're shaking?'

Bertrand Russell claimed that the law of causality survives 'like the monarchy, only because it is erroneously supposed to do no harm'.[9]

---

8. Here we mostly refer to William James and pragmatists in general.
9. Bertrand Russell, 'On the Notion of Cause', in *Mysticism and Logic and Other Essays* (London, 1917).

6. How can things be communicated?

In the material world, the difference between what was written and what was spoken was relatively clear. It was one or the other. Each had its advantages and disadvantages. Each had its partisans and detractors. The former favoured logic, while the latter preferred argumentation and rhetoric. But digital technology has curiously blurred the lines between written language and spoken language. What now belongs with one and what now belongs with the other? Where is the boundary?

On the one hand, in the digital age, the words we utter have never been so often recorded: words remain, as if they'd been spoken in marble. It's as if the spoken word were a form of writing. As soon as an industry leader utters a single word, it is transcribed by witnesses on social media, on twenty-four-hour news channels, etc. It is repeated, shared, analysed as if it had been written by an author. It no longer matters much whether something was spoken or written.

On the other hand, the written word has never been closer to the spoken word, since the explosion of instant messaging. As the number of texts being sent increases, the length of voice calls is decreasing. But this written mass doesn't have much in common with the written word: any literary style has long since gone and its formulations are much more akin to the spoken word. 'Where R U?' This text that everyone has written at least once in their life is a good example. You've written a message to someone but the instantaneous nature of the exchange makes it feel like you've spoken to them, as if they were in front of you. We can now even use voice messages, perfectly blending the spontaneous aspect of chatting and the asynchronous quality of writing.

7. What is true? What is false?

The word 'truth' can be understood in at least two very different ways:

– When I say something that doesn't match reality, I'm wrong, therefore I'm making a mistake. I think that it's Monday, but it's actually Tuesday. In this case, the truth would be the alignment of what I think with reality.
– When I don't say what I'm thinking, I'm lying. I claim that it's Monday, but I know that today is actually Tuesday. In this case, the truth would be the alignment of what I say with what I really think.

'To err is human', yes, but lying also seems to be. The tension between what is true and what is false emerged at the same time as language. They've walked hand in hand ever since, and both have been put to very different uses. The upcoming Venn diagram allows us to distinguish, zone by zone, in the analogue world:

1. What is false, with the intention of causing harm.

There are many examples of those who have wanted to rewrite history: slander and defamation have always existed. Over a century later, the fake handwritten note from the Dreyfus affair, which tore France in half, is still talked about. Sometimes what is wrong inflicts harm with intention, counterfeiting and plagiarism for example.

2. What is false, with no intention of causing harm.

From erroneous figures sent without checking, to hastily written translations, or misunderstood humour, there are numerous cases of false information being circulated without malice. The 1942 movie *Casablanca* was filmed in Rick's café, where you can still enjoy a meal today. But the restaurant was built ten years after the film wrapped. So, true or false? Similarly, Mercator deliberately distorted the map of the world to make it easier to navigate the oceans. As French geographers Sylvain Genevois and Matthieu Noucher put it, 'Cartography is the art of omission'.[10]

3. The truth with the intention of causing harm.

Cases of blackmail are rife, the deliberate publication of private information is the stock of a certain press, and industrial espionage is a common practice between competing companies.

4. The truth with no intention of causing harm.

Out of clumsiness, it sometimes happens that we say things we shouldn't have. But more importantly, telling the truth can be therapeutic, salutary even. At the end of apartheid, the risk of payback was high, given the scale of the abuses committed. Nelson Mandela and Desmond Tutu could neither declare an unacceptable general amnesty nor sentence tens of thousands of people to jail time. They

Figure 15. *Solvay conference, Benjamin Couprie, 1911*

10. Matthieu Noucher, Sylvain Genevois and Xemartin Laborde, *Le Blanc des Cartes : Quand le vide s'éclaire* (Paris, 2024).

defused the unbearable tension by setting up a 'Truth and Reconciliation' commission and pledged forgiveness in exchange for confessions.

The struggle between what is true and what is false is as old as time, and technology has long been a weapon in this struggle.

In 1911, the first Solvay conference was held in Brussels. The picture from the event is both famous and infamous. The company's CEO, Ernest Solvay, had successfully invited several Nobel Prize winners (or soon-to-be Nobel Prize winners) to work together, including Albert Einstein and Marie Curie, the only woman in attendance. In the photo, Ernest Solvay, with his white moustache, is seen sitting at the end of the table. But he didn't attend the meeting! So fake news, indeed. How? The picture was reworked to make it look like Solvay had worked alongside the attending geniuses.

At the beginning of the digital era, new tools were created to make it possible to fake things. In February of 1982, the cover of the *National Geographic Magazine*, featuring two Egyptian pyramids, was particularly compelling. But once again, it was a ... fake! The original size of the picture could not meet the vertical constraints of the cover, so the early adopters and pioneers of Photoshop nudged the pyramid at the back to the right, so that it fit on the cover! The photographer unsurprisingly complained, and the publication later apologized.

The struggle is as old as time, but with the emergence of the internet, the battlefield has changed beyond recognition. New weapons are now available, new strategies are popping up all over the place and new types of fighters are being recruited. New concepts are even being invented, such as 'alternative facts' or 'post-truth'. On the internet, in just one click, someone's lie becomes a million others' mistake.

A rift is occurring nowadays because four major innovations mean that it's possible to create weapons of mass persuasion on the internet. These innovations relate respectively to the camouflaging of algorithms, their customization, their efficiency and their pace.

- It is possible today to produce very subtle fakes called 'deep fakes', or when the most advanced technology is used at the service of forgery. A good developer can today make whomever they want say whatever they want, and say it the whole world over ...
- It is generally difficult to know where a rumour starts and where it ends. The second innovation of cyber-liers provides a solution for this weakness. The internet basically knows everything about everyone, so it is now relatively easy to aim a tailored rumour to group A and a completely different but just as targeted rumour to group B.
- Not only do rumours now know who to target on the internet, they also know how to target their weaknesses. The third innovation is the presence of cognitive science specialists alongside the algorithm designers. These attention pirates have put psychology at the service of technology in order to create a new form of dependency, or even of addiction, to screens.
- The fourth innovation is the fact that computers can be programmed to send millions of lies, continuously.

5. *These four new elements have all come together and mean that It's now possible to produce perfect, custom-made, efficient fakes, automatically, 24/7. The centre of our Venn diagram is a busy place!*

The three remaining areas of the Venn diagram, like its centre, pertain to our digital world, and can easily be illustrated by current affairs:

6. The truth with the intention of causing harm.

Combining information from different algorithms is more powerful than ever and will provide the information to the highest bidder, as was the case with the Cambridge Analytica scandal. Spyware in smartphones allows for a whole new level of surveillance. Another simpler example, repeatedly showing Joe Biden catching his feet in the carpet is also a way of harming him, without even lying.

7. The truth with no intention of causing harm.

This could for example be a clumsy email, in which you answer in a very personal way and accidentally hit 'Reply to all'. At best, it's embarrassing, at worst, the consequences can be disastrous. And sometimes it is done with good intentions: Assange and Snowden revealed true information hoping it would do good.

8. What is false, with no intention of causing harm.

Many artists find themselves in this situation. Étienne Klein once posted online an image of a slice of chorizo, claiming that it was a new photo of the Proxima Centauri star! That was his way of inviting everyone to be a bit more critical in their thinking.

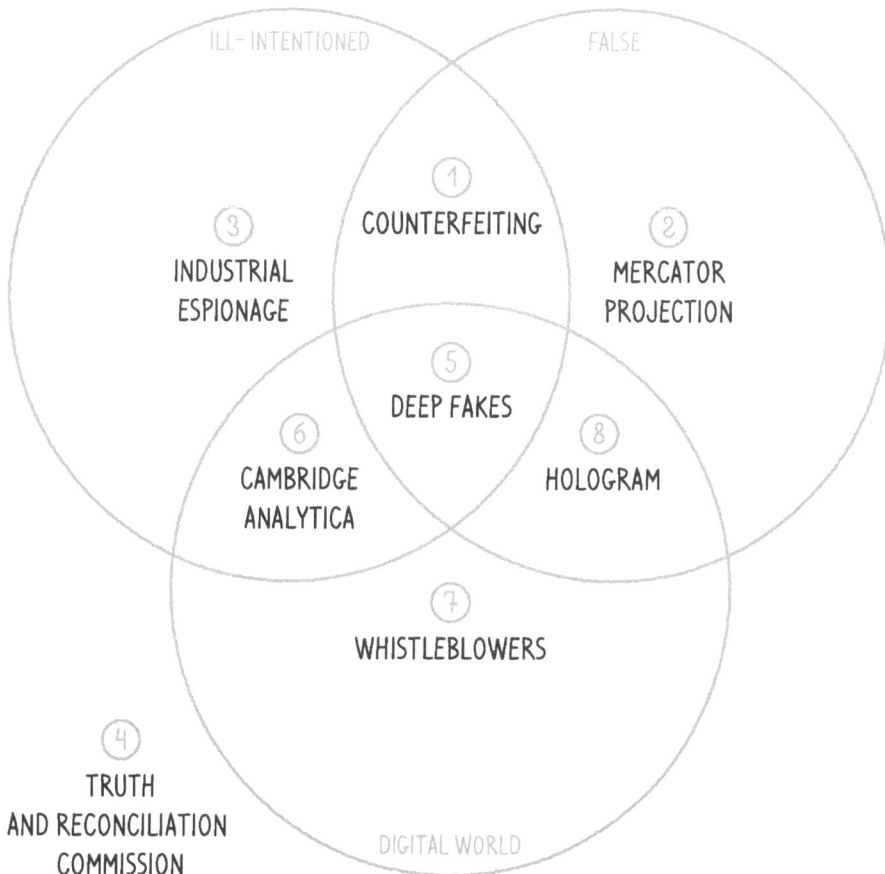

ILL-INTENTIONED

FALSE

① COUNTERFEITING

③ INDUSTRIAL ESPIONAGE

② MERCATOR PROJECTION

⑤ DEEP FAKES

⑥ CAMBRIDGE ANALYTICA

⑧ HOLOGRAM

⑦ WHISTLEBLOWERS

④ TRUTH AND RECONCILIATION COMMISSION

DIGITAL WORLD

Chapter 4 – 'It's only words'

The language of Europe is translation.
– Umberto Eco

The title of this chapter is an ironic reference to something which is often said about a declaration, when it is deemed to be insignificant and not constraining: 'it's only words'. But of course, as the Bee Gees understood, words are all we have![1] Saying 'it's only words' is always true, regardless of what is being said: this type of declaration is called a tautology. There are also declarations which are always false, like 'Je dis ça, je dis rien' in French (which translates literally to 'I'm saying this, I'm not saying anything'): they're called contradictions. We will come back to them in Chapter 6, when we talk about logic.

4.1. Misnaming things in a digital world

When I arrived at a hotel the other night, the receptionist handed me a small white plastic rectangle and kindly said: 'Here is your key'. What a coincidence. I had spent my day at a company where that very same morning, a security agent had also handed me a small white plastic rectangle but had kindly said: 'Here is your badge'.

How strange. Here were two identical objects with completely different names!

This makes me smile, but it also makes me think, because words always mean something, they are not neutral. Language is a frame of reference through which we interpret the world and can therefore influence our actions. Bitcoin is a good example of this! Simply calling it 'virtual money' would have sounded like nothing more than a global game on the internet. Calling it 'cryptocurrency', however, gives the illusion that there is an underlying monetary policy conducted by responsible people. This was not the case: when bitcoin started out, the programmers were indeed very knowledgeable, but also uncontrollable. They developed an amazing algorithm, but it was mysterious and secret.

To paraphrase Albert Camus, who we've already cited, misnaming technologies adds to the unhappiness of a digital society.

At least five specific cases quickly become apparent:

Missing words

Anyone who has seen a 3D printer in action can clearly see that it is in no way a printer. So why do we call it that and not a 'cyber sculptor', for example? Because of analog laziness again. A new object is born nameless and is put into an existing category loaded with a specific difference. In 1985, I named my first book *Les Infoducs*[2] to describe how a sluggish metaphor unfortunately gave its name to the information highways.

---

1. Bee Gees, *Words* (1968).
2. Cited above.

Blurry words

Some words are new but have no clear definition! The 'cloud' is a good example of this. The so often quoted digital 'cloud', not the fluffy white ones we see in the sky, is in fact made up of thousands of energy-consuming servers, contractually well-anchored on the ground. It is actually more of a thick commercial fog where no one really has a clear view of what is being paid for. But we must congratulate the creative people who came up with the name,[3] it's very poetic! Even though the cloud is actually just someone else's computer.

Inappropriate words

I'm sure you've already heard of autonomous cars, but let's be honest, has there ever been a less autonomous object? This car runs thanks to a network of sensors, a sophisticated GPS system, complex software and a whole lot of algorithms ... The car might be automatic but is certainly not – and luckily not at all – autonomous. Let's not forget that when we grant autonomy to a territory, it is then allowed to make its own laws ... We could also wonder why we call 'wireless' a global 'wireless' network which relies almost entirely on physical undersea cables.

Words translated too quickly

'Free' in English can be translated into French as *libre*, meaning 'no longer confined', but also as *gratuit*, meaning 'without cost or payment'. Is 'free software' available for everyone to use, or is it free of charge? We talk about artificial intelligence, but aren't the letters CIA the initials of the Central Intelligence Agency? Because yes, 'intelligence' also means 'surveillance' in English, or even 'espionage'. That sheds a new light on internet intelligence, does it not? When a fridge beeps because we forgot to close the door, we call it intelligent. Would you like to be called intelligent like a fridge?

Words that age badly

Some words have been stripped of their original meaning. Is it not surprising that we still measure engine output in 'horsepower'? Files are no longer actual files and being a 'friend' on Facebook has nothing to do with actual friendship. After all, journalists still write 'papers' and work in an industry called the 'press'. Gutenberg must be smiling about the continued use of this vocabulary.

When we say we're 'connected', in fact, it is quite the opposite! Let's take the example of scientists who study the planets and the Solar System. In ancient times, Thales, Aristarchus or Ptolemy looked up at the sky with a naked eye. Nothing interfered with their relationship with the planets or the stars. During the Renaissance period, Galileo used a telescope and saw what no one had seen before, such as the phases of Venus or Jupiter's satellites. Halley was even able to observe his comet and verify Newton's law. Undeniable progress in science has been made, but were these sleepwalkers[4] connected to the stars or to their telescope? Today's astrophysicists don't even look out of the window, they are glued to their screens, completely disconnected from the sky and all it contains.

3.   Antonio Regalado, 'Who Coined "Cloud Computing"?', *MIT Technology Review*, 31 October 2011, <https://www.technolog yreview.com/2011/10/31/257406/who-coined-cloud-computing/> [accessed 29 May 2024].
4.   Arthur Koestler, *The Sleepwalkers: A History of Man's Changing Vision of the Universe* (London, 1959).

There is much talk about connected objects, but when it's a watch or a pacemaker, shouldn't it be 'connected subjects'? Shouldn't the IOT, the internet of things, be called the IOP, the internet of people?

Apparently, we live in a 'real time' world. But if this is the case, how did we qualify time fifty years ago? Unreal? Virtual? Deferred? Artificial? We talk about an augmented, virtual, blended reality. And since Covid-19, the term 'new reality' has emerged as a topical talking point! But who can define all of these for us?

Big data is not simply more data. It should be called 'other data' because it is all the traces we leave on the internet and there is no equivalent in the past.

4.2. A system of sentences

Philosophers only work with words, so it should come as no surprise that this book contains hardly any numbers. But words are 'within' us and are therefore subjective and arbitrary simplifications. The words in our model are all compromises, trying to get as close to reality as possible.

Amongst all the words that take part in the induction process is the word 'language', as shown in the full I/D model. This is normal since a language is indeed a way of representing oneself and simplifying the world. Two people who speak different languages therefore think in different ways!

Depending on the context, the French word 'aimer' can be translated into English as 'like' or 'love'. The English word 'power' can be translated into French, again depending on the context, as *'pouvoir'*, *'puissance'*, *'énergie'* or even *'force'*. And any engineer will be able to tell you just how much the meaning of these words differs!

The word 'language' could therefore be placed on the left and on the right in the diagram. Words are indeed part of the reality that we face but they also reflect it.

To grasp the concept of language, we will work in four stages.

Sign

Our starting point will be the concept of 'sign', which we will define as follows:

a sign tells us something that isn't linked to itself.

At first glance, this definition is slightly mysterious but becomes clearer thanks to the use of everyday examples, until it is fully transparent and clear. When a referee whistles and waves a red card, the aim isn't to make the player think of the colour red. Instead, the referee is using a sign that refers to the foul and the player's exclusion from the pitch.

Signs are omnipresent. When we gesture to indicate a direction, we don't mean to draw attention to our hand. There seems to be a moment of forgetfulness with signs.

As the proverb goes: 'When a wise man points at the Moon, the imbecile examines the finger'.

Language philosophers may disagree on a number of topics but the concept of signs is inescapable, and no author or thinker can disregard it. We can conceive a language without speech, without communication, without words, without tools, even without humans. But a language without signs is impossible.

Word

If I ask you how many colours there are on a chessboard, your immediate answer will be two. But if the question is how many words are in the expression 'hand in hand'? Your automatic answer will probably be three, but the correct answer is actually two.

This brings us to a second definition:

> *a word is a linguistic sign.*

The common trait of all words is that they mean something. Whether they are compound words, adjectives, pronouns, prepositions or verbs, each and every one of them has a meaning.

But this definition doesn't solve all problems. What about 'wow' for example: is it a word or a sign? But at least we're moving forward!

Sentence

Just as a brick is a building block of a house or an atom is a building block of a molecule, the word is a building block of language. That being said, a group of words still doesn't make up a language. A word, when isolated, is relative. Its full meaning isn't apparent until it is placed alongside others, which is the definition of a system. If I say 'wind turbine' I'm not actually saying anything, which is paradoxical. If I were to say 'look at the wind turbine' or 'why is there a wind turbine?', these become two expressions of language. The word is most certainly an element but it's only the sentence that gives a real dimension to language. We can therefore say that:

> *the sentence is the minimal unit of language.*[5]

There is no randomness in what ties words together since the links obey combinatorial rules. In a language, words are the raw material, and rules allow them to be joined together in sentences.

A child who knows a few words of French doesn't speak French. The same can be said for a tourist who learns a few necessary words for their trip. At best, they will be able to get by, but they don't know the rules.

These rules can be:

- Grammatical: proper spelling, conjugation and past participles shall be enforced.
- Logical: look out for logical fallacies and poorly constructed argumentation.
- Stylistic: sentences ought to be elegant, crafted holistically from harmonious parts that fit together like the stones of a wall.

---

5.   This is a point made in John R Searle, 'What Is Language? Some Preliminary Remarks', *Etica & Politica/Ethics & Politics*, XI/1 (2009), 173–202.

Language

Let's boil it down. Amongst all signs, only a portion is made up of words, and they will only achieve language status once they come together thanks to rules. The minimal combination resulting from this coming together is the sentence. A fourth definition can therefore be put forward.

language is a system of sentences.[6]

But we're far from done covering the subject! Do you speak *English?* Or do you speak *in English?*

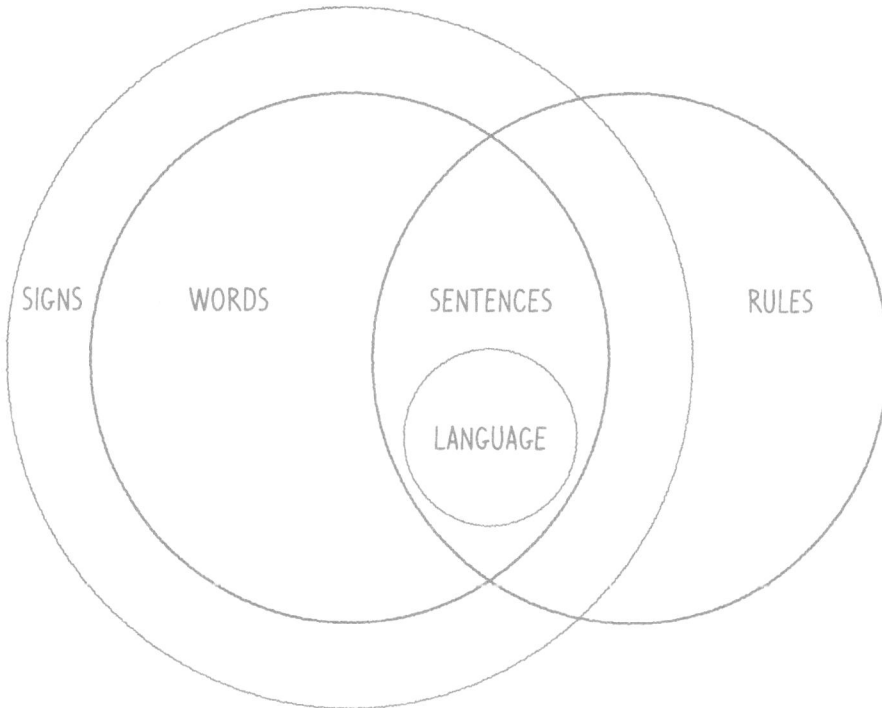

---

6.   This definition and part of the approach taken here are very similar to that exposed in Noam Chomsky, *Syntactic Structures* (The Hague, 1957).

4.3. A definition of a definition

If it were possible to write 'The ten commandments of philosophy', one of them would be about the necessity to define things properly. Philosophers are waging a never-ending fight against approximations, against blurry ideas, and they're always on the hunt for false synonyms. If you think of a philosopher as a photographer of concepts, they are constantly adjusting their lenses so that they have a clear image of a word, with nice neat edges. This imperative of definition is inseparable from philosophy ... as is the difficulty of complying with it! The great thinkers faced this challenge and some of them ran into great difficulties.

In order to define courage, Socrates was happy to put it somewhere between cowardice and recklessness. Saint Augustine claimed to know what time is, but recognized that he couldn't define it if asked to do so. Descartes, who argued for the need to have 'clear and distinct' ideas, never explained how to achieve this. And more recently, Wittgenstein has said that 'the object of philosophy is the logical clarification of thoughts'[7] ... only to then give up on his project!

Different ways to do

In order to describe, comment and explain what things are, we use two main methods. Defining a dog as 'an animal that barks' or a hammer as 'a tool used to drive in a nail', is the first of them, that of genus and specific difference. The definition is therefore made up of two parts: a whole that the thing belongs to (the type) and what differentiates the thing from the other items in the whole (specificity).

By using this method, we're behaving like surveyors. When defining a terrain, it is necessary to specify where the area is, and to trace a line that separates it from neighbouring terrains. And the same applies when defining a concept: clearly mark out what belongs in the perimeter of the definition and what is outside. In French, *définir* is literally showing where the end is, as the word contains *fin*, 'the end'.

But we're not this rigorous in everyday life. When a child asks 'what's this?', we answer in different ways. If they hold up an ingot, the answer will be 'that's gold'. If they hold up a geometrical figure with four right angles, the answer will be 'that's a rectangle'. If the child is in Paris and pointing at a large pointed steel tower, the answer will be 'that's the Eiffel tower'. And if the child is intrigued by a kettle, they'll receive an explanation about how it heats water.

These four types of questions all relate to four different perspectives. The first is about matter, the second about shape, the third about origin and the fourth about finality. Philosophy enthusiasts will recognize here Aristotle's four causes, and when they're considered together they can be seen as a definition. But most of the time we only use one of the four causes to define something, and rigour takes a serious hit.

---

7. 'Der Zweck der Philosophie ist die logische Klärung der Gedanken'. Ludwig Wittgenstein, *Tractatus Logico-Philosophicus*, trans. by Charles Kay Ogden (London, 1922).

These first two methods aren't contradictory, they even overlap in places. Amateurs will have noticed that the material cause often acts like a type, and the shape cause acts like a difference. Aristotle, why is it always Aristotle ...

The first two methods may be relatively simple and common, but they don't always work!

Ludwig Wittgenstein gives the example of a game.[8] Even if we admit that the concept of 'game' belongs to the very wide category of 'human activity', the Austrian philosopher admits that it isn't possible to determine the specific differences that make these activities 'games', as opposed to other types of activities.

Let's consider Monopoly, musical chairs, table tennis, Fortnite, a puzzle, war games and power games. What are their common characteristics? The question can't be answered. A game of cat and mouse has nothing in common with sudoku.

According to Wittgenstein, if everything that we call 'game' can indeed be put in the same whole, it's not because of a common characteristic, but because of a chain of analogies that link them all together.

- There are common points between Monopoly and table tennis: a clear place where the game takes place (a board and a table), one or more opponents, ...
- More analogies appear between table tennis and a game of poker: intimidation techniques, trying to put your opponent off their game, ...
- Poker shares a dimension of non-verbal communication with a power game, ...

When moving between games, similarities appear, some traits appear as common whereas others disappear. In order to characterize these analogies, Wittgenstein used the expression 'family resemblance'.

It therefore becomes possible to define things without putting them into homogeneous and rigid boxes. Thus we move from a system that is limited to categories to an infinite network of classes, from a clumsy and vain process of classification to a process of belonging that is rich and creative.

It can be harder sometimes: some concepts are called 'primitive notions' when they can't be defined in terms of previously defined concepts. For example, in geometry, *point* and *line*.

In this case criteria are needed. Rather than define suffering, let's instead characterize a person who is suffering. If it isn't possible to define justice, let's at least define what allows us to know whether a judgement is just or unjust.

Criteria of a good definition

Regardless of the method used, some definitions are better than others. A definition should be short enough to be memorized easily. It should go straight to the essence. Being able to laugh is indeed a

---

8.   Ludwig Wittgenstein, *Philosophical Investigations*, trans. by Gertrude Elizabeth Margaret Anscombe (1953).

difference that is specific to human beings, but it's better to define them as animals that are capable of thinking.

A definition can only deal with universality. I can try to define what a woman is, but I'll never be able to define Marilou, my grand-daughter.

A good definition can't contain the word that is being defined. Saying that a country doctor is a doctor who practises their medical activity in a rural setting isn't an efficient definition. The extreme case is pure circularity: we could define a letterbox in a circular manner as 'a box into which letters are deposited'.

Moreover, it's best to avoid definitions which:

- contain negatives: hobbies are activities that humans do when they're not working.
- are built on analogies and metaphors: a brain is a very powerful computer.
- are subjective: alcohol is one of the biggest dangers for drivers.
- are based on etymology, because the origin of a word is never certain and the meaning of concepts can evolve over time.

If defining a tree, a trip, geometry or happiness is seemingly an easy exercise, let's push things even further and take a shot at defining … a definition!

A definition is the statement of the meaning of a term whose action is to make it distinct and clear.[9]

---

9.   This definition is partly taken from Wikipedia's entry for 'Definition'.

4.4. The life of words

When observing the words in the I/D model, it becomes clear that some of them have retained the same meaning for centuries. If we define a value as: 'an idea of what is desirable', or if we define a belief as: 'a certitude without proof', then this could already have been done before we entered a digital world. And the same can be said for the word 'concept', which is worthy of a closer look.

If everything that is produced by our minds can be called ideas, then concepts are in a way the reusable and recyclable part of this production. 'Brexit', 'start-up', 'hobby', 'global warming' or even 'magazine' are all concepts because they come up regularly in conversation.

There are two different types of concepts:

– Some are a specific assemblage of elements. They are unique and singular concepts. For example, Brexit and global warming.
– Others on the other hand are an assemblage of specific elements. They are general concepts that become tools for categorization. Within the concept of hobby, you'll find bridge but also beekeeping.

Both types of concepts are useful but in the land of concepts, nuance is an important factor. It intervenes in the link that unites the whole and the parts. The Economist is an example of a magazine, but border control isn't an example of Brexit.

So you can abstract without generalizing, but you can't generalize without abstracting. In this second group here, when a concept contributes a criterion for classification, and therefore gets given the name of the category.

We should take each word of the I/D model and ask ourselves if the digital world has transformed their topicality, their meaning or their significance, and whether the technological context we find ourselves in should lead to a 'reset' of their understanding.

For Plato, creativity, for example, simply did not exist – 'eureka moments' are just 'I remember moments' –, and when he spoke about reality, nobody was talking about *real* time, nobody was mentioning virtual or even augmented *reality*. When Aristotle was looking for the causes of movements, he used a kind of logic which encapsulates only a fraction of the reasoning scope.

A philosopher's work is never-ending and relentless. We have already looked at how words such as 'model' have seen their meaning fundamentally change with the arrival of digital technology. The same can be said about most words in the I/D model. Let's take a closer look at five more examples.

Category

As we've seen in Chapter 3, this might just be the greatest idea of all time! In response to Plato, who denied all theories of thinking, Aristotle suggested a compromise. We should browse through reality, he said, and organize it into categories. We will definitely leave some information behind – the diversity of the particular – and a new general science called 'logic' emerged. But who can choose the appropriate set of categories? According to Aristotle, this is the responsibility of human beings. Kant agrees with him, even though he places categories within the subject and no longer within the object. Causality for example, is *a priori* a category of understanding.

Have humans lost their monopoly on defining categories?

Identity

'Who is Charlie?' This question can have two possible meanings, depending on the context.

Either you're looking to identify Charlie, so you want to establish who Charlie is amongst a crowd of people in front of you. It's his quantitative identity that you're interested in. His date of birth, his first name, his address.

Or you're looking to establish what *type of person* Charlie is. You're after what characterizes him, in other words his qualitative identity. You want to know more about how he lives his life, his tastes, his values, his dreams and his shortcomings.

These two meanings reflect two very different disciplines, respectively logic and psychology, which cohabitate on the internet.

If someone malicious wants to pretend to be you, they'll usurp your 'logical identity', which can sometimes boil down to a password. On the other hand, what people say about you, your 'digital identity' is more hazy and subjective.

Experience

Where does human knowledge come from?

Philosophers traditionally give two possible answers. According to rationalists, the starting point of all reasoning is knowledge. Without prior categories, we are not able to organize and interpret any of the information that our senses dispense. Empiricists, however, claim the opposite. They maintain that the experience of the senses alone is the source of all our knowledge. Before coming into contact with the world, the human mind is a blank canvas, a *tabula rasa*, completely devoid of ideas.

But today, most scientists do not belong to either of these groups. They use computers. And mathematical models have mostly replaced test tubes in the pharmaceutical industry too, in the same way they have replaced wind tunnels in the aerospace industry. But what kind of experience will you ... experience in a flight simulator?

Attention

Attention is a rare and valuable resource. Just like water, it can be polluted, misused or troubled. But it can also be protected and encouraged. With the advent of the internet, it's at the centre of everyone's ... attention. The value of an application is judged on the time that users spend on it. Terms such as 'attention economy' and 'attention capitalism' have even been coined.

Astonishment

According to Socrates and his followers, *thaumazein* (translated as 'to wonder') is a key pillar in thinking. They used it to name the ability to be astonished, which is the gateway to any great idea. According to Aristotle: 'science begins when you are surprised that things are the way they are'. This attitude is still fruitful today but should be accompanied by a second type of astonishment: to be surprised because something is NOT! The digital economy is an unlimited space for creativity and, upon closer inspection, many products and services do not exist today because offering them WAS not a possibility.

Chapter 5 – This is not thinking

If you come to a fork in the road, you must take it.

5.1. The tree of thinking

Researchers in various disciplines have long tried to understand how human beings think. Most of them seem to agree that the brain works in two very different ways.

And that is exactly what we have just done! As far as we're concerned, the first phase of thought imagines, diverges and unlocks the field of possibilities (induction). The second phase judges, converges and chooses (deduction). But if we were to stop there, that would give the impression that thought is essentially an individual effort which seldom depends on context. This is however not the case. Whether you're a champion in creativity, so primarily in induction, or a master in logic where you're confronted with reality, the ideas that are elaborated are indeed destined to be presented to third parties. They should therefore be presented, defended, communicated, negotiated or even sold ...

The third mode of thinking

Irrespective of the quality of the concept that is being forged and the judgements that are being formulated, these ideas will one day be confronted with those of others. We must therefore speak well but also know how to listen, explain and understand other people's points of view. We have to convince or persuade them. The discussion's context must be taken into account.

What is the point of having brilliant ideas if you're then faced with people who don't want to listen, have hidden agendas or worse, are acting in bad faith?

When the context is unfavourable, thought must focus on eluding semantic traps, it must distinguish the truth from the lies, be suspicious of oratory effects and even trace misleading arguments such as begging the question or false dilemmas.

With today's internet offering sophists the tool they've always dreamed of, being logical and creative is no longer enough. The mind must also be critical, which is the third way of thinking.

Unexpected logic

Let's take a step back and give ourselves a new perspective. The spectrum of thought is vast: we're thinking when we're multiplying, but we're also thinking when we're dreaming at night! These are indeed very different cognitive steps but it's still the same brain that is in action. If certain forms of thought such as mathematics can claim to be fully disciplined, it seems that science, however, cannot explain the logic of nightmares!

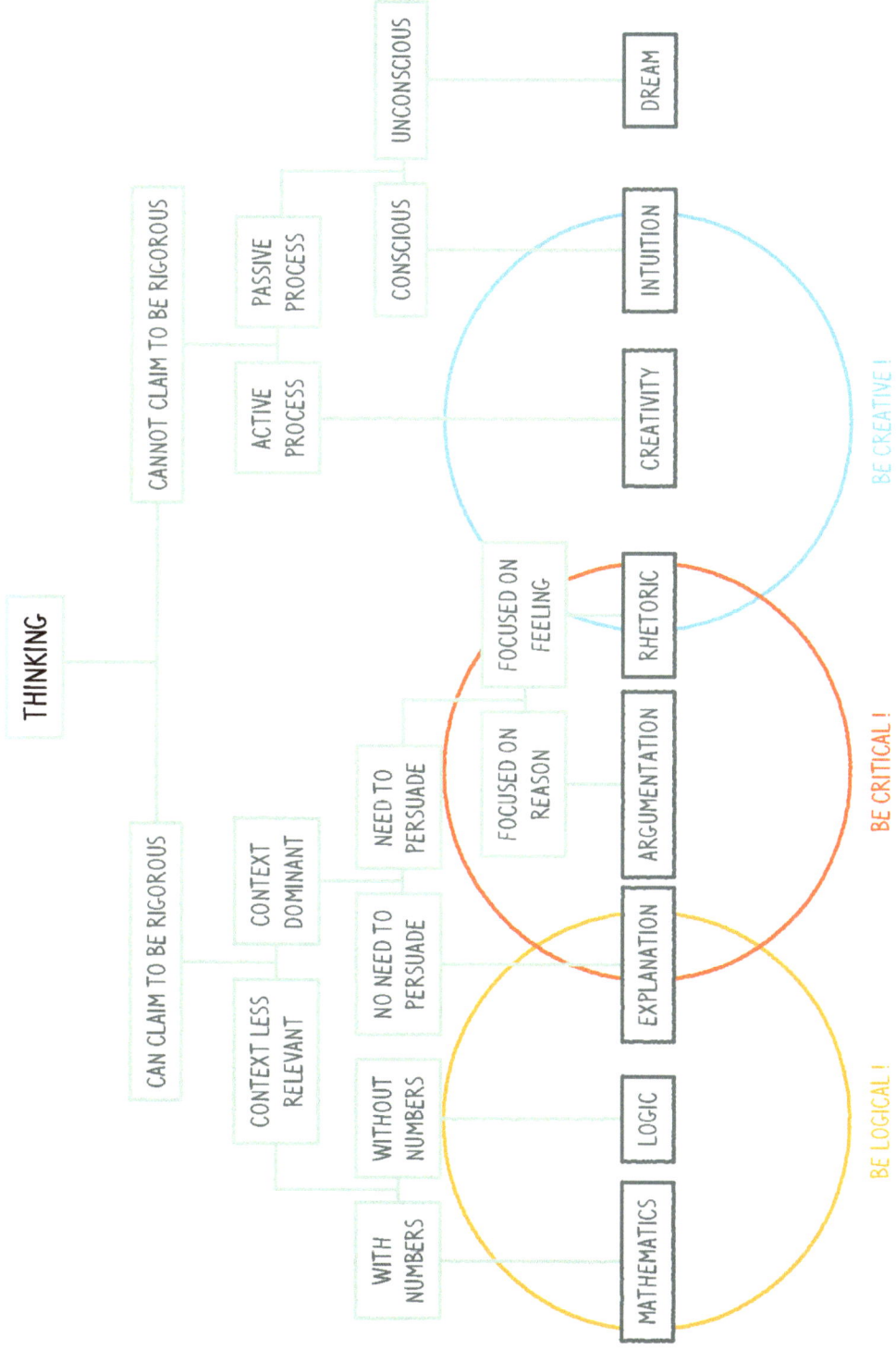

THINKING

CANNOT CLAIM TO BE RIGOROUS

- PASSIVE PROCESS
  - UNCONSCIOUS
    - DREAM
  - CONSCIOUS
- ACTIVE PROCESS
  - CREATIVITY
  - INTUITION

BE CREATIVE !

CAN CLAIM TO BE RIGOROUS

CONTEXT DOMINANT

NEED TO PERSUADE
- FOCUSED ON FEELING
  - RHETORIC
- FOCUSED ON REASON
  - ARGUMENTATION

BE CRITICAL !

CONTEXT LESS RELEVANT

NO NEED TO PERSUADE
- EXPLANATION

WITHOUT NUMBERS
- LOGIC

WITH NUMBERS
- MATHEMATICS

BE LOGICAL !

CAN BE TAUGHT AND LEARNED

−

+

Different forms of reasoning are identifiable between these extremes and can be merged into three groups, as explained in the tree of thinking. On the left, we have mathematics which mostly feeds off numbers (even though there are graphical demonstrations of some theorems) and logical thought which manipulates only concepts.

Logic is the field which studies the conditions of valid reasoning or, more commonly, the conditions of the correct use of the word 'therefore'.

The group on the right merges two other forms of conscious thought: creativity and intuition, which are very distinct. Intuition is the 'reasoning before reasoning', which means that it is difficult to explain what led to it. Creativity on the other hand isn't a logical approach but has a hidden logic that is unexpected, that we only understand in hindsight. A finding is the result of reasoning but it's only identifiable after the new idea has emerged. That's why we often hear 'why didn't we think of this sooner?'

Critique and criteria

The third group is called 'critical thinking'. It doesn't claim to be a science, doesn't state any truths, doesn't prove anything, but leads us to constructive doubt and judgement. It pushes us to stay awake, to be open to context and to constantly better ourselves. It is the condition of useful discussions. Without it, we cannot really 'get things done'.

This form of thought, which only exists in interactions, can be divided into three very distinct areas:

- If the counterpart presumably agrees with the proposed thesis, it's an *explanation*.
- If they need convincing, then *argumentation* is built.
- If the presentation requires little reasoning but focuses more on emotions, it's *rhetorical*.

An argument is a series of claims (assertions, allegations, etc.), the last of which is the conclusion. The others are called premises. There are two possible cases: either the reasoning is valid because it complies with the laws of logic, or it has been built voluntarily to mislead the interlocutor and is then called 'misleading' or 'fallacious'. It gives the impression that the reasoning is correct but this isn't the case. It has a dazzling and jaw-dropping side, but the argumentation is flawed, ambushed, rigged.

Critical thinking can therefore be defined as the vital toolbox that is needed when we're confronted with misleading arguments. It allows us to establish whether there are sufficient reasons to believe or do what others would like us to.

The purpose of critical thinking isn't to provide certainty but rather to protect ourselves from brainwashing and to drive debate and decision. Its main tool is – etymology is no coincidence – the criterion, which we can define, at first approximation, as the 'rule or principle for judging'.

The purpose of the tree of thinking was definitely not chronology, it is nevertheless what we ended up with. Maybe this is not a coincidence; it reflects humankind's desire to push science forward in order to understand its own very nature. Mathematics appeared sometime around 3000 BC and Plato believed it to be the archetype of perfect Ideas. Aristotle introduced logic and connected explanation with argumentation and rhetoric. Creativity was up next but was not accepted as a possibility until Kant and the Enlightenment. Intuition and dreams were only explored by Bergson and Freud at the beginning of the twentieth century.

The possibility of learning – and in French, the same word means 'to learn' and 'to teach' – decreases as you move from left to right on the tree of thinking.

Double bind

Regardless of the quality of the concepts that are being crafted ('Be creative!') and the inferences that are being built ('Be logical!'), we will one day or another be confronted with people whose beliefs, opinions and ideas differ from ours ('Be critical!').

It's worth pointing out that only one of those three imperatives is non-paradoxical. If we ask somebody to walk us through valid reasoning, what follows is logically compatible with our own order. But the other two imperatives are a kind of 'double bind' injunction leading to a logical stalemate.

By definition, you shouldn't blindly agree to comply with a given rule if you are in creativity mode. And that includes the one telling you to be creative!

By definition, you shouldn't blindly agree to comply with a way of thinking if you are in critical mode. And that includes the one telling you to be critical!

5.2. Three ways of not being a pipe

You've probably noticed a contradiction in the previous paragraphs, or at least a discrepancy, a gap between the model and the text. And you would be right since we have claimed that creativity somehow follows a logical process but, on the model, the two imperatives have no common area ...

But this shouldn't come as a surprise: a model is never true and only pretends to be useful! And seen from another perspective, the same three clusters can be organized as a Venn diagram, as shown below:

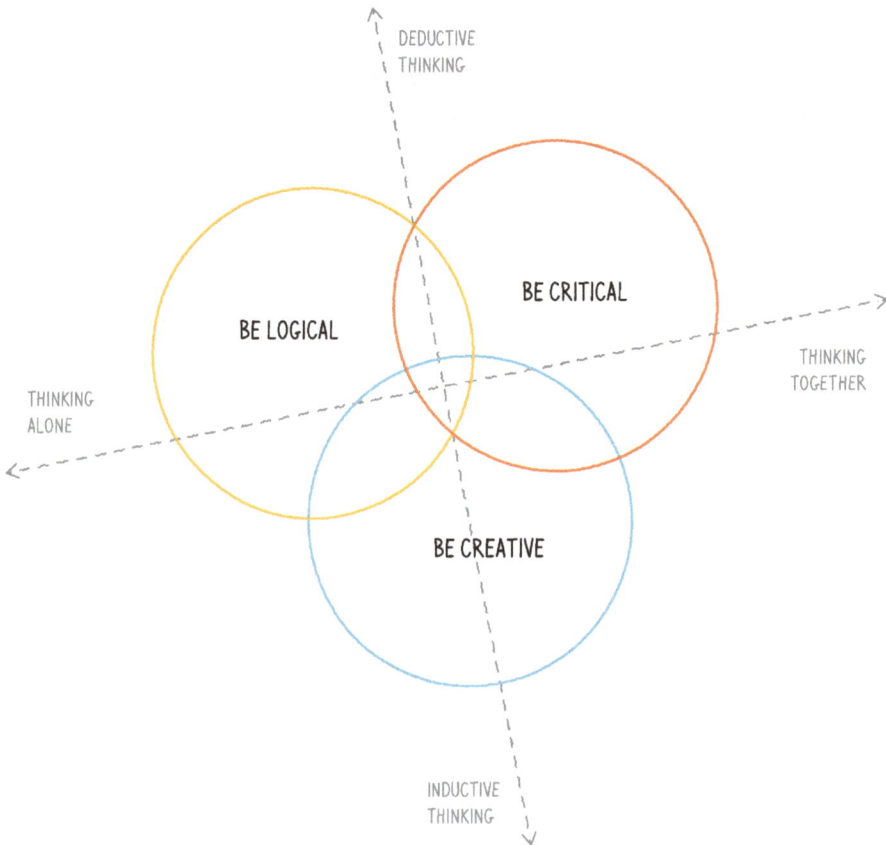

Seen from this perspective, the three groups have blurred boundaries and partially overlap each other. Nevertheless, they allow us to distribute the forms of reasoning that are identifiable in everyday life according to their salient features.

There are different models for different purposes, and none of them are true! Let's take another look at Magritte's painting: the various depictions of the same pipe look very different despite them all being derived from the same object. The pipe is the same and the points of view vary but none of the images represents a pipe, just three ways how not to be a pipe!

* This is not a pipe.

* This either.

* And this either.

A whole chapter will be devoted to each of these three ways of thinking. But we should first say a few words about what they share and the markers they have in common. Let's explore these shared zones and their blurred boundaries.

5.3. Duelling modes

Be logical and be critical

Logical thinking and critical thinking have a common ancestor: Aristotle. The Greek philosopher used a three-storey structure to explain how the mind works. And he used it both to test the formal validity of a line of reasoning and to denounce false arguments. In a way, his model was the first algorithm in the history of artificial intelligence!

According to Aristotle, thought unfolds in three stages:

Conceptualization	'I'm thinking of something'	A student
Judgement	'I think something about it'	Students are tomorrow's decision-makers
Reasoning	'I conclude something'	I need to consider my long-term strategy
		Students are tomorrow's decision-makers
		Therefore I need to think about students

We'll take a deep dive into this in Chapters 6 and 8, but this three-storey model shared by logical and critical thought allows us to put forward the following comparison:

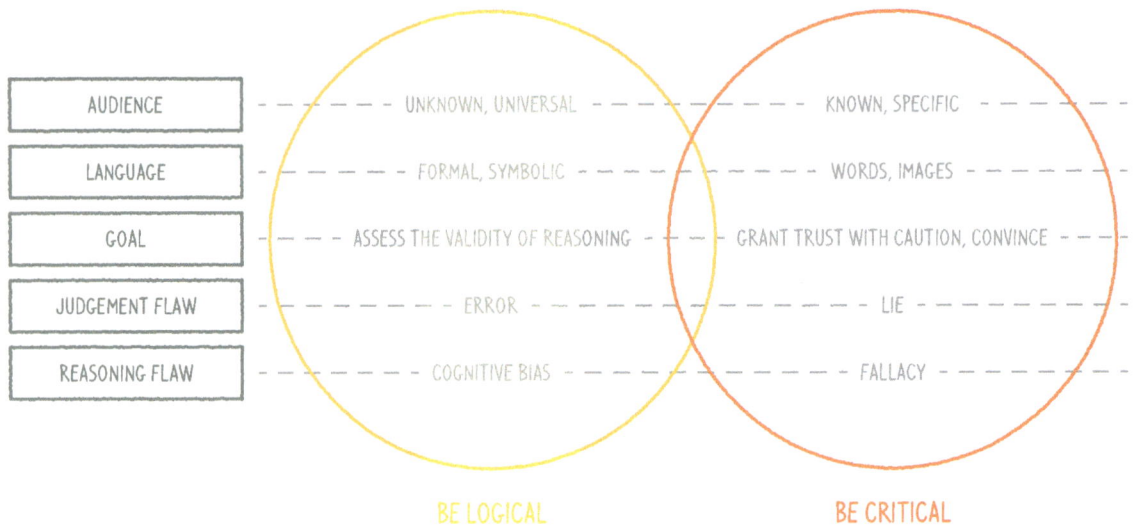

	BE LOGICAL	BE CRITICAL
AUDIENCE	UNKNOWN, UNIVERSAL	KNOWN, SPECIFIC
LANGUAGE	FORMAL, SYMBOLIC	WORDS, IMAGES
GOAL	ASSESS THE VALIDITY OF REASONING	GRANT TRUST WITH CAUTION, CONVINCE
JUDGEMENT FLAW	ERROR	LIE
REASONING FLAW	COGNITIVE BIAS	FALLACY

Be logical and be creative

Mathematics and logic are often pitted against creativity. But to do so is to forget that these two disciplines which seem to leave no place for imagination have been developed thanks to the exceptional creativity of brilliant thinkers. In mathematics, the invention of zero, of the decimal point and of complex numbers have made outstanding developments in calculation methods possible. And the same goes for logic, like for example with Aristotle's development of syllogism, the three-storey structure that was mentioned a few lines ago.

Let's now illustrate this in mathematics first, and then in logic.

Mathematics

You've been asked to pick some numbers from the list below, and their total sum must be 100.

51	36	3	15
9	17	63	6
53	42	33	72

You may think that calculating and trying is enough. Yes and no. Yes, because you'll find the answer, and no, because you could probably have reached the answer a lot faster.

This exercise highlights two types of potential approaches:

– A logical approach which requires trying all of the possible combinations and will eventually result in finding the answer, as long as you have the time to do it this way.
– A more creative approach to this exercise requires noticing something *before* you start your calculations. Have you noticed that all of the numbers, aside from 53 and 17, are multiples of 3? The problem is therefore suddenly considerably simpler because 100, the total needed, is not a multiple of 3. 100 is equal to 99 (a multiple of three) plus 1. The solution will necessarily include 53 and 17 because they add up to 70, that is to say 69, a multiple of 3, plus 1. In this case, they are the only numbers allowing us to do this. The remaining 30 is then clearly the sum of 6, 9 and 15.

This second, more 'creative' approach remains nevertheless perfectly logical. And this short metaphorical exercise reminds us just how indispensable the synergy of these two ways of thinking is, as long as they are used at the right time. After all, isn't intelligence defined as the ability to manage one's own aptitudes?

Logic

Euler established a graphical method to validate a syllogism!

Let's take three groups, S, M and P, and organize them graphically in order to obtain eight possible scenarios. In the following diagram, each zone holds elements with specific properties. Zone 2, for example, holds the elements belonging to both P and M, but not to S. The centre zone, which belongs to all circles, holds elements belonging to all three circles.

It then becomes possible to transform statements into drawings, and to demonstrate visually the validity of a syllogism.

Let's take an example. Is this syllogism valid ?

All S are M

All M are P

Hence All S are P

The answer is yes. Let's visualize the two premises.

'All S are M' would mean area 1 and 7 are empty, 'All M are P' would mean area 3 and 5 are also empty

We could then see whether all S are confined in area 4, in other words see whether... all S are P !

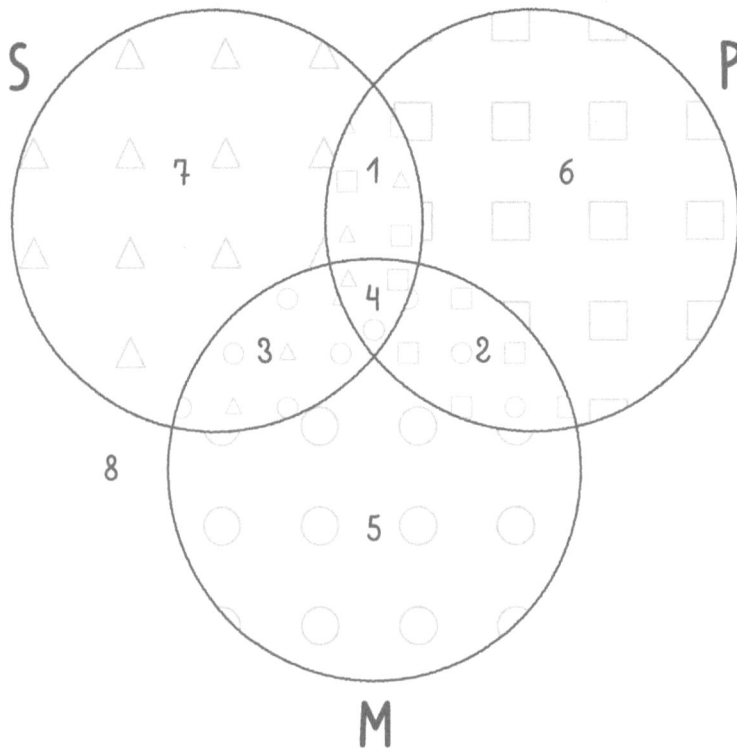

There are many links between creativity and logic. In Chapter 7 we'll look at how creativity isn't in any way illogical. Indeed, as we have said before, a creative idea is still produced by a certain logic.

Be creative and be critical

A speaker who wishes to put across their point of view can choose between two approaches.

They can try to convince their audience by using mostly logical reasoning, but they can also try to persuade them and play with the emotions of those listening in a creative way. In the first case, the speaker is in argumentation mode and in the second, in rhetorical mode. The latter is often treated separately from argumentation because there is little interaction when speaking to an assembly. We sometimes even leave critical thinking behind since some great speeches don't use any arguments!

According to Aristotle's analysis, the *logos* is the tool of conviction and can be defined as the rational capacity to continue with propositions which should lead to a conclusion. But the Greek philosopher thought it necessary to add two other elements of 'proof'. First, the *ethos*, which is using moral character as an argument, by painting themself or another as a reference, as an authority, as an element of probity. And then the *pathos*, which is the ability of great speakers to resonate with their public, choosing the words that will move them.

The *logos* is rather cold, it is the stuff of scientific evidence. *Ethos* and *pathos*, on the other hand, add a human dimension in quite a symmetrical way – *ethos* on the side of the speaker, and *pathos* on the side of the audience.

Some forms of persuasion don't use any form of *logos*. When Martin Luther King Jr. proclaimed his famous *I have a dream* speech in front of an emotional crowd in Washington, DC, no argumentation followed. That was probably the right choice.

It's not unusual to add a fourth element to the rhetoric: *kairos*. This is knowing when the time is 'right'. The *kairos* is a dimension of time that has little to do with the linear notion of *chronos* (physical time).

Critical thinking and creative thinking are both pursuing the same objective: to change perception. The aim of a speech is above all to change the perception of those listening, and a creative person is capable of easily changing their own; this will even be our way of defining creativity in Chapter 7.

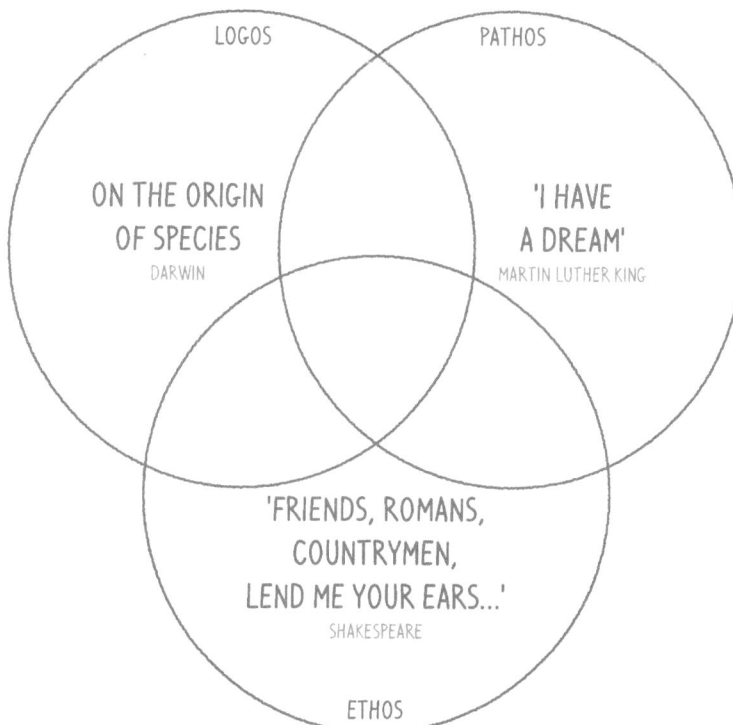

5.4. Wittgenstein's humour

As French Renaissance writer François Rabelais famously said, 'to laugh is proper to the man'.[1] Animals and machines don't laugh. Laughter has many characteristics, and one of them is of particular interest in this book: laughter can help us to understand how the mind works. If we understand why we laugh, we have a better understanding of how we think.

Lots of things can make you laugh, but we'll take a closer look at just two of them: jokes and cartoons.

Jokes

Ludwig Wittgenstein is said to have declared that it should be possible to do very serious philosophical work using only jokes. This may seem surprising coming from the Austrian genius whose life was more of a tragedy than a comedy. It's less surprising when you know how crucial the analysis of words and language was to his work.

Wittgenstein was convinced that small well-chosen jokes could clarify powerful philosophical messages. But he left it at that, leaving the reader wanting more. He only gave a few examples to support his thesis, like this one which he took great pleasure in telling whenever he discussed infinity:

Two friends meet up:

- *... 9, 5, 1, 4, 1, 3. Phew!*
- *You look exhausted.*
- *You bet! I've just recited π backwards!*

It's a great shame that Wittgenstein was so stingy with his examples. So many philosophical works are repetitive and dull, and there are so many boring texts, that a touch of humour wouldn't have gone amiss. And what if Wittgenstein was right after all?

Apart from infinity, many other philosophical concepts can be cleared up with a well-chosen joke. Here are a few hand-picked examples:

Logic

A professor asks a student:

- *What's your name?*
- *Harry without a P.*
- *But there is no P in Harry!*
- *Exactly, that's what I said!*

---

1. 'Le rire est le propre de l'homme'. François Rabelais, *Gargantua* (Lyon, 1535). Translation by Thomas Urquhart, in *The Works of Rabelais*, Books I and II, 1653.

Meta-level

– *What do you think of Western civilization?*
– *It would be a very good idea!*[2]

Linguistics

– *In a circle, what's the difference between a diameter and a radius?*
– *A radius.*

Lost in translation

– *Why did the golfer wear two sets of pants?*
– *He got a hole in one!*

Paradox

– *Are you the new guy?*
– *I don't know, I just got here ...*

Ambiguity

– *Is it true that there's a drug problem in the army?*
– *No, no. Everyone has plenty enough!*

Let's take a closer look at this last joke, because it takes us straight to the heart of the matter. In some of its uses, the word 'problem' refers to a lack of something: 'I have a cash flow problem', 'I have a time problem'. But sometimes, the word 'problem' refers to an excess of something: 'I have a cholesterol problem', 'I have a rat problem'.

As explained in our I/D model, there are therefore two inductive logics to explain the same concept. Humorists know where our comfort zone is, they know that we will induce something in one direction, and they'll be waiting around the corner. Laughter is therefore the result of this shock of perception when we suddenly understand the other logic. That's why a joke never makes you laugh twice.

Cartoons

Many cartoons are built like the one below which was published in a Belgian newspaper.[3] Everyone remembers the courage of the Chinese student who faced the tanks in Tiananmen square. The article however had nothing to do with this historic event, it was instead defending the position of books against the invasion of screens. The cartoonist therefore chose to merge the two strong mental images into the same drawing.

---

2. This answer is attributed to Gandhi.
3. Jérôme Viguet, *La Libre*, 21 November 2019, <https://www.lalibre.be/debats/opinions/2019/11/21/face-a-internet-lindisp ensable-pensee-critique-JEEK3TLZURBK3FDOQMM3KRJALA/> [accessed 30 May 2024].

Figure 24. *Tiananmen book resistance, Jérôme Viguet*

Figure 25. *CatGPT, Vince (Vincent Dubois)*

The same method was used a while later, to illustrate the launch of ChatGPT.[4] In this cartoon, a laptop is merged with a bulldozer.

The novel connections that a new idea forges must often overcome resistance to the initial ideas being mixed. Hungarian author and journalist Arthur Koestler used the word 'bisociation' to denote this action which is more audacious and more deliberate than simple association. Bisociation is at the heart of creativity and we will look at it further in Chapter 7.

The work of press cartoonists is sometimes particularly delicate.

In 2001, shortly after the attacks that felled the Twin Towers in New York City, claiming thousands of innocent lives, cartoonists were faced with a seemingly impossible challenge.

How could they make readers laugh, or at least smile, when faced with such a tragedy? Luckily for cartoonists, nothing is ever definitive. A few days after the attacks, one of them published a cartoon in the *New Yorker*[5] depicting two friends meeting in a bar. Upon seeing the other's vividly patterned suit jacket, one of them says: 'I thought I'd never laugh again. Then I saw your jacket'. This cartoon came as a relief, allowing grieving cartoonists to 'catch their breaths'.[6]

Humour vs irony

It's difficult to decode humour without losing its power. According to E. B. White and Katharine S. White,[7] analysing humour is like dissecting a frog: no one is interested and the frog dies. Henri Bergson couldn't have been too sensitive to the plight of amphibians as he took a stab[8] at producing a first theory of laughter: you might be surprised to learn that it took until 1900 before a philosophical thesis was published on the topic. One of the reasons, it seems, is that no one had ever seen Jesus Christ laugh, and that humour must therefore have satanic origins …

For Bergson, what makes us laugh is a certain mechanical stiffness when we expect to see the flexibility and adaptability of living things. This is the case for example when habits become rigid instead of adapting to a changing environment, as demonstrated by the disjointed way Charlie Chaplin walks.

By wanting to define humour, you run the risk of being boring. So beware! One way of doing this is undoubtedly by contrasting it with irony, the other side of the mountain that makes us laugh.

4. Vince, *La Libre*, 12 January 2023, <https://www.lalibre.be/debats/opinions/2023/01/12/jai-teste-chatgpt-SCGXZAPDXJCIBLRKY6VN7HHECI/> [accessed 30 May 2024].

5. Leo Cullum, *The New Yorker*, September 2001, in Robert Mankoff, 'September 11th: Ten Years, with Robert Mankoff', *The New Yorker*, 6 September 2011, <https://www.newyorker.com/news/news-desk/september-11th-ten-years-with-robert-mankoff> [accessed 29 May 2024].

6. See Mankoff (2011).

7. 'Humor can be dissected, as a frog can, but the thing dies in the process and the innards are discouraging to any but the purely scientific mind'. Elwyn Brooks White and Katharine Sergeant White, *The Saturday Review of Literature*, October 1941, as quoted in Garson O'Toole, 'Humor Can Be Dissected, As a Frog Can, But the Thing Dies in the Process', *Quote Investigator®*, 2014, <https://quoteinvestigator.com/2014/10/14/frog/> [accessed 29 May 2024].

8. Henri Bergson, *Le Rire : Essai Sur La Signification Du Comique* (Paris, 1900). Translated as *Laughter: An Essay on the Meaning of the Comic* in the 1911 translation by Cloudesley Bereton and Fred Rothwell.

Humour isn't intended to hurt, to laugh at the other, it is all about laughter. Irony on the other hand develops in the face of an adversary with a clearly defined aim. Irony is first and foremost a weapon, sometimes used wisely, like Socrates against the sophists, and sometimes with a less commendable aim, like Voltaire against those who overshadowed him.

Humour lightens the mood, whereas irony makes things tense. Humour has neither fixed goal nor reference system ... Humour is humble, irony is humiliating.

'Irony is a mind game, whereas humour plays on the heart strings', according to French writer Jules Renard.[9] Many public jesters display their political convictions in this way. Humorists use humour about people who have their sympathy, and are ironic about people on the other side.

If irony is ambitious, humour has zero pretension. Jankélévitch reminds us that: 'humour has no kingship to re-establish, no throne to restore, no title deeds to assert; it hides no sword in the folds of its tunic'.[10]

9. 'L'ironie est surtout un jeu d'esprit. L'humour serait plutôt un jeu du cœur'. Jules Renard and Claude Barousse, *Journal: 1887–1910*, Babel, 152 (Arles [Bruxelles] [Lausanne] [Montréal], 1995).

10. 'L'humour n'a aucune royauté à rétablir, aucun trône à restaurer, aucun titre de propriété à faire valoir, ne cache pas d'épée dans les plis de sa tunique'. Vladimir Jankélévitch and Béatrice Berlowitz, *Quelque Part Dans l'inachevé* (Paris, 1978). The title seems to have been translated as *Somewhere in the unfinished*.

5.5. Thinking with algorithms

Punch cards

My first encounter with algorithms dates back to the end of the 1960s, during my studies in Applied Mathematics Engineering, at the catholic university in Leuven. Computer science was in its infancy and the internet hadn't yet been invented. We used to line up to drop off our punch cards and we would each have a few minutes on the one and only computer in the building, which ran mostly at night. With no other machines available, our lessons were more theoretical than practical. This meant that we had to calculate less and think more. What a privilege!

What we called 'algorithms' at the time were a series of instructions fed into a computer that would then do what we expected of it. This set of coded specifications was called a 'computer program'.

An algorithm is a way of doing something, a procedure, a method. Our inspirational professors, to whom I am still very grateful to this day, would explain to us that in order to achieve the same goal, some algorithms were more efficient than others.

I thought of them on my very first day at work in 1974. I was working in the IT department of a bank and the machine I was working on was so basic that it couldn't even do a simple division! I therefore had to design my first algorithm in order to carry out a division using only subtractions.

Fifty years later, I asked ChatGPT how to do the same thing. In impeccable French, the answer appeared on screen instantly, crystal clear, structured, ready for use. So today, algorithms can elaborate, explain and program other algorithms, in the language of your choice.

ChatGPT and other 'generative' software bursting onto the scene is only the latest lightning acceleration in a revolution which is far from over. The twentieth century was the century of mathematics, and the twenty-first century is the century of algorithms. And I am forever grateful that life has allowed me to bear witness to and accompany this transition. When I started out as a programmer, I had to program in binary language, using only ones and zeroes. I realize today how lucky I was, especially when I compare my career with those who caught the computer train on the move.

Irresponsible algorithms

Very early on in my career, I started to wonder what the massive use of computers would mean for society, and I have wanted to share these ponderings. In 1985, in my first book, I envisioned the advent of the internet – even though I did not call it that. I named the book *Les Infoducs*,[11] based on a suggestion from Anne Mikolajczak as an analogy to aqueducts, convinced that one day a single network would transmit all types of information.

---

11.   Cited above.

When I look back at those pages, where digitalization and artificial intelligence were already present, I'm quite proud. Especially as I already stated that it was impossible for a computer to be creative, and that it would be a mistake to attribute any kind of responsibility to it.

I haven't changed my mind in the years since. Having studied philosophy in the 1990s, I have slowly been able to turn my intuitions into arguments. Philosophy has equipped me with the theoretical tool-box that I needed in order to structure, give perspective, clarify and make more accessible decades of thought about technology.

I haven't changed my mind. No matter how powerful the machine it's running on, an algorithm cannot be creative, because it can't escape its own logic. And it can't be held responsible because it's a tool and all responsibilities fall to its creator. Most questions which we call 'technical' aren't really that. They are instead societal questions caused by the emergence of increasingly powerful techniques. But these questions relate to law, to health, to education, to communication or to ethics.

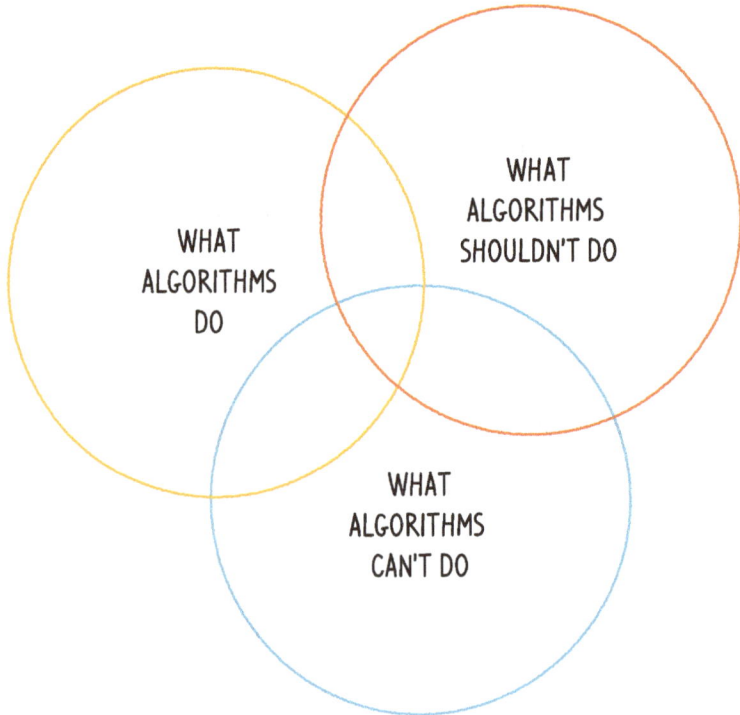

The three types of thought that constitute the backbone of this book will allow us to examine, over the course of the next three chapters, what it is that algorithms do, what they can't do and what they shouldn't do.

At the heart of the Venn diagram is the explosive cocktail of data and algorithms. In high-end restaurants, the ingredients are as important as the recipes. And the same goes for data and algorithms. Yet at the heart of the Venn diagram, there is also a paradox. Strictly speaking, this zone of the diagram should be empty, as it isn't possible to have something that the algorithms can do and can't do at the same time. This is probably one of those times where a sprinkling of humour is required, as we've just discussed.

In the 1980s data and algorithms were already present when we first started discussing artificial intelligence.

But back then algorithms were explicit, they were logical rules that were clearly described and made it possible to choose, at each node of the decision tree, which branch should be taken. In other words, it was possible for humans to follow them.

So how is it possible for an algorithm to pick out the photo of someone from a large amount of photos? In this case it's very different, there is no method available. When it comes to what we call 'learning' algorithms, we don't know exactly what's happening, as they are implicit, experimental and probabilistic.

So there's a lot going on with algorithms, but the same can also be said about data. There are four types of data, of which only the first existed before the internet:

- The data that we communicate consciously (name, date of birth, etc.) whenever we're handling an administrative or commercial transaction.
- The data that we communicate unconsciously, for example by clicking 'I accept the cookies', even though we don't actually understand what we're accepting. Or more generally, all of the breadcrumbs that we leave across the internet.
- The data that others provide about us, by tagging us, retweeting or forwarding information to us because they think that it might interest us.
- The metadata which is made possible by the massive processing of all the traces that we leave as soon as we log on, of which the infamous cookies.

The fourth group of data has been coined 'big data'. Billions of pieces of seemingly insignificant information that are turned into files and sold for a small fortune. If you were to invent a pill that makes small dogs fluorescent, you would have no problem turning it into a commercial success thanks to big data, which will provide you with a list of people who not only have a chihuahua but are also afraid of the dark.

5.6. Being a corporate philosopher

In 2001, when I introduced myself to the Boston Consulting Group (BCG) as a corporate philosopher, I got some very surprised looks. And I can understand this reaction, because back then googling 'corporate philosopher', you didn't get any results! Nowadays I'm delighted to see the profession becoming more mainstream, so I'm going to take this opportunity to answer the question that I have been asked so many times: what on Earth is a corporate philosopher?

After my first career as a manager, I was left with a simple observation: in all companies, there are areas where numbers are available (accounting, stocks, energy consumption, market shares, etc.) but a lot of important areas are neither quantified nor quantifiable (brand management, stress, creativity, team spirit, ethics, client proximity, etc.).

Corporate philosophy is a tool that allows you to be more rigorous when there are no numbers.

I started out my professional career as a mathematics teacher and I was happy at the end of every lesson if I had managed to transmit some knowledge to my students. Since becoming a philosopher, things are very different. I want to pass on my surprises, my questions, my experience and my values. There is no useful philosophical 'knowledge' to be passed on to those in charge.

Most of the time, we don't even know what the participants in our workshops do for a living. And it doesn't matter, because our role is not to tell them what to think, but to explain how we think.

The spectacle of change[12]

Thanks to the I/D model presented at the start of the book, I remind them over and over that our brain is a two-stroke engine, and has its own strengths and weaknesses. Let's repeat it once more: the first movement, induction, simplifies reality and allows us to build categories and other models. The second one, deduction, allows us to use these simplifications. Deduction has its own strict rules, but there is no science of induction. And I always enjoy reminding people that a market segmentation is not the market ...

When you teach geopolitics in a company, you're providing intellectual nourishment. When you teach accounting, you're passing on recipes. The aim of philosophy is to make people hungry, to whet their appetite for 'clear and distinct' ideas.

A corporate philosopher invites participants in their workshops to organize their discussion according to three movements.

The first one consists of zooming out, of seeing the bigger picture and putting things into perspective, of spotting fertile analogies. It's also important at this stage to detect what would be good to

---

12. This is a reference to a sentence by Jeanne Hersch in *L'étonnement philosophique: une histoire de la philosophie* (1981). The title seems to have been translated as *Philosophical Astonishment*.

change, as opposed to what we don't want to change. Was philosophy not born from the spectacle of change? In a company this translates as a question: how can we articulate what stays (values, DNA, purpose, etc.) and what needs to change (more robustness, reorganization, etc.)?

The second movement is the complete opposite, we take a deep dive into facts and semantics, we clarify, we demand definitions, we hunt down false synonyms and we try to understand the semantics at play. Creativity isn't innovation, regulation isn't reglementation, balance isn't stability and comfort isn't luxury. There is much talk about business models, but what exactly is a model? We talk of customer experience, but what exactly is an experience?

So where do we begin?

The third movement takes a tangent and involves taking an oblique look at the situation, by using Kant's third maxim, and think by putting yourself in the other's shoes.[13] This is the best route to creativity and critical thinking.

These three movements all seemingly go off in opposite directions, but they only appear to contradict each other. Philosophy isn't about thinking better, but rather about thinking more.

One day a manager asked me to facilitate a brainstorming workshop around big data. 'I don't even know where to start', he told me. The workshop went ahead and was a success. At the end he said 'Thank you, I can now see where I'm going to start'.

This is what a corporate philosopher does. We help leaders to draw maps that allow them to first see where they are, and then decide where they want to go.

---

13.   Immanuel Kant, *Groundwork of the Metaphysics of Morals* (Riga, 1785).

Chapter 6 – Be logical!

Everywhere is walking distance if you have the time.
– Steven Wright

BE LOGICAL

WITHIN US

IN FRONT OF US

PREMISE
CATEGORY
AXIOM
THEORY
ETC.

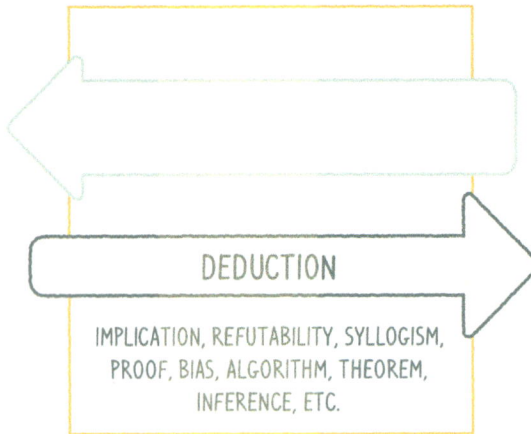

DEDUCTION

IMPLICATION, REFUTABILITY, SYLLOGISM,
PROOF, BIAS, ALGORITHM, THEOREM,
INFERENCE, ETC.

6.1. A very short history of logical thinking

The history of artificial intelligence didn't start eighty years ago when the first computers were built. The principles, laws and concepts that guide computer sciences as we know them today, date back to a time when mathematics and logic were developed alongside each other around their emblematic thinkers, respectively Plato and Aristotle.

The history of computer science can be described as the dream of reuniting those two sister branches. This dream was mainly that of Gottfried Wilhelm Leibniz, a German philosopher who couldn't figure out why these two disciplines had been evolving in parallel since Antiquity, despite both apparently aiming for the same thing. After all, don't mathematicians and logicians want to understand how to establish unquestionable truths? They're all fighting against reasoning errors and want to determine laws for correct thinking.

To reuse Koestler's term, as explained earlier, Leibniz wanted to 'bisociate' mathematics and logic!

We know today that Leibniz's dream would never come true, and that what is true and what is demonstrable will always be two distinct things. But three other bisociations, admittedly less ambitious ones, have previously proven to be very fruitful: René Descartes managed to reconcile algebra and geometry, George Boole, the British logician, combined algebra and syllogism, and the American engineer, Claude Shannon, brought binary calculations and electronic relays together.

When presented in this way, the history of logical thinking feels like a slightly pared down version of *Four Weddings and a Funeral* ... let's take a closer look.

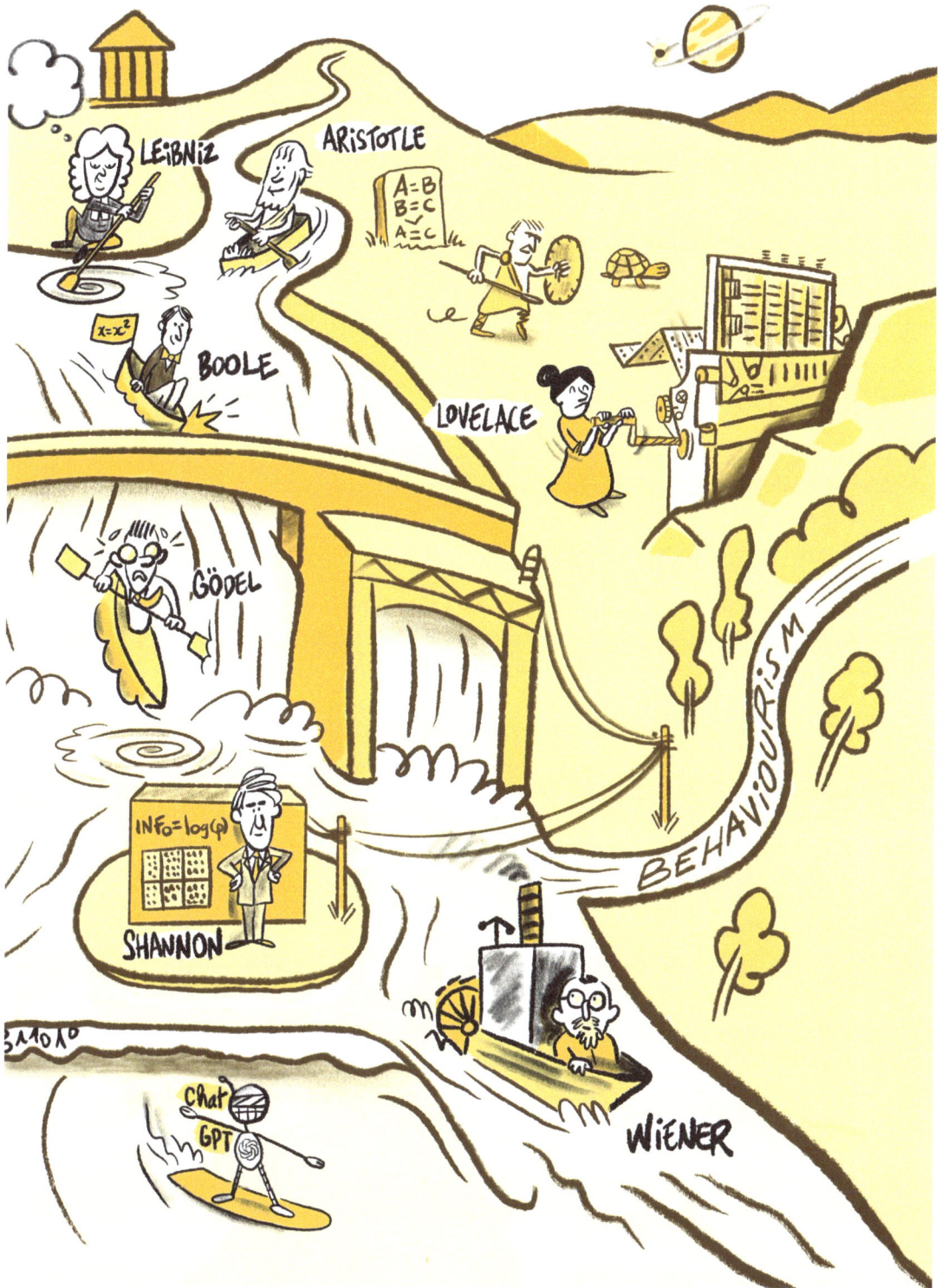

Analytical geometry

In the Middle Ages, Arab mathematicians arrived in the West. This was an important event, because with them came al-Khwarizmi, whose name is the origin of the word 'algorithm', and who came bearing a whole new way of doing maths. Whilst according to the Egyptians and Plato, geometry was the dominant paradigm, the Arabs explained the principles and the advantages of algebra (a word which comes from the name of one of al-Khwarizmi's books). In their conceptual luggage, these mathematicians also brought the number zero. Hard to imagine, but the Romans hadn't included it in their numbers! How on Earth did they add XXXV and XV? How did they explain that the result was L?

Descartes reconciled geometry and algebra thanks to his x and y axes, abscissa and ordinate, and the construction of the reference frame known, unsurprisingly, as Cartesian. His algebraic geometry was renamed analytical geometry and was mostly used as a tool for whomever wanted to model a curve. A circle can now be drawn or can be represented by the following equation: $x^2 + y^2 = r^2$, and the one enriches the other. Descartes and his passion for maths subsequently motivated a handful of geniuses to explore unknown territories.

Blaise Pascal is a prime example of this. He lived several lives, and the one that interests us in this case was his efforts to calculate probabilities. Pascal contested the existence of Aristotle's final cause, and admits de facto that of chance. Moreover, he actually wanted to calculate it. Given the cause, what is the probability of the effect?

A few years later, Thomas Bayes, a particularly curious English pastor, decided to ask the question the other way round. Given the effect, he wondered, what is the probability of the cause? We will come back to this later on because Bayes' ideas are at the heart of quite a few of the internet's biggest algorithms.

And then we have Leibniz of course, whose dream to bisociate mathematics and logic lies at the heart of this fresco. Whenever an argument arose during a conversation, Leibniz would say: 'Let's calculate!' But Leibniz is at the heart of our particular story for another reason. He established, at the same time as Newton did, despite never discussing the matter, the bases of differential calculus. In other words, equations of the infinitely small.

Binary algebra

Mathematician Leonhard Euler lived in Königsberg (known as Kaliningrad today). The town is split across two islands that both sit on a river. They are connected to each other and to the mainland by seven bridges. Euler wanted to find a walk that would allow him to go over each of them only once, but he never found this perfect path. His interest in graph theory, the science of networks, was born from this frustration about bridges.

Kant also lived in Königsberg, that's why he's on our map. But not for his contribution to logic or to mathematics, disciplines that he didn't consider to be worth his time. He even wrote: 'Isn't Aristotle's logic a complete science?' He wrote that with humility of course, but also with an astonishing lack of insight for such a genius!

George Boole is at the centre of the fresco and that's also not by chance, because he is the hinge between two worlds. He pushed Leibniz's dream as far as it would go, and developed binary numbering, to bisociate Aristotle's syllogism and algebra. In other words he wanted to find equations for reasoning, which meant that he could verify an argument in the same way you would a theorem.

Boole's idea was initially quite simple. In arithmetics, we talk of addition and multiplication. In logic, we talk of 'OR function' and 'AND function'. So why not combine both approaches? His research led him to the equation $x^2 = x$ that can only be verified for two x values, respectively 0 and 1. And thus binary calculation was born, 100 years before computer science.

For the record (pun intended), Boole found two errors in Aristotle's logic, and paradoxically reinforced his status as being the absolute reference.

The theory of information

In 1931, a fuse blew. Kurt Gödel published his incompleteness theorem in which he proved that what is true and what is demonstrable are two very distinct things: the fourth bisociation would never happen.

It is possible to look at Gödel's theorem in the following way:

- *Take proposition P, which says 'P is not demonstrable'.*
- *If P is false, that would mean that P is demonstrable. But this makes no sense because a false proposition can by definition never be demonstrated.*
- *Therefore P is true, and P is not demonstrable.*

It's this theorem that allows us to confirm that Leibniz's dream would never come true. Bertrand Russell made the most of the shock wave to overhaul the whole logic, and thus sorted out a problem that had been troubling people for over 2000 years: according to Epimenides, a Cretan himself, 'all Cretans are liars'. Was he right?

Bertrand Russell wasn't afraid of much. He wrote simply about Aristotle: 'the logic of the syllogism is completely wrong, and the small part that isn't wrong is useless'. And he was actually right. He then embarked on a long voyage with his professor Norbert Whitehead that he called *Principia Mathematica*.[1] Farewell to the logic of propositions, and hello to the logic of relations. The adventure wasn't a complete success because language is logically faulty, as shown by Ludwig Wittgenstein, his disciple, colleague and opponent at Cambridge.

Paradoxically, it was actually Boole who would leave the world of antique logic behind with his head held high, thanks to Claude Shannon and the third major fruitful bisociation that structures our tale. The American mathematician and engineer, who shared his life between MIT and the Bell laboratories, decided to combine the binary system with the first electronic relays (back then they were electronic tubes!) in order to materialize logical functions and to create the first circuits. Shannon intended to build the foundations of a theory of information. We'll take a closer look at some of the elements of this at the end of the chapter.

---

1. Bertrand Russell and Norbert Whitehead, *Principia Mathematica*, 1st edn, 3 vols (Cambridge, 1910).

Black box and black swan

Simply put, Anglo-American psychology in the twentieth century has consecutively seen two schools of thought that both appear on the map: one on the right, and one on the left of the main river.

You'll find the behaviourists on the right, they were psychologists who were convinced that the essence of humankind could be understood by analysing reactions to specific stimuli. This is a 'black box' approach: we don't know what's in your head, but we're watching how you react. This approach heavily influenced Norbert Wiener when he set out to study regulation and piloting mechanisms. In 1948 he called this new discipline 'cybernetics'. He carried out a thorough study of the automation possibilities and is the undisputed precursor of those who today dream of robots and artificial humankind.

During the Second World War, behaviourism slowly but surely gave way to a new approach towards humankind. Under the influence of the computer metaphor, the cognitive scientists (on the left), believed that thought could be modelled and that reasoning is made up of a succession of steps. Alan Turing was certainly inspired by this way of seeing things. It probably motivated him to design the virtual machine that he gave his name to. And he was the first to imagine the possibility of artificial intelligence. It obviously isn't a coincidence that, on the map, the cognitive scientists are on Plato's side and the behaviourists are on Aristotle's side.

So it turns out that nothing is ever definite, even in logic! In November 2022, the arrival of ChatGPT in a way hailed the great return of Aristotle, and the victory of Wittgenstein 2, the old man, over Wittgenstein 1, the young man. Researchers in AI have given up trying to understand the rules of thought. Paradoxically, logic is today no longer the preferred approach in computer sciences, with the statistical approach having taken over. The philosopher's pendulum, which was stuck for a long time on the side of rationalism, has swung back towards empiricism!

A critique of automatic reason

The IT world is currently in turmoil, but all of the new developments continue to be made on the shoulders of giants, as Newton said, and the overview suggested here reminds us of that. What is happening today is part of a conceptual continuum that started in Antiquity. But what's next?

In the 1980s I worked in telecommunications and I read almost all of the forecasting books on the topic. That's when I wrote my first book, *Les Infoducs*,[2] in which I tried to imagine all of the possible options: the possibility of distributed or interactive networks, either low- or high-speed, analogue or digital. I tried to think of everything, but I missed the most important part: the advent of wireless phone service. That's what we'd call a black swan today, a highly unlikely event, with a huge impact. So be careful!

Leibniz's dream never came true. Are we heading towards a nightmare instead? There are reasons to be worried. In Silicon Valley many conversations now revolve around a fifth – and last? – bisociation which would merge the living and the machine …

---

2.   Cited above.

6.2. The unbearable lightness of being logical

Mathematics vs logic

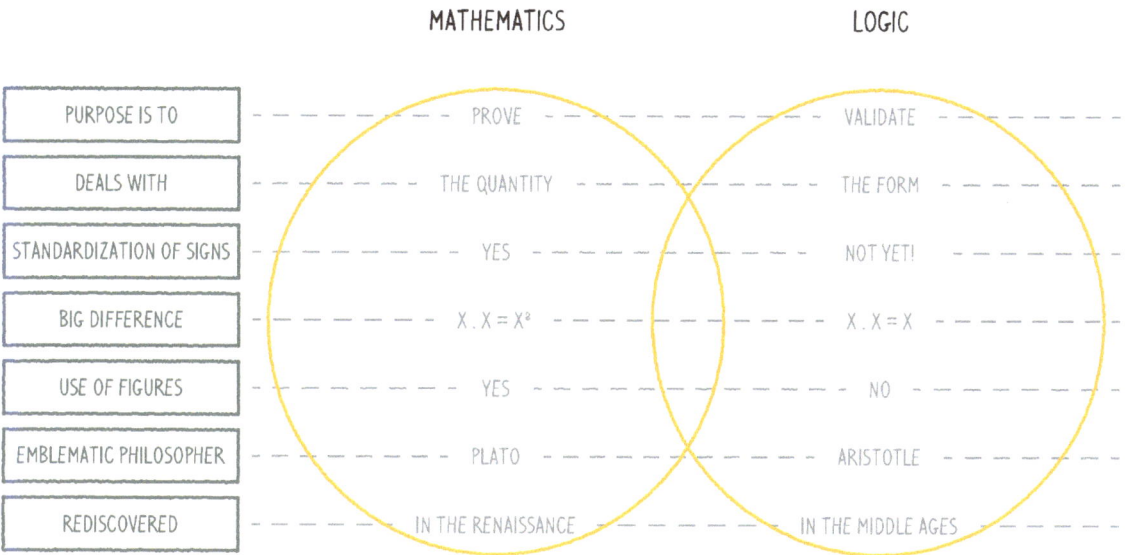

	MATHEMATICS	LOGIC
PURPOSE IS TO	PROVE	VALIDATE
DEALS WITH	THE QUANTITY	THE FORM
STANDARDIZATION OF SIGNS	YES	NOT YET!
BIG DIFFERENCE	$X . X = X^2$	$X . X = X$
USE OF FIGURES	YES	NO
EMBLEMATIC PHILOSOPHER	PLATO	ARISTOTLE
REDISCOVERED	IN THE RENAISSANCE	IN THE MIDDLE AGES

Even though there is a radical difference between mathematics and logic, there is a common blurry zone that both disciplines share. Indeed:

- There are purely graphical demonstrations of mathematical theorems where the presence of numbers isn't always a reliable marker.
- In contrast, some logical algorithms involve the vast processing of numbers. Cryptography is a good example, where prime numbers play an essential role.
- Set theory was born in mathematics, but introduces logical concepts such as the difference between the 'inclusive or' and the 'exclusive or'.
- At the beginning of this chapter we introduced you to Thomas Bayes who revolutionized the mathematical theory of probabilities. But he also deals with the logical form known as abduction, which is explained below.

So we could ask ourselves why is 'mathematics' plural and 'logic' singular? The influence of Aristotle once again?

Main definitions

As previously announced, it's time to introduce a few definitions of already mentioned concepts.

Proposition

Factual content expressed by a declarative sentence, which can be true or false. The same proposition may be expressed in different sentences.

Inference

Process of drawing a conclusion from a set of propositions, hypotheses or assumptions called premises. Inference is the mental operation that underlies all reasoning.

The goal of logic is to codify kinds of inference, and to provide principles for separating valid from invalid inferences. Inference is thus the most general term, and of which reasoning, deduction, induction, abduction etc. are special cases. If an inference is valid, it becomes a proof.

Proof

A sequence of statements, each of which follows logically from what is already known to be true.

A bag of beans

Aristotle's stroke of genius – modelising thought in a three-storey structure, as presented in the previous chapter – gives us a tool to understand the following exercise. Let's look at three propositions: A, B and C, and let's line them up in three different ways. We will thus see three types of reasoning:

- DEDUCTIVE reasoning goes from the general to the particular (or to the general).
    A. All the houses in this street are beautiful
    B. This house is in this street
    C. This house is beautiful

- INDUCTIVE reasoning goes from the particular (or the sum of particulars) to the general.
    B. This house is in this street
    C. This house is beautiful
    A. All the houses in this street are beautiful

- ABDUCTIVE reasoning goes from the particular to the particular.
    C. This house is beautiful
    A. All the houses in this street are beautiful
    B. This house is in this street

Let us distinguish these three forms using an example adapted from American scientist and philosopher Charles Sanders Peirce.[3] In front of you is a white bag on a table in a shop, and you think it only contains coffee. This conclusion can come from three different reasonings:

---

3. Charles Sanders Peirce, 'Deduction, Induction, and Hypothesis', *Popular Science Monthly*, 13 (1878), <https://en.wikisou rce.org/wiki/Popular_Science_Monthly/Volume_13/August_1878/Illustrations_of_the_Logic_of_Science_VI> [accessed 31 May 2024]. Replacing 'hypothesis' by 'abduction' is done, among others, in Umberto Eco and Thomas A. Sebeok, eds, *The Sign of Three: Dupin, Holmes, Peirce*, Advances in Semiotics (Bloomington, 1983).

- DEDUCTION: it's a coffee shop and the shopkeeper is trust-worthy.
- INDUCTION: I plunge my hand into the bag and it's filled with coffee beans.
- ABDUCTION: there are coffee beans on the table that have escaped from the previous bags.

One final remark, in our I/D model, for clarity, we have presented abduction as a frequent way of inducing.

The fall of Aristotle's logic

As we've seen, the history of logic only contains two chapters! The first ended in the nineteenth century with the downfall of Aristotle's theory, and the second is still being written ...

The meagre level of syllogism leads us to wonder how it could have remained a reference for so long, and wonder even more how Kant could ever have declared it a 'complete science'?

Aristotle's project of founding a science of reasoning was doomed from the start, for two reasons.

First, Aristotle decided not to examine a series of situations that were problematic for reasoning, such as Epimenides' liar paradox mentioned above. Another famous paradox that he ignored was Zeno's, who claimed that Achilles could never catch up with the tortoise from the moment that it was given a slight head start. It wasn't until the eighteenth century and the invention of infinitesimal calculus that an answer was found and the paradox dissolved.

Second, to build his three-storey model, Aristotle had to consider untenable hypotheses:

1. One and only one word corresponds to each thing.
2. Any proposition can be in the form 'A is B'.
3. Any reasoning can be in the form of a syllogism.

The three hypotheses very quickly appear false because:

1. 'Paul Mc Cartney is the author of *Yesterday*' is then logically equivalent to 'Paul Mc Cartney is Paul Mc Cartney'.
2. These relational propositions such as 'Lausanne is south of Brussels' or 'Lou is Nicolas' daughter' cannot be in the form of 'A is B'.
3. Some valid reasonings cannot take the form of a syllogism:
   A horse is an animal.
   Therefore a horse's head is an animal's head.

Despite its structural defects, the syllogism construct still survived for nearly two millennia! The answer to why this occurred is paradoxical: people aren't logical! Aristotle's prestige blinded brilliant intellectuals for 2000 years, as shown by Immanuel Kant. Welcome to the world of cognitive bias where it seems that when we reason, we are not as rational as we think we are ... and our level of intelligence doesn't affect this much. But before we do that, let's take a look at how a British aristocrat kicked off the second chapter of the history of logic.

Everyone loves someone

At the end of the nineteenth century, after over two thousand years of relative peace, a new logic is about to wipe the old one from the board. As we've established, Gottlob Frege kicked off the demolition. Whereas Aristotle had built his logic by distinguishing the subject (Socrates) and the predicate (mortal), Frege wants to rebuild everything by focusing on the relationship that unites the two.

He starts by introducing new symbols:

- x, y, and other letters are used to designate both concepts and attributes.
- ∃ (that is read as 'it exists'), that is, the 'existential quantifier', took the place of 'some', 'certain', and 'ones', all vague words used to refer to a part of a whole.
- ∀ (that is read as 'irrespective of'), that is, the 'universal quantifier', took the place of 'all', 'any' or 'each', all terms used when referring to the totality of a set.

The use of quantifiers is particularly effective and, at first glance, easy to understand. These three examples should convince you of this:

1. The proposition 'everything has a cause' becomes

    $(\forall x)(\exists y)(y \text{ causes } x)$
    that can be read as 'regardless of x, there exists a y such that y causes x'.
    And the proposition 'everything has the same cause', becomes
    $(\exists y)(\forall x)(y \text{ causes } x)$
    that can be read as 'there exists a y such that, regardless of x, y causes x'.

By comparing these two expressions, we notice the permutation of the first two elements of the logical expression. The difference is fundamental, because the first one is true, regardless of what the fans of first uncaused causes say, whilst the second one is false, regardless of what those who believe in the omnipotence of God may think.

2. The use of quantifiers also means that some ambiguous points can be solved. The proposition 'everyone loves someone' can be interpreted in two ways:

    Either $(\exists y)(\forall x)(x \text{ loves } y)$
    That can be read as 'there exists a y, such that, regardless of x, x loves y'. That is to say, 'there is someone that everyone loves'.
    Or $(\forall x)(\exists y)(x \text{ loves } y)$
    That can be read as 'regardless of x, there exists a y such that x loves y'. That is to say, 'everyone loves at least one person'.

3. In both of these examples, the same quantifiers remain attached to the same variables: ∀ remains attached to x and ∃ to y. But they can of course move around.

    $(\forall x)(\exists y)(x \text{ hates } y)$ can be read as 'regardless of x, there exists a y such that x hates y', or 'there is someone that everyone hates'.
    $(\exists x)(\forall y)(x \text{ hates } y)$ can be read as 'there exists an x such that, regardless of y, x hates y', or 'some people hate everyone'.

6.3. The logical thinker's toolbox

If you want to think logically, you can base yourself on solid theory, even if it's incomplete. But you will have to accept that logic can't cover everything. As we saw, perfect induction is impossible. So if you want to think logically, you will have to accept a few things: that your premises will always remain hypotheses, that you'll have to do a certain amount of letting go, and that the risk of being wrong cannot be completely eliminated. Welcome to the world of cognitive bias!

Let's take this set of propositions as an example:

Artists are creative.
Among creative people, some of them are funny.
Therefore, some artists are funny.

Do you think this reasoning is correct?

In other words, if we accept that the two first propositions are true, can we then say with certainty that there are artists who are funny?

At first the answer seems to be yes. And yet, the answer is no, this reasoning isn't valid. Not convinced? Let's examine the second case:

Trumpets are musical instruments.
Among musical instruments, some have strings.
Therefore, some trumpets have strings.

The reasoning here is undoubtedly incorrect. And yet, it has the exact same structure as the first one!

A are B.
Among B, some are C.
Therefore, some A are C.

Then why is it that we tend to react differently?

I'll say it again, the answer is simple: we are not logical beings and we let ourselves be wrongfully influenced by what differentiates the two reasonings. In the first instance, we know the conclusion to be true. In the second one, we know it to be false. The logical flaw lies in believing that reasoning is inevitably correct if it leads to truth. Even a broken clock is right twice a day ...

Our errors in reasoning are varied and numerous, and they are what we call 'cognitive biases'. They show and remind us that a number of our deductions are not fully rational. In order to go faster, and very often we don't have the choice, thought takes shortcuts that sometimes lead to short-circuits and blow our logical fuses.

One example of these fatal shortcuts is called 'confirmation bias'. All too often, newspapers will gather two defenders with two opposing essays on a societal issue. As readers, we will pay more attention to the opinion that matches our own, whether we are conscious of it or not. We may not even try to understand the other point of view! To put it in more general terms, we spend more time reading newspaper articles that we agree with than articles that we don't.

Cognitive bias has been discussed for a long time. In the sixteenth century, Francis Bacon pointed out that we always prefer to believe what we hope to be true. This is why we tend to believe the more positive weather reports than the negative ones, even though the reliability of the Meteorological Institute has nothing to do with which kind of weather it predicts. But we still rejoice when good weather is announced, and if bad weather is on the horizon, we think back to past erroneous predictions and think 'surely it can't be that bad'.

Homo sapiens were never – and will never be – homo logicus, and two major elements have placed cognitive bias back at the heart of today's preoccupations:

- First came the works of Kahneman and Tversky, discussed at the beginning of this book, and which were awarded the Nobel Prize for Economics in 2002. Ever since then, cognitive biases are better identified and continue to be the object of significant research and publications.
- Secondly, cognitive bias and social media are a particularly explosive combo!

Bias can be categorized into two large groups and we shall do so following the I/D model that has accompanied us since the start of this book.

Deduction bias

Deduction bias is particularly worrying because the mistakes we make are obvious. Try and answer the three following problems:

- *Bernard is looking at Julie, but Julie is looking at Antoine. Bernard is married but Antoine isn't.*
  Question: is a married person looking at an unmarried person?
  A: yes
  B: no
  C: cannot be determined

Most people reply with C, because we don't know whether Julie is married or not. And yet, the answer is A since only two cases are possible. Either Julie is not married, and Bernard, who is married, is looking at her. Or Julie is married, and she is looking at Antoine, who isn't. This means that, regardless of Julie's status, a married person is looking at an unmarried one.

The reasoning is foolproof, the answer undeniable, and yet ...

- Take two people chosen at random. Without giving them any time to calculate, ask the first person to estimate the value of: 2 × 3 × 4 × 5 × 6 × 7 × 8. In the same short amount of time, ask the second person to estimate the value of: 8 × 7 × 6 × 5 × 4 × 3 × 2. The answer to the first one will generally be lower than the second one – and by far![4]

There is no discussion possible there, and yet ...

- How many people need to be in a room in order to have a 50 per cent chance of two of them sharing the same birthday? Surprisingly ... only 23!

Induction bias

Induction bias is of a different kind since there is by definition no 'right answer' to be found. What is obvious is that we've stopped thinking too quickly!

If we ask you what this is:	**T**
You'll probably say that it's the letter T.	
Now tell me what this represents:	**T T**

Two Ts? It could be. But if the first question hadn't been asked, you'd have more readily thought of poles, a balance sheet, bar stools ... or even something else, than if it had been asked. The answer to the first question influences the answer to the second question. Why?

If we ask you to draw a little dog, without giving it much thought there is a strong chance his head will be on the left. Why is that?

If we ask you which word is the odd one out in this series:

cathedral – prayer – mosque – Eiffel Tower

You might give a different answer if the same series of words was presented in a different order:

mosque – Eiffel Tower – cathedral – prayer

Why?

These short exercises highlight the fact that part of our thought process is out of our grasp. We continuously take on hypotheses without really deciding to, and we often set ourselves limits and constraints without having been asked to.

---

4.   Amos Tversky and Daniel Kahneman, 'Judgment under Uncertainty: Heuristics and Biases: Biases in Judgments Reveal Some Heuristics of Thinking under Uncertainty', *Science*, 185/4157 (1974), 1124–31.

If we ask you to carry on the series *apple – melon – cherry*, it would be logical to say 'banana'. But it would also make sense to say 'Moon', since the Moon is also spherical.

The most famous exercise of this type is called the 'nine dots' puzzle, where nine dots arranged into three parallel rows of three have to be linked together using only four strokes and without lifting the pen off the paper.

This can only be achieved by stepping outside of the imaginary box formed by the nine dots. This exercise probably underlies the popularity of the saying 'outside the box' which has become intrinsic to all brainstorming sessions. In the next chapter, we will ponder creative thinking, and we'll also see that thinking outside of the box isn't the real challenge! But first, let's celebrate two legends of the digital revolution.

6.4. Being logical in a digital world

Contrary to creative and critical thinking, logical thinking mostly concerns a limited circle of insiders. We will not go deeper here into the challenges faced by professional logicians when it comes to digital transformation. But we will take a few lines to pay a heartfelt tribute to the researchers who have made it possible. Thomas Bayes and Claude Shannon, introduced at the beginning of the chapter, are unknown to the general public, yet their work is both fundamental and accessible.

Thomas Bayes, the true Cyberstar

Alan Turing, Steve Jobs and Sam Altman are always referred to as the leading players in the digital revolution ... Yet, if the internet can recommend books or plan a vacation with baffling precision, and if big data is close to transforming your everyday life, it is down to another man who is as astonishing as he is unknown: Thomas Bayes (introduced in the fresco).

Upon his death in April ... 1761, this British theologian and philosopher left a few incomplete articles behind. One, entitled 'An essay towards solving a problem in the doctrine of Chance', reached the Royal Society two years later thanks to the diligence of a friend as unknown as Bayes himself: Richard Price.

In this essay, Thomas Bayes takes the opposing view to Blaise Pascal's words. The French scholar started his 'geometry of chance' by studying the probability of an effect given a cause. In other words, what are my odds of winning if I gamble at the casino? The British mathematician turns it around and suggests a formula that can compute the probability of a cause given an effect. In other words, if I draw three aces in a game of poker, what is the probability of the deck being rigged and holding five aces? Pascal and Bayes shared our I/D model between the two of them: Pascal took deduction and Bayes took care of induction!

Bayes' formula, demonstrated 300 years ago, is at the core of today's major algorithms, which I would like to prove thanks to a short exercise.

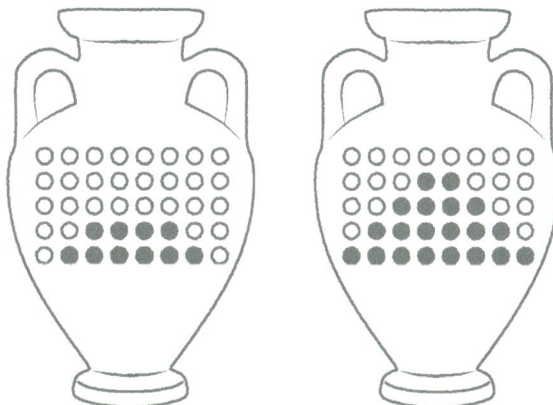

Imagine two identical urns, each containing forty stones. The first holds thirty white stones and ten black stones. The second contains twenty white stones and twenty black stones. You must choose one of the two urns at random and then pick out a random stone from that urn. The stone you picked is white. What is the probability that that stone is from the first urn?

Intuitively, we get a sense that it was most likely to come from the first urn since the proportion of white stones is higher there. But what is the exact probability?

To assess this, let's first compute the probability *a priori* that the stone is white AND was from the first urn. There are two ways of going about this:

- either computing the global probability of picking a white stone, multiplied by the probability of having chosen the first urn, knowing that the stone is white.
- or computing the probability of having chosen the first urn, multiplied by the global probability of picking a white stone, knowing that the stone comes from the first urn.

Both methods should provide the same answer, since they are two ways of computing the same thing. If A corresponds to 'choosing the first urn' and B 'picking a white stone', and p() indicates probability, then we can write this equivalency as follows:

$$p(B) \cdot p(A/knowing\ B) = p(A) \cdot p(B/knowing\ A)$$

Let's now go back to our initial problem. Randomly select one of the two urns and then pick a stone at random from that urn. What is the probability that that stone is from the first urn?

The answer is instant.

$$p(A/knowing\ B) = \frac{p(A) \cdot p(B/knowing\ A)}{p(B)}$$

We owe this formula to Thomas Bayes. Demonstrating this theorem is almost instantaneous and it is all the more impressive because of the boundlessness of its consequences! But instead of getting ahead of ourselves, let's get back to our problem and compute the three probabilities of the right-hand side of the equation.

- p(B/knowing A) is given in the statement = 75 per cent (as there are ¾ of white stones in the first urn)
- p(A) is also given in the statement = 50 per cent (as the urn is chosen at random)
- p(B) is a bit more complicated to establish as we can obtain a white stone in two different ways.

As both are mutually exclusive, we therefore need to add the probability of having B in hypothesis A, which is 30/40, that is, 75 per cent, to the probability of having B in hypothesis non-A, which is 20/40, that is, 50 per cent.

$$p(B)\ is\ therefore\ (50\% \cdot 75\%) + (50\% \cdot 50\%) = 62.5\%$$

The original question now has an answer: the probability that the white stone is from the first urn is:

$$p(A/knowingB) = \frac{75\% \cdot 50\%}{62.5\%} = 60\%$$

In other words, if we go back to the question, the probability of having taken the stone from the first urn, which amounts to 50 per cent before you look at the colour of the stone, increases to 60 per cent as soon as you know that it is white.

The calculation does indeed confirm our intuition, but it also attributes an accurate value to it. Although extremely simple, this example is highly enlightening as it enables us to understand the underlying current of Bayesian philosophy.

This is how recommendation algorithms work. If you've bought the latest bestseller (effect), which recommendation is most likely to make you buy another one (cause)? The same goes for spam and scam detectors: if you receive a message (effect), how likely is it that the sender has bad intentions (cause)?

Today's algorithms take enormous amounts of information into account, and the Bayesian approach is modelled in the form of a network that allows us to apply this probabilistic reasoning to a field of uncertain knowledge.

Yet, of course, all of this is mere conjecture. If Thomas Bayes had computed the probability that he would still be talked about 250 years after he died, he would probably … have gotten it wrong!

Calculating probabilities is very counter-intuitive and is at the origin of many deductive biases. Thomas Bayes can help us to better grasp this:

A mother has two children. One of them is a boy (B), what is the probability that the other one is a girl (A)?

No, the answer is not a 50/50!

Let's take a look at the formula:

$$p(A/knowing B) = \frac{(1 \cdot 1/2)}{(3/4)} = 2/3$$

If you're curious to find out more about this, why not take a look at the Monty Hall problem, also known as the three door problem?

Claude Shannon and infodynamics

Claude Shannon is – by far – the leading figure in computer science that we never hear about. He is the most famous unknown individual in our history. Shannon is the 'coding magician', as he was described by the organizers of the Paris CNAM exhibition, in celebration of his hundredth birthday.[5]

5.　'Le Magicien des codes', temporary exhibition by CNAM (Paris, 2016).

Shannon is the Lavoisier of computer science, the Darwin of telecommunications. 'Brilliantly simple and simply brilliant', according to his collaborator Bob Gallager. Shannon spent most of his professional life at Bell Labs, the legendary laboratory that ATT (American Telegraph and Telephone) financed in its heyday and at the height of its monopoly. Bell Labs worked with thousands of researchers, had just about all of the desired qualities of a research centre and produced no fewer than eight Nobel Prizes: not bad for a non-academic institution!

People came from the four corners of the world to visit Bell Labs. In 1943, Shannon welcomed Alan Turing with whom he wanted to explore the possibilities of an 'artificial intelligence'. He also invited his master Norbert Wiener, the creator of cybernetics. All three are on the fresco.

Claude Shannon passed away in 2001 after a battle with Alzheimer's. He was born before electronics and died a few years after Google was created ... What a life!

Just as Carnot had theorized energy by publishing the two principles of thermodynamics in 1824, Shannon published in 1948 the two theorems that made him the founder of what we could call 'infodynamics', since one involves the quantity of information and the other its quality.

The first theorem is based on *compressing* the information and seeks to answer the question: what is the minimal number of signs needed to code information?

The second theorem is based on *transmitting* this information and sets out to answer the question: what are the necessary conditions to end up with the *exact* same information as the information at the beginning?

To answer both of these questions, he started by choosing a unit of measurement.

In the same way a calorie is used to quantify heat exchange, he suggests the notion of *bit* to measure a volume of information. The bit is a binary number that will take the values 0 or 1. The chosen name is particularly elegant: it is both a contraction of *binary digit* and a pun, playing with the expression *a little bit*.

But beware because the theory of information is formal, just like logic. It is completely unaware of the sense and meaning of the messages it analyses. According to Shannon, questions such as 'Does God exist?' and 'Did Chelsea qualify for the FA cup final?' belong to the same category. In both cases, if the probability of the answer being either yes or no is the same, the answer to the question contains one *bit* of information.

Once he'd chosen the unit of measurement, Shannon started researching the mathematical law that links the quantity of information to the part of uncertainty that makes it disappear. It reasons in the following manner.

If we consecutively throw a coin into the air, and then roll a dice, the spectator watching the object after it has been thrown will receive information twice. But the sight of a 'tails' on the coin provides less information than a 'five' on the dice, because the probability is a one in two chance in the first case, and a one in six chance in the second.

If the coin and the dice are thrown at the same time, the spectator will find themself in a slightly paradoxical situation.

– On the one hand, the probability of a given pair, for example 'heads, four' is 1/12.
– On the other hand, hearing the result does not provide more information than the two objects thrown separately.

The measurement of the information must therefore satisfy a demanding relationship:

$$f(1/2) + f(1/6) = f(1/2 \cdot 1/6)$$

And f must be a logarithm type function since the sum of logarithms is, by definition, equal to the logarithm of the product.

With Shannon, the *bit* became a quantity of information which, regardless of the given problem, matches a halving of uncertainty. If you are looking for a house in the street, and you know it is an even number, you will only have to look on the one side. The information 'even number' is worth one *bit* because it splits the possibilities into two.

The *bit* is therefore the 'elementary' information. It is not possible to provide information that is smaller than the result of an experience which only has two possible and equiprobable outcomes. In all other cases, the information provided is superior, since the reduction of uncertainty is also superior.

Imagine that you are looking for a book in a library that contains 4,000 books. If 500 of them are blue, the information 'the book you are looking for is blue' is worth log(4000/500) = log 8 = log 2^3 = 3 bits. Information worth three bits divides by eight the time it takes to search for the book.

This is how Shannon was able to evaluate the redundancy of the English language, by calculating the probability of having a specific letter right after another. H is more probable after a T than after an S, and even more so after a C, etc.

If there was no logical or linguistic link, each new letter would have a probability of 1/26 and would provide 4.7 bits (since log 26 = 4.7) of information. But in English, a letter only contains around one bit of information and the redundancy is therefore around 75 per cent.

Shannon's theory made it possible to pay a powerful posthumous tribute to Samuel Morse. In 1832, having created the alphabet that he named after himself, he had intuitively grasped the link between information and probability. He assigned the most frequent symbols of our alphabet to the shortest codes in his alphabet. E is a simple dot, T is a single dash, but the less frequent Q is – – · –

Shannon's formula made it possible to calculate *a posteriori* that Morse code was 85 per cent efficient! We can only bow before the incredible intuition of its inventor.

Chapter 7 – Be creative!

We don't know who discovered water, but we're pretty sure it wasn't a fish.

BE CREATIVE

WITHIN US

ANALOGY, ASTONISHMENT, CURIOSITY,
HEURISTIC, CREATIVITY, INTUITION,
OBLIVION, PERCEPTION, QUESTION, *ETC.*

IN FRONT OF US

FINDING
PARADIGM
HYPOTHESIS
BOX
INSIGHT
NEW BOX
PATTERN
TABOO
IDEA
ETC.

INDUCTION

DEDUCTION

INNOVATION, ALGORITHM, *ETC.*

PARADOX
BIG DATA
FAILURE
NEED
WEAK SIGNAL
FACT
MEGATRENDS
ETC.

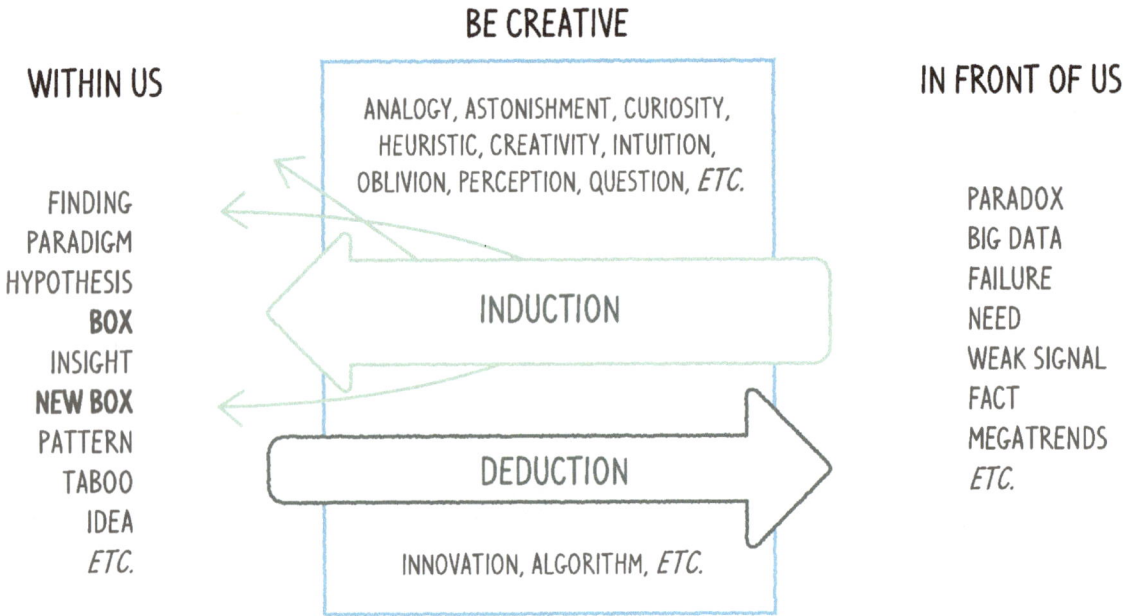

7.1. A very short history of creative thinking

When illustrating the history of creative thinking, the metaphor of a roller coaster seems fitting! It takes us through a world of fun, is in perpetual movement, and is dotted with calm interludes before throwing us up in the air, but with no real danger.

This story doesn't have the best of starts! According to Plato, creativity is quite simply impossible, pointless even. The perfection of Ideas is given *a priori* and all Ideas exist in a world of their own. There is therefore no point trying to imagine anything, as new Ideas don't exist and only an effort of memory can provide better ideas. In reality, unlike the cave in Lascaux, and despite being much more recent, Plato's cave therefore doesn't contain paintings.

Aristotle predictably takes the opposite standpoint to that of his master Plato. He claims that imagination produces images, thus highlighting the essential function of 'phantasia'.

Archimedes decided to put imagination at the service of technique and of science, and can therefore be qualified as the first engineer. All those who have since succeeded him have dreamed of also being able to one day say: 'Eureka! I found it!'

Reason has dominated since Socrates, pursuing its journey with Saint Thomas Aquinas, and triumphing with Descartes. But imagination remains, irreducible, disturbing. As proven when this very Descartes talks of chimaeras and chiliagons (a polygon with a thousand sides).

Pascal states that imagination is 'that mistress of [...] falsity, the more deceptive that she is not always so'.[1] All the more surprising coming from the inventor of the first calculating machine, who also held experiments to measure the atmospheric pressure atop Puy de Dôme and ... founded the first public transport company in Paris!

Pascal later adds nuance to his claims, giving the example of optical illusions, which can only fool those who know nothing of geometry.

And here comes the ... creative leap in this brief history of creativity. It comes from Kant, who thought of himself as the Copernicus of thought.[2] His revolutionary hypothesis was that we build our own way of seeing the world, and thus Kant opened the second chapter in creative thinking. According to him, imagination is a centrepiece of understanding because it enables the mapping out of categories.

Kant was ambitious, he also wanted to be seen as the Newton of the 'good life'. The German philosopher was fascinated by the simplicity of the law of gravity discovered by the Englishman, and suggested his *categorical imperative* be considered as one of the laws of morals.

Creativity is cranked up a notch in the following century. The novel, a pure product of imagination, *le roman* in French, gives its name to a new era: 'Romanticism', that conveys a new vision of the world. It establishes the primacy of subjectivity. Imagination becomes almost like a heightened visual sense that makes present what is absent. Alongside the clarity and the quality of ideas, Romantics also value the quantity and originality of ideas. It becomes useful, even necessary, to dream, and it becomes possible, desirable even, to create.

Imagination can now mobilize the other intellectual faculties and invade the fields of psychology, philosophy and natural science. Imagination is no longer the faculty of forming images of reality, it becomes the faculty of deforming images to change reality.

Freud gives the unconscious a privileged place in the psychic life of the individual. Imagination becomes therapeutic. Jung stands out from his master by affirming that individual imagination is rooted in a common fund, which he calls the 'collective unconscious'. Even from the depths of his cave, where he had to return to, Plato's Ideas continue to be influential ...

The French Henri Bergson is the philosopher of intuition and the author of *Creative Evolution*;[3] he is also one of the first Europeans to take an interest in pragmatism, a new philosophy from the United States.

Education finally makes way for a child's creativity thanks to Maria Montessori and her world famous method. The Italian teacher and doctor insists on the importance of creativity and experimentation throughout the learning process.

---

1. 'cette maîtresse [...] de fausseté, et d'autant plus fourbe qu'elle ne l'est pas toujours'. Blaise Pascal, *Pensées* (Port-Royal des Champs, 1670). English translation by William Finlayson Trotter, title translated as *Thoughts*, in Charles William Eliot, ed., *Blaise Pascal* (New York, 1910).
2. Immanuel Kant, *Critique of Pure Reason*, trans. by Norman Kemp Smith (London, 1929). The analogy is developed in the Preface to the second edition of 1787.
3. Henri Bergson, *L'Évolution Créatrice* (Paris, 1907). English translation by Arthur Mitchell, *Creative Evolution* (New York, 1911).

As demonstrated by Frida Kahlo, creativity can be political. In her mural frescoes, the Mexican artist expresses her feminist convictions and has since become an icon for all women who are fighting for something.

Thomas Kuhn suggests considering the history of science as a succession of 'paradigm shifts'. The passage from one to another is necessarily a shock, only made possible by a creative leap.

As explained in the beginning of Chapter 6, Arthur Koestler claims that a new idea often originates from a new link established between two old concepts. He calls this 'bisociation', as was the case when Gutenberg's version of printing was born from a forced union between a press used to make wine and lead characters.

The already mentioned works of Daniel Kahneman and Amos Tversky, demonstrated that we aren't as rational as ... we imagine. Together they contributed to the popularisation of the idea of cognitive biases, and revealed that the feeling of having an idea and that of making a mistake both come from the same mechanism: a change in perception. From a cognitive point of view, eureka and caramba are the same thing!

As is the case with the history of logic, the history of creativity is also made up of two major chapters. And both times, Kant is at the heart of change. But not on the same side! As we've just seen, he is at the beginning of the second chapter of creativity, but the same Kant gets bogged down at the end of the first chapter of logic, because he considers Aristotle to be incomparable. *Eureka* in one case and *caramba* in the other!

The word *créativité* only made an appearance in French general dictionaries in the early 1970s, but in English 'creativity' existed well before that! And it immediately proved to be very successful! Numerous business models, currents and theories started including and exploring it.

The concept of brainstorming itself owes a lot to the works of Alex Osborn[4] and Graham Wallas. Systems thinking dates back to Ludwig von Bertallanfy. The techniques involved in scenario planning put creativity at the service of foresight and have been used by Shell since the 1970s. More recently, the approach known as design thinking has seduced many entrepreneurs who are convinced that co-creativity is the key to success.

---

4.   Alex Faickney Osborn, *How to 'Think Up'* (London, 1942).

7.2. The stairs and the slope

From Clermont-Ferrand to Santiago de Compostela

Ask someone in which book category they would put the Michelin guide and without much hesitation, they'll probably answer that it should be put with either travel or gastronomical guides. In other words, they'll end the sentence 'the Michelin Guide is an example of ...' with '... a guide to find a good restaurant'.

In the beginning though, this wasn't at all the case. Flash back: in 1900, the Michelin brothers were on the lookout for a way to incentivize drivers to use their car more, wearing down more tires in the process. Even in a changing world, business is business (another tautology!).

It was during the year of the Universal Exhibition in Paris, when cars were frailer. Car-related incidents were a frequent occurrence and poor-quality roads were the cause of numerous flat tires. In that context, how could drivers be encouraged to drive more?

And then the idea hit them. Why not graciously offer a guide listing all garages ready to rescue drivers in distress? And so, the *Guide Michelin* was born!

The guide quickly became a big success and was improved on every year with the addition of photos, more precise maps and even more useful information about the featured towns. New ideas were added with every edition, and the guide started to be sold instead of handed out.

One day, someone pointed out that a tire repair could take a while and that suggesting some places to eat would be an interesting concept to keep the driver occupied while they're waiting for their car.

Just another innovation? Yes and no. Yes, since it was an improvement on the existing product and no, because for the first time the same guide belonged to a whole new category.

It may seem at first glance that adding restaurant addresses to a garage guide is only an extra detail. But it changes everything, a bit like in the example below: when you add the two dots above the line of zigzags, you will suddenly see a word which can be read in many languages ...

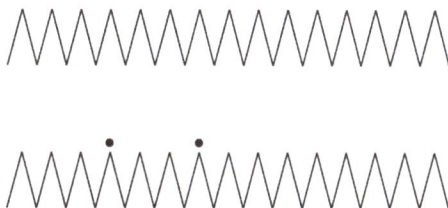

This double movement – continuous improvement on one end and discontinuous creativity on the other – perfectly illustrates the fundamental mechanics of creative thinking which, in the long run, must necessarily alternate between 'better of the same thing' and 'something else'. This mandatory back and forth looks like a zigzag.

If we could draw the Michelin story on the playing field of thought discussed in Chapter 2, it would look something like this:

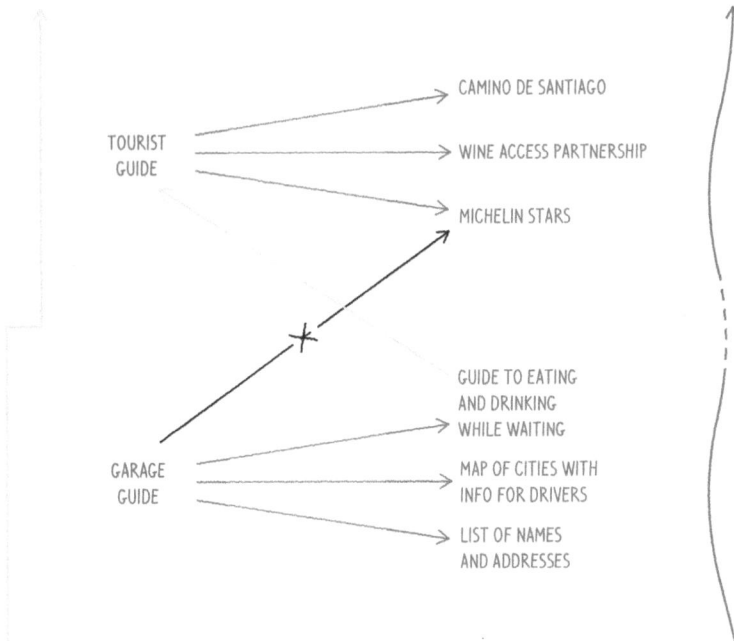

Instead of thinking of the book as a garage guide with tips on restaurants, it is now possible to end the sentence 'The Michelin guide is an example of' with 'a tourist guide'.

At this point in time, we're not changing the guide but a new field of improvements suddenly becomes possible. One example is the famous Michelin star created in 1926 and reputed, *a posteriori*, as (very) good.

But we'll notice that this gastronomic star idea:

- Couldn't have stemmed from an improvement on a garage guide.
- Couldn't be derived from the Michelin brothers' first idea in 1900.

And so, the story continues. Today, Michelin's Zoom map 161 details the routes of the Camino de Santiago. The idea is surprising since what was first created to help drivers is now also a useful tool for walkers! A guide for pilgrims isn't an improvement on a garage guide!

Writing innovation

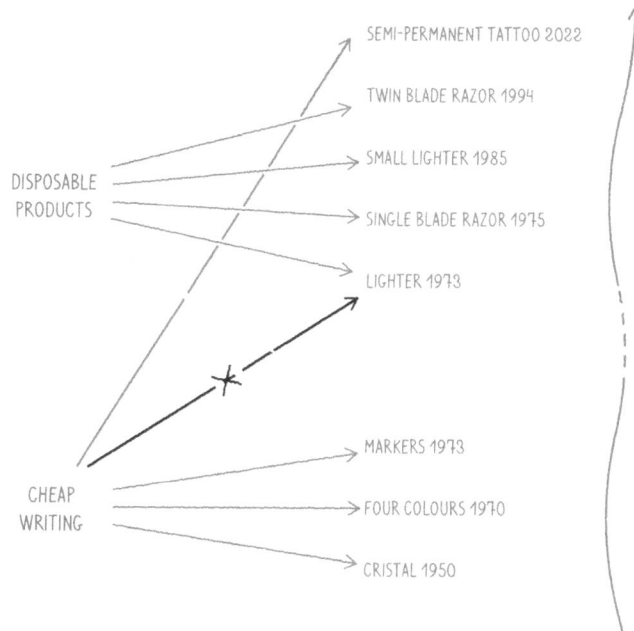

In the 1950s I learned to write with a quill that was dipped in an inkpot embedded in the school desk. One day, a certain Mr Bich decided that enough was enough (so many tautologies!) and so he came up with a new idea: 'I'm going to make writing tools that are easy to use and that are cheap'. This idea (which we will call Strategy 1, or S1) remained his strategy for many years. As soon as an idea is formed, the brain kicks into deduction mode. And that's what happened in the brand new BIC company. They found investors, buildings, writing professionals and salespeople. In 1950 the very first BIC Cristal was commercialized. Over the next thirty years, BIC improved and diversified their product. But after a while, their source of inspiration and improvement started to run dry.

BIC understood the importance of induction. After thirty years of 'the BIC Cristal is an example of a cheap writing tool', they switched to 'the BIC Cristal is an example of a disposable product'. This simultaneously changed nothing and everything. S2 was born. BIC's business was now in the 'disposable' business.

By deduction, it then became possible to branch out into producing lighters and razors. All this without giving up on S1, as BIC proved in 2022 when they bought two companies which specialized in semi-permanent tattoos!

Ambiguity and paradoxes

The Michelin and BIC examples are comparable. In both cases, innovation invited a change in categorization. This is what we called ambiguity in Chapter 2. Let's summarize what we said.

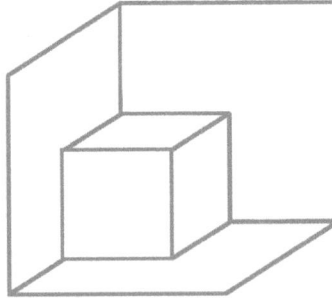

You'll often hear: 'this situation is ambiguous'. But that doesn't make any sense. A situation is what it is. The feeling of ambiguity comes from the presence within us of several mental models that can give coherence and meaning to what is in front of us.

In the example above, it's almost as easy to see a small cube in a corner as it is to see a big cube with a missing chunk. But this isn't always the case, like in the famous image where you usually spot the profile of a young woman first, before spotting the face of an old woman. The same goes for the 'rabbit-duck' image made famous by Wittgenstein.[5] No matter the straightforwardness of these optical illusions, they share one common trait: it is impossible to see both images at the same time.

Here's another example. Can you read this?

Paradox and ambiguity are sometimes represented in a symmetrical manner. The feeling of a paradox appears when a pre-existing mental model doesn't allow two different observations to be made at the same time. This is an invitation to creativity.

Einstein found himself in this situation. In front of him were two incompatible theories: Newton's theory, in which speeds add up, and Maxwell's theory, where the speed of light is constant. So what is the speed of the light beam emitted by the headlight of a flying aircraft?

A paradox can't be solved in the way you'd find a solution to a problem. It dissolves into a new representation of something. Einstein's theory of relativity is a new framework for thought, it's a new way of looking at the world, even if it doesn't actually change it. Einstein reframed physics, without saying that either Newton or Maxwell were wrong. What was incompatible is no longer, the paradox has disappeared, it has vanished in the German-born genius' findings.

---

5.   Ludwig Wittgenstein and Gertrude Elizabeth Margaret Anscombe, *Philosophical Investigations* (1953).

You'll often hear 'this situation is paradoxical'. But that doesn't make any sense. A situation is what it is. Often, the mind doesn't know what to do about two contradicting pieces of information, and it then tends to ignore both of them.

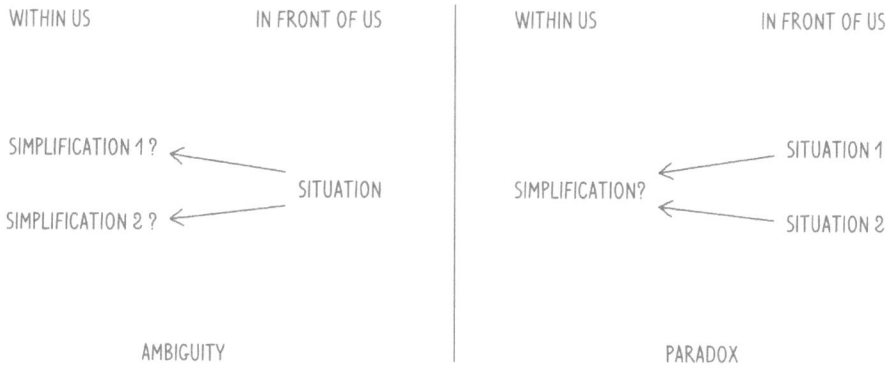

WITHIN US	IN FRONT OF US	WITHIN US	IN FRONT OF US
SIMPLIFICATION 1 ? ←			SITUATION 1
	SITUATION	SIMPLIFICATION?	
SIMPLIFICATION 2 ? ←			SITUATION 2
AMBIGUITY		PARADOX	

7.3. The zigzag imperative

Based on the BIC and Michelin models, it becomes possible to conceptualize and ... induce a wider model.

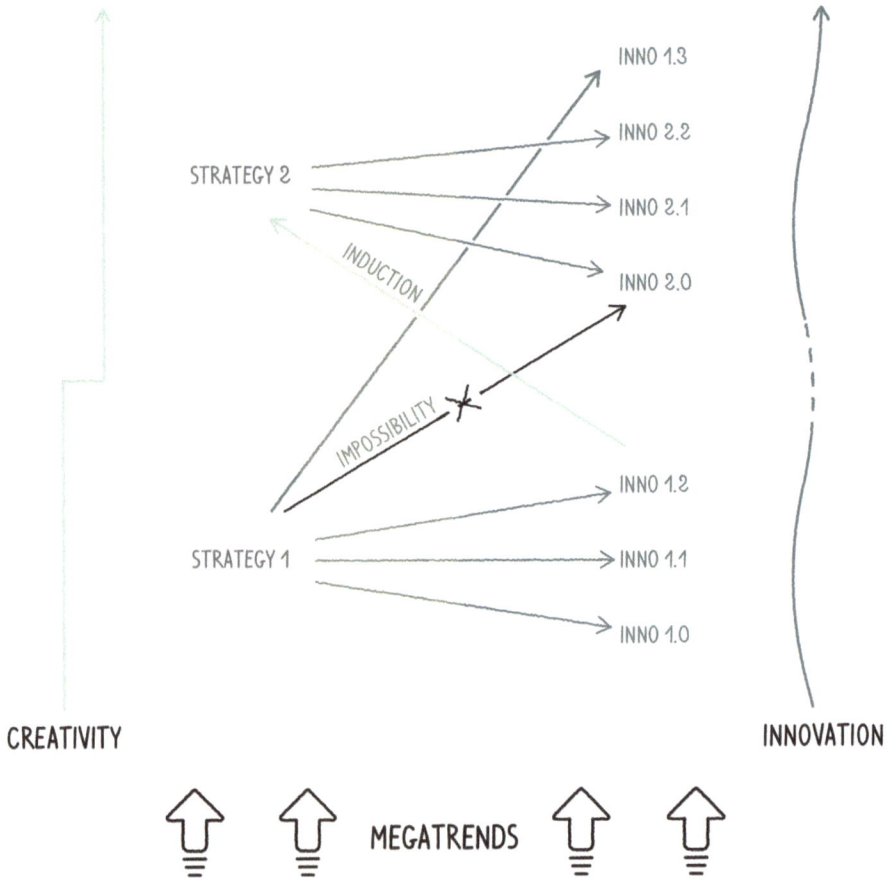

Innovation (on the right-hand side of the diagram) can be defined as the ability to do better, cheaper, more developed, more elegant or more fashion-forward, but essentially to do the same thing.

Creativity (on the left-hand side of the diagram) can be defined as the ability to think about something else while reorganizing our perception. It's not a coincidence that the verb 'creativate' doesn't exist.

		CREATIVITY	INNOVATION
CHANGE OF	---	PERCEPTION	REALITY
DRIVER	---	INDIVIDUAL	ORGANIZATION
PROCESS	---	DISCONTINUOUS	CONTINUOUS
IMPACT	---	NON MEASURABLE	MEASURABLE
TYPE OF THOUGHT	---	DIVERGENT/INDUCTIVE	CONVERGENT/DEDUCTIVE
CONSULTANT ROLE	---	MAKE PEOPLE THINK	MAKE PEOPLE PERFORM

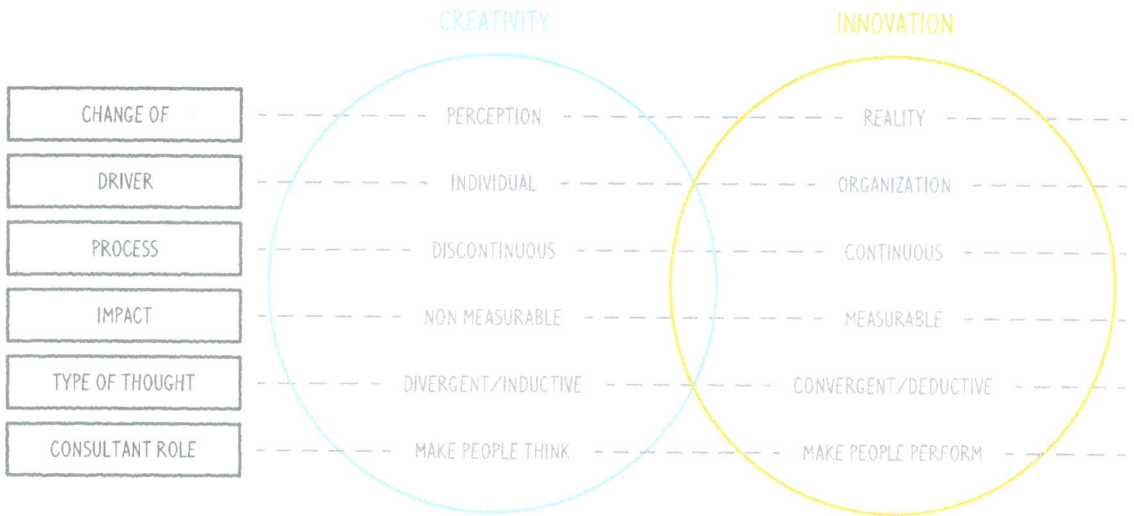

Innovation means continuously improving on things and is derived from a strategy which itself doesn't change. Strategy 1 spurs the first burst of innovation. But a wave of innovations cannot go on indefinitely, precisely because the strategy doesn't change. We cannot endlessly add colours to a pen, blades to a razor, functions to a search engine, or different flavours to a cappuccino.

This is when the creative jump must happen, and it is induced by another perception of things. Strategy 2 is new and sets off a new wave of innovations which could not have been derived from the initial strategy.

S2 doesn't change anything, yet it changes everything. The objects before us remain the same, but they're suddenly perceived and categorized differently. This mental jump allows us to go back to deduction. This change in perception is beneficial to the company because the new strategy offers a means of developing new innovation.

The defining moment of the path which led us to this second wave is the inductive arrow. This creative moment is purely mental. It might only be a break in our way of seeing things. But it's the necessary condition to resume innovation.

Garage owners long employed mechanics who could work with electronics. But today, they hire programmers who aren't afraid of getting their hands dirty …

On a personal note, my midlife crisis also boils down to a change in polarity, so to speak. I'd usually introduce myself as a creative engineer, preferring then to describe myself as a creative person who studied engineering. The doors then opened for me completely. I was a consultant in innovation who studied philosophy to better understand the Ideas and, thirty years later, I am examining how to initiate students into critical thinking!

No one can avoid the zigzag. For a long time, the two main computer providers were Hewlett Packard and Dell. From a user point of view, the differences were minimal. But the way the companies were organized wasn't at all the same. Why? Once again, because of two words being swapped. HP's strategy was to 'manufacture and sell', whereas Dell's goal was to 'sell and manufacture'.

Innovation is possible without creativity. Like a restaurant owner who constantly copies their neighbour's ideas.

Creativity is possible without innovation. The solar system is exactly the same today as it was before Copernicus.

Let's remember law number 6: creativity is the only way to resume innovation and the ultimate responsibility of a CEO is to articulate these back and forths between the two.

No strategic vision is eternal. Under the pressure of megatrends, competition, customers, or regulations of all kinds, one day S1 will give way to S2. And it's in the CEO's interest to have chosen that S2 themself, rather than having it imposed by an external element.

7.4. Thinking in new boxes[6]

When we hear 'think outside the box', what does it actually mean? What is this box that we need to get out of? The zigzag diagram helps us, firstly, to answer this question that we should have asked ourselves a long time ago and, secondly, to realize that it's not actually the right question!

If you're in a bank and you're asked to think outside the box, you're not asked to think outside of the bank. You're asked to leave behind the way you've been simplifying a banker's job for years. And that's not the same thing at all.

The BIC example is clear. The boxes are on the left and are a representation of things, a group of working hypotheses from which we can work out actions. No idea of a product is possible without a box. All products inevitably come from a given box and the important question is knowing how old the box is. Because if a hypothesis is too old, it will eventually stop producing anything interesting. It's time for induction and to choose a new box to jumpstart innovation. It's a double strategy, because a decision must be made on which box to choose and on when to set it up. But once it's known and announced, anyone can help fill it.

Executives must therefore articulate creativity and innovation. The required skills are very different and the big challenge is that the better we are at one of them, the more difficult it is to be good at the other ...

Renault is considered to be a very innovative car manufacturer. But the more the company keep changing their models and cars, the more they are remaining in a posture of not changing, that of a car manufacturer.

In a way, everything is a zigzag in the life of ideas. Amongst all iconic creative inventions, the lightbulb got so much attention that it now symbolizes the eureka moment for a character in many comic strips.

The invention of the electric lightbulb is actually the result of a particularly interesting zigzag: Thomas Edison – we'll say that it's him because twelve other inventors (at least) actually claim that the idea was theirs! – didn't invent lighting. Ever since Prehistory, lots of tools have produced light but they have all been based on a hypothesis: something must be burned to make light. A great deal of inventions were inferred from this supposed necessity. It's indeed possible to burn wax, alcohol, oil, etc.

It's this partially oblivious hypothesis that Edison contested. He decided to produce light without burning anything. The lightbulb became possible, as well as neon tubes, and many new lighting technologies. Today, an LED strip creates light without any burning at all.

Even though there are a lot of common traits between the most sophisticated petrol lamps and the first lightbulb prototype (a glass globe, something luminous on the inside, an on/off switch, etc.), it is impossible to go from one to the other in continuity. Even if they are objectively quite similar, a lightbulb is absolutely not an improved petrol lamp.

6.   Luc de Brabandere and Alan Iny, *Thinking in New Boxes: A New Paradigm for Business Creativity* (New York, 2013).

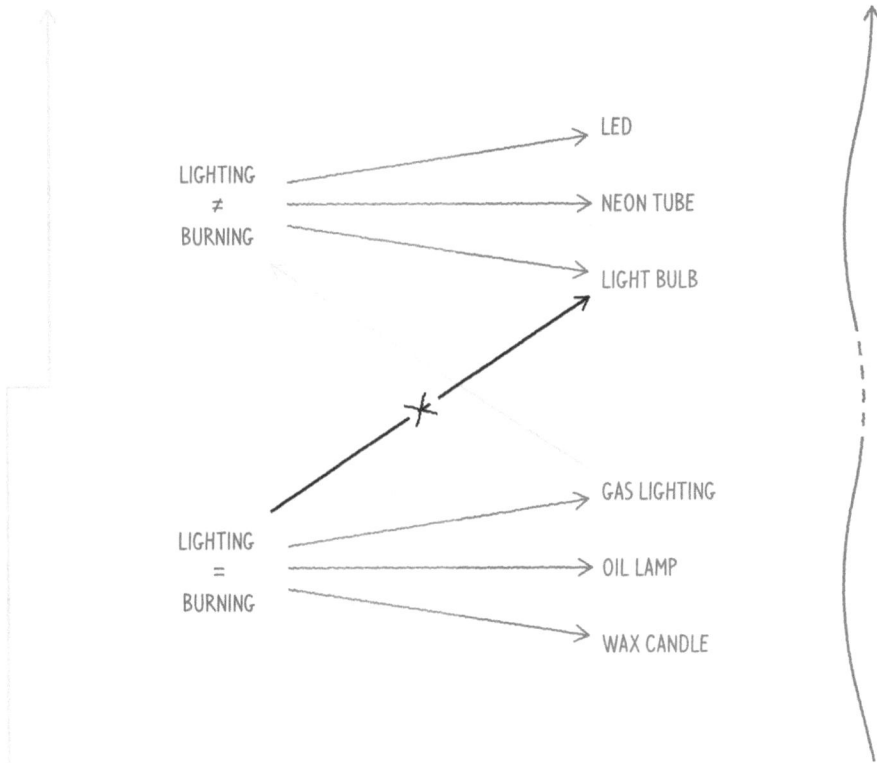

LIGHTING ≠ BURNING → LED
→ NEON TUBE
→ LIGHT BULB

LIGHTING = BURNING → GAS LIGHTING
→ OIL LAMP
→ WAX CANDLE

This chapter highlights the importance of words and especially the order in which we line them up. We've seen that a simple permutation of two words can change the way we see the world. This happened to me while I was studying philosophy.

For a long time, I thought that new ideas were necessary in order to change the world. I changed my mind. I believe we must change our vision of the world in order to pinpoint the existing ideas for which the time is right, out of all the ideas put forward.

A successful brainstorming session is rarely a meeting during which someone suggests a brand new idea. A successful brainstorming is usually a meeting where a new representation of things allows us to understand the potential of a pre-existing idea, which has sometimes been present for a long time.

We can learn a lot from creativity if we understand how Apple made the iPod and iTunes, for example. But we'll understand creativity even better if we look at how Sony managed to NOT do it. And yet they'd had the idea since the 1980s: it was called the Walkman ...

Lots of ideas exist but we can't see them. We all think, all of the time. The production of ideas is therefore a continuous and immense flow, and too often the new idea we're looking for already exists somewhere. When the automotive industry first started out, General Motors and the other giants had a lot of customers who were farmers. And one of the first things that these first buyers did was to take out the back seats because they needed more space to transport straw bales and bulky tools. It took years for the pick-up truck to be 'invented' even though the idea had always been there.

Creativity is therefore a double entry process. On a strategic level, we choose the new box and everyone can then contribute to filling it in the best way possible.

As a more recent example, picture this: a meeting of Mattel's executive committee, number two in the toy world, behind Lego, owning brands like Barbie. One of the items on the agenda is a project for a movie bearing the name of the famous doll. The person who has had this idea describes a script in which the doll's image takes a serious hit and the executive committee looks ridiculous. They're asking for a production budget of over 100 million dollars, and even more for the promotion of the movie. The idea is met with a frosty silence, and most of the people present are thinking 'Got any other stupid ideas like that one?'

In this kind of situation, everything is in place to kill the idea instantly, and its bearer alongside it.

And yet the film was produced, and the zigzag is the explanation. For the past fifty years, at Mattel, the sentence 'Barbie is an example of ... ' had been finished with 'a doll'. This had allowed them to fuel fifty years of innovations, adapting the doll to the changing world. But one day the sentence ended with 'modern-day heroine' and it then became deductively possible to make a movie about promoting her values. S2 is impressive, and Mattel suddenly find themselves competing with Netflix!

The reward came in the form of success. But the merit is great. And S1 still isn't dead: proof being that in 2024, Mattel released a Barbie of Queen Camilla!

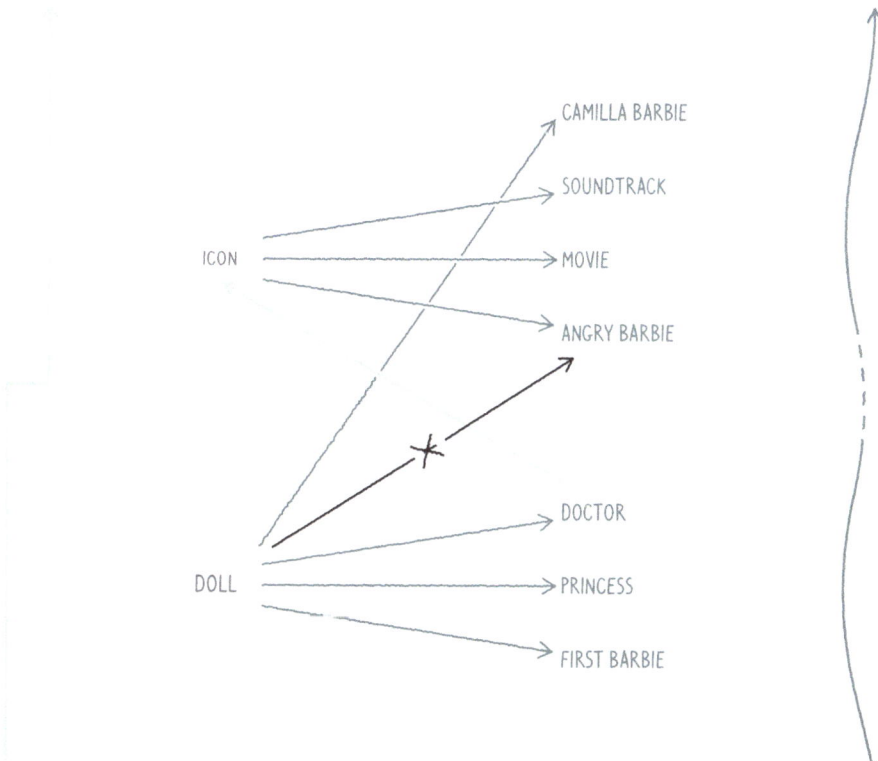

7.5. Obeying the laws of ideas

Let's summarize the forces at play in the world of Ideas that Bacon recommends we obey.

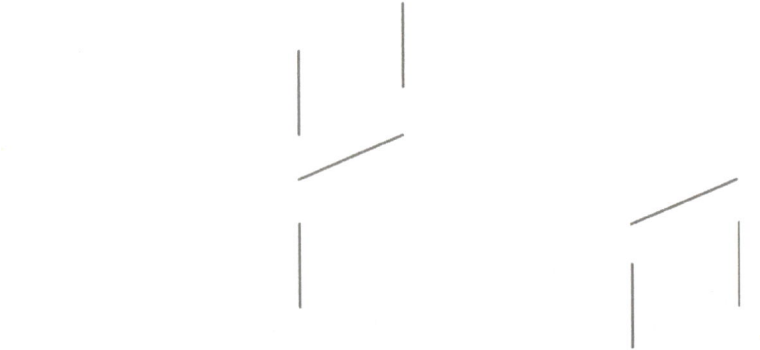

1. *An idea is a construct of the mind*

Take a look at these seven lines. Maybe they remind you of rugby goalposts. But what about if you see them as a whole? What do you see now? Can you see a bed? If so, something has happened: there has been a shift and something has clicked. By trying to understand the image, your mind has built an explanation to put together the different pieces. This is a proactive cognitive process, even though it is partly unconscious, and relies on what we have within us (images, memories, etc.) to interpret what is in front of us. It's this kind of mechanism that produces ideas.

2. *An idea is necessarily a simplification*

Whether it is a start-up project or a vacation, whether it is a new vision of social security, the outline of a political speech, the subject of a novel or the principles of computer architecture, at first glance an idea is necessarily a simplification. It can be expressed in a few sentences. An idea is an abstraction produced by the spirit that catalyses a few concepts and rushes them into a small mental structure.

3. *An idea is a working hypothesis*

The consequence is immediate. Just like a model, an idea is never true or false. 'Science is the asymptote of truth', claimed Victor Hugo.[7] Newton's theory isn't exact and neither is Einstein's. But relativity is a more useful idea than the law of universal gravitation. Any idea, regardless of its brilliance, is only ever a hypothesis. In science, it can help to explain the world better; in business, it means that change is sometimes possible. In science, a big idea is often called a theory; in business, it's often called a strategy.

---

7.   'La science est l'asymptote de la vérité'. Victor Hugo, *William Shakespeare* (Brussels, 1864).

4. No idea lasts forever

For an idea to pay off, it can't be touched. To start shooting a movie, the script must be set, and if we want to travel, we have to know where we're going. The same can be said for not thinking about a strategy in order to set it into motion. But the world doesn't stop turning. There will inevitably be a gap between an idea that has been wisely set and a world that is constantly evolving. One day, we'll need a new idea and to simplify things in a different way.

5. No idea began as a good idea

There is no example in history of an idea that was good from the moment it came to mind. An idea is firstly new, nothing more. The ideas behind bread, democracy, James Bond or WhatsApp were born vague and inaccurate in someone's mind. A new idea begins in a raw state and only, eventually, becomes a good one after a long period of discussion with other thinkers and being confronted with reality. 1 per cent finding, 99 per cent work …

6. The best way to have a good idea is to have many

The brain is a two-stroke engine capable of diverging by forgetting about the constraints, and then converging by taking them into consideration. But any attempt at operating both hemispheres simultaneously will result in disappointment, even frustration. Imagination and judgement operate on a different logic: imagination is assessed by the quantity of ideas produced, while judgement is assessed by the quality of the ideas chosen.

7. Moving from one idea to another is always a shock

This next law is the result of others indeed, but it is however useful to highlight it. Since an idea is a simplification, changing ideas means moving from one simplification to another, which can't happen smoothly. On a vast majority of subjects, we think today in the same way we thought last week, last month, even last year. A change in opinion or perception is therefore rare and sudden.

8. All ideas inevitably come from a box

A box is a framework of thought: a group of assumptions, stereotypes, hypotheses, etc. In other words, it's a sort of lens through which we observe the world. When we talk about creativity – as we saw before – the expression 'outside the box' isn't really appropriate because any idea inevitably comes from a framework. By changing one or several original hypotheses, we're creating a new framework which can be used to spot the potential of an old idea which will suddenly be qualified as new. Being creative requires not so much leaving the box as creating several new ones to better choose the right one.

And it becomes clear that the difficulty doesn't lie in having new ideas; the difficulty lies in the necessity of giving up on old ideas.

7.6. The creative thinker's toolbox

Many books have been written on creativity methods and techniques, and I recommend you seek out those that fit with your interests and your strengths. But it is useful to summarize here a few of the fundamental and unavoidable concepts that are essential for anyone who wants to develop their creativity – and that of others – while making a link with the zigzag model, more precisely by zooming in on the 'step' on the left which represents the eureka moment sparked by a change in perception.

'Yes, and ... ' vs 'Yes, but ... '

As explained above, there is no point in wanting to jump in one go from an existing idea to the next good idea, no one has ever managed that leap.

The creative leap happens on the first half of the step, the one where we move from an existing idea to a new idea. At this point, two reactions are possible: it's either a variation on 'yes, but ... ' or it takes the shape of 'yes, and ... '. Only the second reaction makes sense.

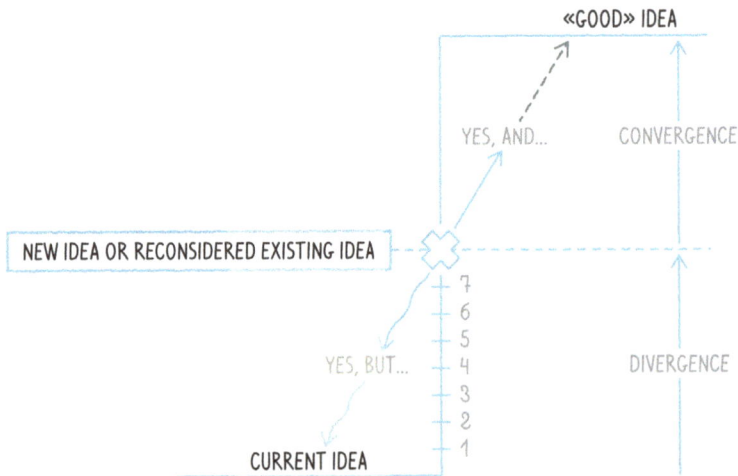

Three types of new ideas

There are three possible types of new ideas: discovery, invention and creation. The table below summarizes the main differences between the three.

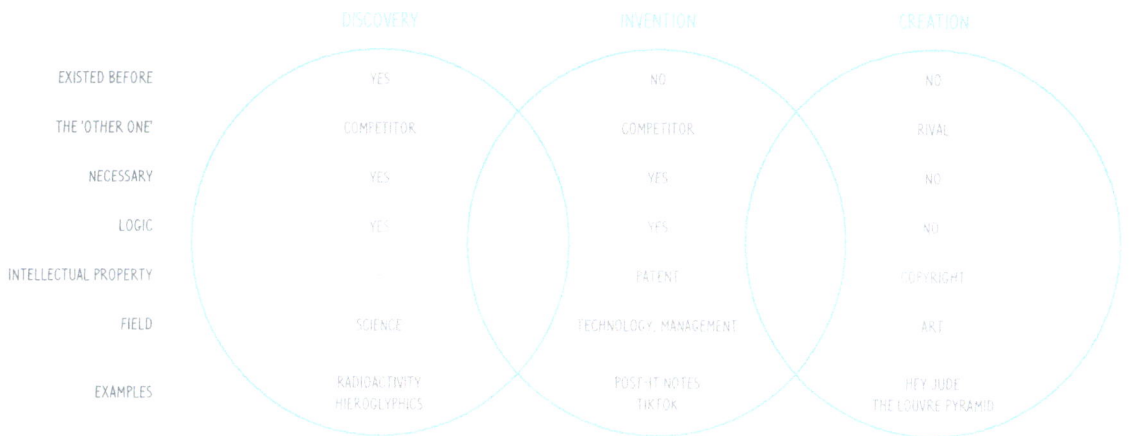

	DISCOVERY	INVENTION	CREATION
EXISTED BEFORE	YES	NO	NO
THE 'OTHER ONE'	COMPETITOR	COMPETITOR	RIVAL
NECESSARY	YES	YES	NO
LOGIC	YES	YES	NO
INTELLECTUAL PROPERTY		PATENT	COPYRIGHT
FIELD	SCIENCE	TECHNOLOGY, MANAGEMENT	ART
EXAMPLES	RADIOACTIVITY HIEROGLYPHICS	POST-IT NOTES TIKTOK	HEY JUDE THE LOUVRE PYRAMID

Eureka!

In order to reach a new idea, a series of seven steps is possible, without all of them always being necessary. The first six moments are all major subjects of study in philosophy and cognitive science, and they all take part in the inductive thought part of the I/D model. We've already mentioned astonishment in Chapter 4, and we will talk about attention again in the next chapter, but here they are, lined up chronologically (and therefore from the bottom up on the diagram showing the steps from 'current idea' to 'good idea').

1. Attention
   'The taking possession by the mind, in clear and vivid form, of one out of what seem several simultaneously possible objects or trains of thought'. – William James[8]
2. Curiosity
   An eager wish to know or learn about something.[9] A response to an information gap.[10]
3. Astonishment
   Emotion caused by an event that leads to questions because of its being unusual, unexpected, strange, and difficult to explain.
4. Doubt
   State of neither believing nor disbelieving a proposition.[11]
5. Intuition
   The ability to acquire knowledge, without recourse to conscious reasoning or needing an explanation[12]
6. Questioning
   Utterance which functions as a request for information.[13]
7. Brainstorm/Creativity methods (optional)

8. William James, 'Attention', in *The Principles of Psychology*, American Science Series, 2 vols (New York, 1890), i.
9. Cambridge dictionary.
10. George Loewenstein, 'The Psychology of Curiosity: A Review and Reinterpretation', *Psychological Bulletin*, 116/1 (1994), 75–98.
11. Oxford Dictionary of Philosophy.
12. This definition is taken from Wikipedia's entry for 'Intuition'.
13. This definition is adapted from Wikipedia's entry for 'Question'.

The seventh step is of a different type, it's the brainstorming process that can be enriched by a number of creative methods. The most well-known are the combinatorial, associative, analogue and random methods.

We need to remember that the toolbox doesn't make the handyman, and that the best facilitator has equal amounts of ideas and energy, and as much rigour as ability to release the creativity of the participants.

7.7. Constraints and creativity

Niccolò Paganini was an exceptional violinist. And as if playing the violin wasn't hard enough as it is, the Italian artist would occasionally snap a string or two in order to make playing the piece even more difficult.

He was also a composer. In his famous piece for a single cello string, the musician isn't given a choice! But the minutes spent listening to this single string are pure enjoyment.

Regardless of whether it was imposed or chosen, a constraint made the artist push his boundaries even further. And there are many examples of this type: Maurice Ravel took up the challenge of composing a piece where the same double melody is repeated without any development. The result, with 169 repetitions, was *Boléro*!

A year later, Paul Wittgenstein, famous pianist and brother of the philosopher Ludwig, even asked Ravel to compose for him a piece for left-handed musicians. The pianist had lost his right arm during the First World War and suffered terribly from not being able to play his favourite instrument anymore.

André Gide once said: 'Art is born of constraint, lives of struggle, dies of freedom'.[14] Does the missing, the needing, the absence of something lead to more creativity than the having, abundance or comfort do?

Django Reinhardt confirmed this theory. He was a gifted guitar player but was severely burned when his caravan caught fire and he lost the use of two fingers. After neverending rehabilitation treatment, he devised a new musical playing technique that was so fascinating that some fans went as far as binding their own fingers in order to copy his disability!

Constraint and creativity! These two words that we're not used to seeing together. And yet! Imagination takes kindly to discipline. And creativity sometimes even feeds off rigour, as long as it isn't trapped by it, but rather framed by it. As is the case in jazz, where musicians improvise one after the other, following a pre-established set of rules known in advance. Creative thought unfolds like a jam session, imagination is let loose because there are limits to this freedom.

Greek tragedies and Cicero's speeches, Renaissance frescoes and Bach's concertos, temples, tapestries, sculptures, all of these works of art are considered to be beautiful or grandiose, yet they all hide a restrictive structure and relentless discipline.

Proving Aristotle wrong

History and science are crawling with examples of how the absence of resources has limited researchers' creativity. One of my favourite examples comes from the Italian Renaissance.

---

14. André Gide, 'L'évolution du théâtre' (Brussels, 1904). The title, which translates to *The evolution of theatre*, is that of a conference. Its text is transcribed in *Nouveax Prétextes* (Paris, 1911), which translates as *New Pretexts*.

Ever since Aristotle, it was accepted that a falling body falls at a constant speed. Galileo wanted to prove that, in reality, the speed increases as time goes by, there is an acceleration.

The Italian scholar couldn't measure time accurately enough, so he came up with the genius idea of an inclined plane: he slowed down the fall by rolling a ball on a long slope. He built the inclined plane with a rail so that he could slide small bells up and down it. By letting go of the ball at the top, he wanted to make sure that the bells rang at perfectly regular intervals. He noticed that, when this perfect pace was respected, the bells were respectively at 1, 2, 4, 8 and 16 lengths from the summit. Not only was there an acceleration, it could even be calculated and put into equations!

But let's be careful: so many examples in so many different disciplines could lead us to believe that we have found the method, the recipe, the secret for creativity! So it's constraint that is unavoidable? Of course not! As soon as a hypothesis seems plausible, the opposite hypothesis needs to be tried ... and it turns out to be just as plausible!

For example, what made the explosion of creativity in painting 200 years ago possible? Why, the disappearance of a constraint of course! The invention of photography suddenly freed the painter of a feeling of obligation, conscious or not: that of copying reality in order to immortalize it.

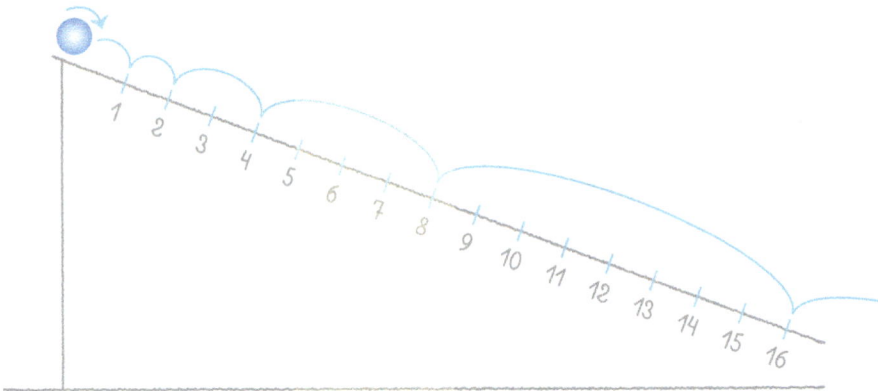

7.8. Being creative in a digital world

Evian vs Spotify

The book that you're holding in your hands defends a very precise claim. We need to go back to the basic principles of thought, we need to be conscious of its strengths and weaknesses in order to see how much it has been impacted by the arrival of digitalization.

In business, digital transformation is at the centre of everyone's attention, but it's often forgotten that a successful transformation is necessarily twofold. As explained above, we need to change both reality and the perception of reality.

To measure the scale of this switch, let's take a business that sells mineral water, and turn our attention to its production. Beside every bottle produced, let's imagine a second, virtual bottle, containing all information and knowledge about the real bottle. We find out where it is, the name of the purchaser, the difference in price with competing bottles, the marketing investment for the brand, etc. We can also find out the expertise used to analyse it, the patents issued for the type of cap, the new business strategy for new bottle sizes, etc.

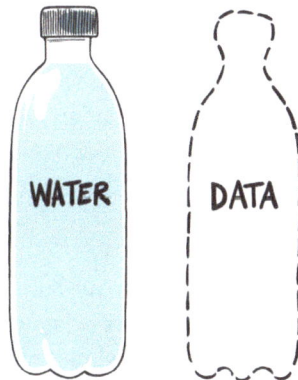

And here comes the question worth 100 bitcoins: which of these bottles has more value? Obviously the second one, with a consequence that Copernic would not have disavowed. The society that conditions and sells bottles is indeed no longer a business that provides the market with mineral water and manages the information related to it. No, this company is a *big data* business operating in mineral water.

What is true for water is also true for coffee, a pen and for the overwhelming majority of consumer goods. The starting point of successful digital transformation is not the current situation of relevant businesses or organizations, but rather a reassessment of the hypotheses and principles that explain it. But for the resulting digital transformation to be a success, we need to simultaneously reinvent concepts, categories and models that society has settled into, and that are all over seventy years old.

The fatal equation is the perception that the future is built by adding new technologies to the present. This is what is going on in Lampedusa's *The Leopard*, mentioned in Chapter 2.

With digital transformation, we are in a similar situation. The change is such that if we want a professor to still be able to teach, if we want an executive to still be able to perform, if we want a doctor to still be able to treat patients, if we want Culture to keep its essential role, if we want magistrates to still be able to guarantee the rule of law, then everything must change!

The challenge is not to 'digitize' all of these essential jobs but rather to reinvent them in a world where disruptive tools are now available.

This fatal equation has been causing trouble for a while now. There are countless examples where we have 'mechanized' or 'electrified' something without giving it enough thought. Here are three examples in the history of transport:

- We did not start out by inventing the bicycle. The first device was equipped with a frame, wheels and a handlebar but had no chains or pedals! It was called a 'velocipede' and, as the word indicates in Latin, was designed to allow the feet to go faster ...
- Why did the first railway carriages have as many doors as they had compartments? Simply because they were thought of as a series of stage coaches placed side by side!
- In the 1960s, some cars were equipped with lateral mechanical arrows that indicated the intention of turning to the driver behind. We invented the turn signal only when we reassessed the initial question, not when we modernized a previous answer.

The future is not the result of an addition of old ideas to new tools. A sober, useful and desirable future will be built by asking the question: 'now that new tools exist, what will I do, and how?' In other words, to use the same vocabulary as above, before thinking about innovating, let's start by being creative!

The zigzag method is particularly suited to face the challenge of digital transformation. In the mineral water example presented at the beginning of the chapter, the result is the following: the executives are extremely surprised to see that their new competitors are not the drinks salespeople, but electricity distributors or social media which also gather information about people who drink mineral water!

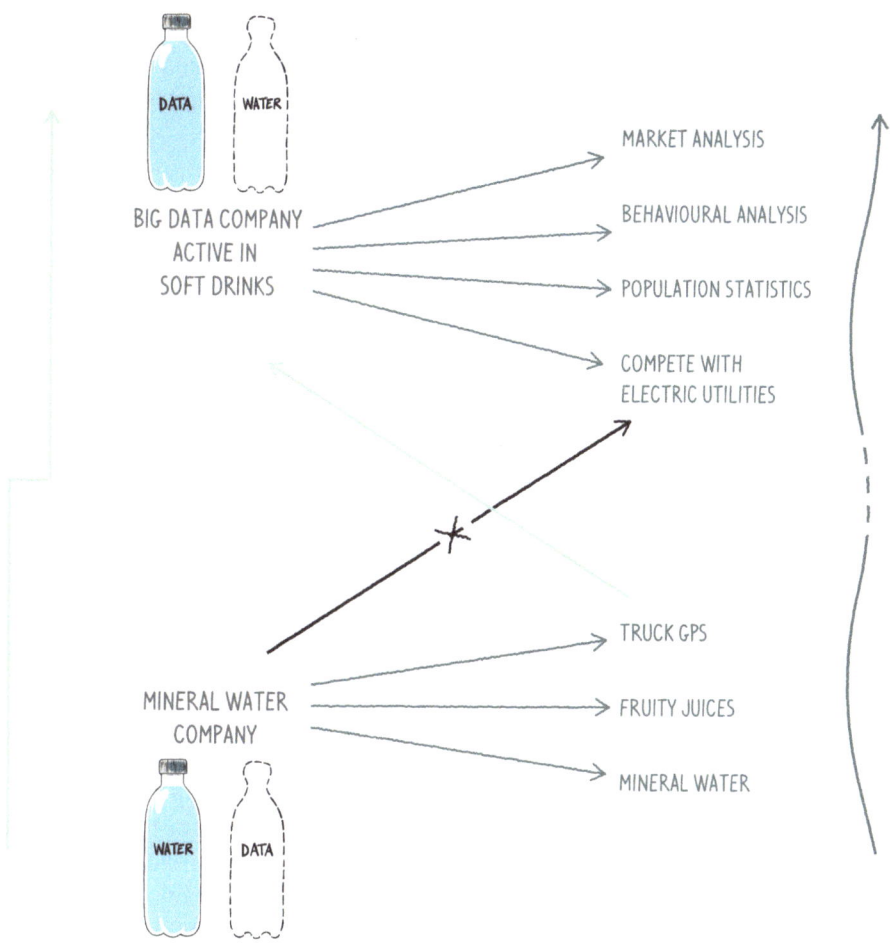

Big problems and big data

At the beginning of this book, we referred to the *Wired* article *The End of Theory* published in August 2008. The author claimed that the accumulation of billions of data points renders the use of models useless, that correlations are enough to make forecasts, that theories have become superfluous and that a machine will know what to decide, even if we don't understand why.

We obviously don't agree with this. Computers are no match for human creativity. I would like to break my argument down into three steps.

To start with, let's take eight people who are world-renowned for their creativity and who have left their mark on history, in different domains: Aristotle in philosophy, Coco Chanel in fashion, Archimedes in physics, Schubert in music, Agatha Christie in literature, Freud in psychology, Charlie Chaplin in the movie industry and Maria Montessori in pedagogy.

They all produced their best work before the advent of computers. But how would a computer have changed their contribution to their respective disciplines? The essence of their creativity didn't rely on existing theories or data. Even the only scientist amongst them, Archimedes, is no exception. His 'Eureka!', that he uttered suddenly when he came up with the first principles of hydraulics, wasn't the result of calculations or infinitely repeated experiments, it came from an insight that only a human being could have.

The essence of human creativity therefore doesn't necessarily require a mass accumulation of data or algorithms, and the thesis put forth in *Wired* already can't withstand this first observation.

Let's concentrate on science and technology for a moment, with nine other profiles that are both emblematic and varied. In doing so, we will look at the link between data and theories, between information and creativity. These nine 'influencers' also all lived in the pre-internet world (and two of them are Belgian, that's no coincidence ...).

The first five used lots of data.

When Johannes Kepler was born in 1571, it was assumed that the Sun was at the centre of the Solar System and that it was orbited by planets set on circular paths. Yet, when he analysed the writings of the Dane Tycho Brahé, who had spent hundreds of nights observing the sky, Kepler spotted an anomaly in Mars' trajectory. Was the Creator bold enough to slightly deform it? To somehow flatten orbits? Progressively, Kepler began to imagine the unimaginable.

Adolphe Quetelet was a Belgian mathematician, naturalist, astronomer and, above all, statistician. The essence of this profession is to analyse extremely large quantities of data. With a keen interest in sociology, he took a scientific look at people and presented his idea of the 'average man' as the central value of the Gauss curve. He also designed the Body Mass Index (BMI), calculated by dividing the weight in kilograms by the height in meters squared (kg/m^2). The concept is still very topical. Some beauty contests, for example, refuse candidates whose BMI is below 18, in an attempt to combat anorexia.

Contrary to the first two scientists, Charles Darwin developed his own big data! During an incredible five-year journey by ship, he took countless notes. He left for a trip around the world when he was twenty-one and observed everything that moved in great detail. In the Galapagos, for example, he identified thirteen different species of chaffinches! He gathered a tremendous amount of scientific data that he regularly sent to the British Museum. When he returned to London in 1836, he started to analyse it ...

Diderot and d'Alembert (a philosopher and an engineer!) lead the writing of the *Encyclopédie*[15] during the Enlightenment. They wanted to accumulate all of the knowledge in the world in one place and make it accessible to as many people as possible.

For the next four, the accumulation of data was not a priority.

French Egyptologist Jean-François Champollion faced another challenge: what was the meaning of these millions of hieroglyphs engraved on almost every Egyptian monument? His predecessors were

---

15.   See Diderot and D'Alembert (1751) cited above. The monumental task of assembling this encyclopedia took them over twenty years, as it was only completed in 1772.

worn out from trying to answer a misconceived question: are hieroglyphs small drawings or are they alphabetical characters? A pictogram or an ideogram? Champollion decided to ask the question in another way.

Ernest Solvay filed a patent for a new process for producing soda ash and founded the eponymous company that would become a multinational.

In 1898 Marie Curie emitted the hypothesis of radioactivity, by observing the way in which radium can burn a photographic plate from a distance.

And we've already seen how Thomas Edison developed the first lightbulb.

All together, these diverse profiles allow us to clarify the role that creativity plays in the digital world. We will of course be building a new Venn diagram, with the following dimensions:

- The difference between discovery and invention, as explained at the beginning of this chapter.
- The use or not of large quantities of information.
- The impact that an algorithm might have had (had they been available).

With no surprise, the following diagram presents eight possible combinations.

Kepler would have been the most impacted by artificial intelligence. He would even have lost his job, as he brought together a concept that had existed for a long time (the ellipse) with a large number of observations of the sky. And this, a computer can do better than anyone.

Darwin brought his theory of natural selection to the table, a new concept that no algorithm could have produced. The same goes for Marie Curie's discovery and Quetelet's invention. Champollion's work would have been made possible with artificial intelligence, Diderot and d'Alembert's would have been considerably helped, even though we've seen by showing the strengths and weaknesses of any classification system that these can never be perfect. Their three-part organization (memory, reason and imagination) was actually later abandoned. Ernest Solvay's story is one of innovation more than creativity, and computers would have helped him considerably to build his empire. This is less true for Thomas Edison, whose real passion was to invent, as shown by the more than 1,000 patents that he filed, which is still an all-time record.

So, contrary to *Wired* magazine's claim, science hasn't reached its end just yet. No, in a digital world, creativity has changed. Artificial intelligence enables us to discover new things every day, but it will never be an exact substitute for a human being who is capable of inventing. The large language models deliver surprising answers but will always depend on the question asked. It's all about 'prompting', as Socrates said a long time ago!

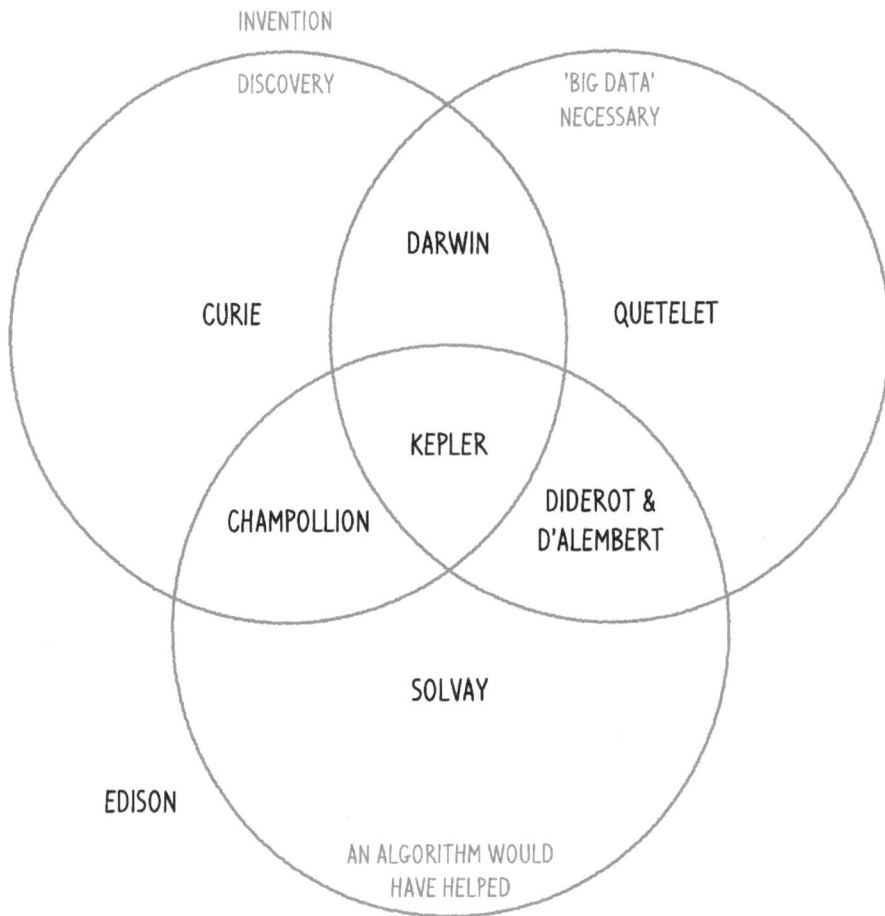

INVENTION

DISCOVERY

'BIG DATA' NECESSARY

DARWIN

CURIE

QUETELET

KEPLER

CHAMPOLLION

DIDEROT & D'ALEMBERT

SOLVAY

EDISON

AN ALGORITHM WOULD HAVE HELPED

A computer does not have ideas

In 2016, a machine named AlphaGo beat the world champion at the game of go, and news spread like wildfire in the media: man had met his match.

But we are still a long way from that, and for at least two reasons: the computer did indeed win, but it is incapable of knowing what it played, why it played, or what a game is.

The computer did indeed win, but this did not make it proud or happy.

Both observations perfectly illustrate the two unsurpassable limits of a computer. Unlike a human being, it cannot be aware of its actions, nor can it have feelings.

Let's take a closer look:

1. A human being can tell the difference between what they are and what they are not. They know that something outside of themself exists. Their intelligence is developed by multiplying points of view and crossing different perspectives.

Stoics already recommended 'climbing the hill' to see things from above and not just through a small house window. This same invitation has travelled through time, as demonstrated by the late Robin Williams who witnessed this in his role in *Dead Poets Society* where he played a professor who climbs on his desk.

Being aware requires being able to take some distance. A machine is unconscious because it cannot step outside of itself. AlphaGo promoters explained that their program's success is based on its ability to learn in depth, something they call 'deep learning'. They made the machine play itself during millions of Go games which were randomly generated. This definitely contributed to improving the software. But the program never did more than the same thing.

A machine cannot step back and no so-called 'intelligent' system is aware of what it is doing, which is paradoxical to say the least. An automatic lawn mower that keeps knocking into things will definitely end up changing its trajectory. But it cannot come up with the idea of replacing itself with sheep.

And in any case, in order for a computer to one day be conscious, we would first need to be able to explain to ourselves what consciousness is and then tell others ... But nobody is capable of doing this yet.

2. Philosophers make a difference between factual judgements and value judgements. 'The Earth is round' is an example of the first and 'the Earth is in danger' illustrates the second.

A computer cannot make a value judgement. A computer does not have feelings. It can recognize a song, but it cannot find it beautiful. It could potentially confirm that a mathematician's reasoning is correct but it cannot say if a football referee's decision is unfair.

A computer can free us from many tedious tasks, but this does not mean that it can make us free. It can help us to predict but not to want. It can help us to find information but not tell us which information to search for. It can analyse the direction of things but cannot know the meaning. It can contribute to science but cannot reach consciousness.

A screwdriver does not have ideas. An elevator does not have ideas. A power plant does not have ideas. It is probably worth reiterating that a computer does not have ideas either.

Later on we'll come back to this fundamental difference between factual judgement and value judgement by opposing descriptive philosophy and prescriptive philosophy.

The Ringtu test

Let's, for a second, imagine a world that is 100 per cent rational.

Imagine a world where each gift is calculated, each friendship is programmed, every purchase is logical, all food is translated into numbers and planned, each emotion is measured, an algorithm decides what is beautiful and what is ugly and another differentiates the good from the bad.

It would be unbearable. The world would be a living hell because this world would simply not be human. Humankind is, thankfully, not 100 per cent rational. We are humans because we can sometimes be melancholic, sometimes be full of energy, because our language is locally defective, because we can have a crush or be crushed, because our memory fails us, because our values motivate us.

Humans are not 100 per cent rational, so we should at least be ... reasonable. Strangely, these two words share the same etymology and yet so many things tear them apart, and technology differentiates them even more. Rationality is programmable, reason is not.

A relationship between two people cannot be 100 per cent rational with its inevitable misunderstandings, context, paradoxes, good and bad surprises, frictions, games and imperfections. A relationship that is obsessed with efficiency is doomed. Refusing to calculate everything is part of human nature. A large portion of what makes up our humanity would dissolve in a world built only on algorithms. The very essence of generosity is that it cannot be calculated because 100 per cent rational selflessness would happen at the detriment of others.

Imitating the machine

Alan Turing is a Second World War hero. His deciphering of the Enigma machine used by the Germans provided the Allies with information that was critical in securing the final victory.

The film *The Imitation Game* tells his fascinating story and his unjust and tragic death in 1954. The title is not directly linked to the decrypting of the German secret code but is an ode to another side of his genius: as a computer science pioneer. Alan Turing was indeed one of the first thinkers of algorithms and of what we call artificial intelligence. He suggested, for example, that we should evaluate an artificial intelligence's sophistication based on its capacity to imitate humans. According to Alan Turing, a computer can be labelled 'intelligent' if it is capable of tricking someone into believing it is a human being. The machine can then be congratulated for passing the Turing test.

But things have changed over the last seventy years and if the news is anything to go by, we could imagine a test working the other way around which would no longer measure artificial intelligence's progress but rather the user's decline. Humans passed the Ringtu test when our vocabulary had become so weak and our critical thinking so elementary that the machine thought it was dealing with another machine!

We need to be careful not to confuse 'being' intelligent and 'seeming' intelligent. In my opinion, a computer will only be considered intelligent when it laughs at a joke that it doesn't know or when it reacts to a cartoon that it's never seen before. In other words, a computer will never be intelligent.

Chapter 8 – Be critical!

The best proof of the existence of intelligent alien life is that they haven't contacted us

BE CRITICAL

WITHIN US		IN FRONT OF US

LANGUAGE, BIAS, DOUBT, SEMANTIC, ETC.

INDUCTION

CLAIM
GOAL
BELIEF
FORECAST
STEREOTYPE
CAUSE
ETC.

DEDUCTION

ARGUMENTATION, EXPLANATION,
ETC.

SOCIAL NETWORK
FAKE NEWS
FALLACY
VIRTUAL REALITY
RUMOURS
'POST TRUTH'
CORRELATION
ETC.

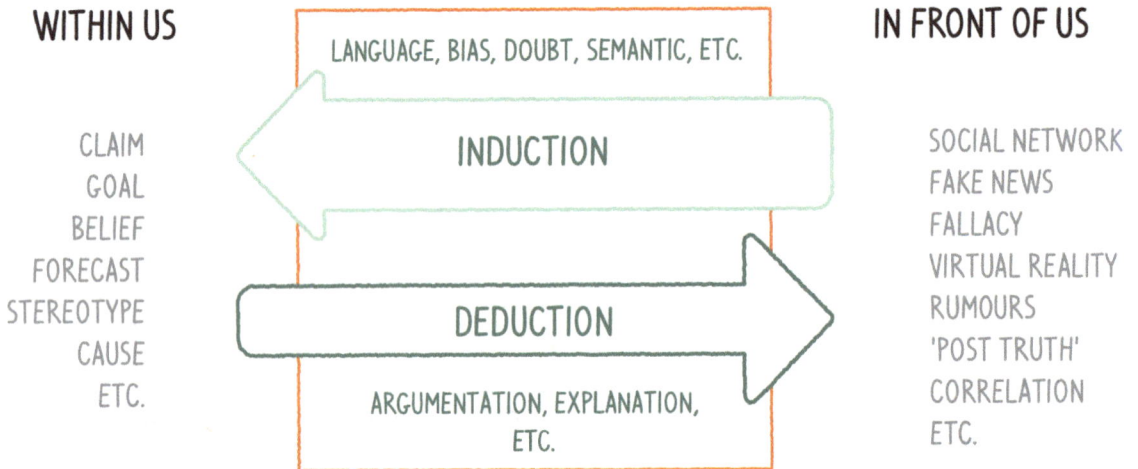

8.1. A very short history of critical thinking

In Ancient Greece, in the fifth century BC, some eloquent professors turned their oratory skills into a particularly lucrative profession. Thanks to lame arguments, they were able to 'prove' something and simultaneously its opposite. Convinced that 'man is the measure of all things', Protagoras was amongst those called 'sophists'.

In the Gorgias, Plato pitted Callicles, a pretentious, maybe even violent young aristocrat for whom success had no price, against Socrates, for whom it was more moral to suffer injustice than to commit it. Socrates dismantled Callicles' arguments one by one.

The first to study the nature and structure of fallacious arguments was – once more – Aristotle. He also wrote the first rhetorical treatise, in which he demonstrated the importance of *ethos* and *pathos*, as well as that of *logos*.

Cicero drew inspiration from him, and his speeches influenced the history of Rome. He remains to this day a reference in the oratory art.

Do we gain access to truth via reason or faith? Thomas Aquinas suggested a way of settling this dilemma and became the leading philosopher of the Catholic Church. William of Ockham fought against useless words and ideas, and wanted to remove all superfluous assumptions with his 'razor'.

During the Renaissance, the critical mind was placed at the heart of scientific debates. Francis Bacon suggested a method for researchers and scholars, telling them to destroy their 'idols', in other words their main prejudices.

In contrast to Bacon's empiricism, Descartes recommends a realistic approach coupled with 'methodical doubt', a posture of systematic mistrust towards everything that we think and feel.

John Locke is to England what Descartes was to France. In 'An Essay Concerning Human Understanding',[1] he reveals the hollow and vain side of Aristotelian logic, since any idea can only be the result of an argument.

Around 1658, Blaise Pascal wrote *The Art of Persuasion*[2] as a preface to a surprising treatise about … geometry! It was never published. This unexpected association of mathematics and rhetoric demonstrates the rigour that the French theologian wanted to impose on the construction of discourse.

Despite being a fan of the ideas from the Age of Enlightenment, Jeremy Bentham dreamt of a science of politics. Convinced that if logic is faulty, then people are too, he became an expert in argumentation. John Stuart Mill finalized his treatise *Book of Fallacies*.[3]

Etymologically speaking, the word 'critical' comes from the Greek 'kriterion' and can be translated as 'the rule by which one judges'. As such, a 'criterion' can therefore be defined as a rule or a principle used to judge something.

And this is how Kant used it. He placed it once again front and centre on the philosophers' workbench. His motto for the Age of Enlightenment was 'Sapere Aude!'[4] This Latin principle meaning 'Dare to know' comes from Horace,[5] and loosely translates as 'Have the courage to use your own reason!'

According to Nietzsche, philosophizing with a hammer means testing the idols or fake gods (moral values) to reveal their true selves. You could also say it's like gently tapping a wall to see whether it's hollow.

Schopenhauer took great interest in the logic of discourse. Eternally pessimistic, he recommended always being initially suspicious of bad intentions from one's counterpart. As a classic of argumentation, and of bad faith, *The Art of Being Right* is a must for whomever takes an interest in sophism.

Karl Popper believed that disciplines such as psychoanalysis or economics could not be considered as scientific as they cannot be falsified.

Born in Warsaw in 1912, Chaïm Perelman emigrated to Belgium in 1925. He became the reference for all matters relating to argumentation, and defined it as 'a discursive technique used to provoke or increase the adhesion of an audience to a thesis presented for their assent'.[6]

1.   John Locke, *An Essay Concerning Human Understanding* (London, 1689).
2.   *L'art de persuader*, translated by Orlando Williams Wight in Charles William Eliot, ed., *Blaise Pascal* (New York, 1910).
3.   Jeremy Bentham, *The Book of Fallacies from Unfinished Papers by Jeremy Bentham* (London, 1824).
4.   Immanuel Kant and Lewis White Beck, 'An Answer to the Question: "What Is Enlightenment?"' (Indianapolis, 1963).
5.   Horace, *Epistularum Liber Primus (First Book of Letters)*, 20AD.
6.   Chaïm Perelman and Lucie Olbrechts-Tyteca, *Traité de l'argumentation, la nouvelle rhétorique* (Paris, 1958). The title can be translated as *Treatise on argumentation, the new rhetoric*.

Following the disaster that was the Second World War, Hannah Arendt defended the need for all strata of society to be thinking critically, not just the elite.

What we nowadays call 'posttruth' is only the modern-day expression of the indifference to truth that the sophists of Antiquity were known for. The emergence and subsequent rise of ChatGPT and other so-called 'generative' intelligences make critical thinking more essential today than ever before.

On the fresco, the attentive reader will have noticed the eight fallacies dotted around the scenery. They have strange names but these will be explained later in this chapter: the slippery slope, the straw man, the bandwagon, the circular, the red herring, post hoc ergo propter hoc, ad hominem and the false dilemma. They're all indicated by a warning sign.

8.2. Resuming the conversation[7]

Trust with caution

Many definitions of critical thinking exist.

But they all agree on one point: they tend to converge towards the idea of a thought that is of a very high intellectual rigour. Critical thinking is a constant vigilance regarding oneself, just as much as regarding others. It aspires to be clear, precise, careful, reliable, coherent, practical. It encompasses the reflexive link of the subject with itself, which then questions itself over its identity, its values, its story, its choices and ... its way of thinking.

Critical thinking is not linked to a particular discipline. It's not a specific body of knowledge, and it must proceed through all disciplines. It's located somewhere between two extreme positions because systematic doubting is no more instructive than blind trust is. Critical thinking wants to preserve the advantages of scepticism without having to pay the price of ignorance.

According to the Pyrrhonian school of scepticism, universal doubt is the path to wisdom. Their thesis is that, when faced with a given hypothesis, there are always arguments in favour of it and arguments against it. In other words, since certainty is inaccessible, we should suspend all judgement and not claim anything! The critical thinker adheres to this premise but not to the conclusion, and, just like the great master Descartes, does not consider doubt to be a principle but a method.

The message for all of us suddenly becomes clear. Rather than renouncing all judgement, we should calibrate our trust, adjust our degrees of belief, and finely regulate our level of support. Believing always includes the risk of making a mistake, so we should accept to review our convictions with every new piece of information, when a new argument is presented.

Thinking in a critical manner means trusting with caution while being wary of four elements: the reliability of the source, the strength of the argument presented, the medium, and too often forgotten, our own ability to judge on the matter at hand.

More specifically, critical thinking is at war with superstition, gullibility, bigotry, confusion, dogmatism, scientism, occultism, esoterism and charlatanism. It helps us to face oversimplified Manichean views, obscurantism and conspiracy theories. Concretely, it cannot believe in astrology, fortune telling, telepathy or the search for extraterrestrial life, though it must seriously envision them as objects.

---

7. This formulation is a nod to Richard Rorty.

Everything written above could have been written 100 years ago, perhaps more. Critical thinking represented as a compass has guided generations in search of clear and distinct ideas. Ever since the internet was created, the dream of intellectual rigour has stayed the same but the rules of the game have changed, and so have fallacious arguments. The 'appeal to majority', for example, is now measured by the number of followers and likes ... This will be the topic of the following pages.

Critical thinking is a set of tools useful to deal with arguments.

The starting point of argumentation is a disagreement between two incompatible positions (which doesn't mean that either is wrong). Argumentation is not the constantly repeated affirmation of a starting point, nor is it the systematic belittling of an opposing opinion. It's an attempt on behalf of both parties to impose their point of view. Two cases are possible.

In the first one, the argument is solid since all three following conditions are respected:

- The concepts used are clear and relevant.
- The premises are true.
- The reasoning is correct.

In the other one, the purpose of the argument is to entice the interlocutor into a trap. The argument is then defined as fallacious.[8] Here, anything goes: the stratagems are numerous and well-known.

A sophist is not concerned with ethics or justice. Truth is of little importance to them, their point of focus is the balance of power. If we must lie to win, then let's lie! If we must cheat to pass, then let's cheat! This does not matter since the purpose is not to prove but to be approved, regardless of the words used. According to a sophist, affirmation is above all self-affirmation, persuasion is above all winning, and a debate is above all fighting. A joust starts with 'may the best man win', but for a sophist, the opposite stands: 'the winner is the best man'.

Switching points of view seems to be common practice among these acrobats of discussion. Sophists do not like ideas they think are true, but claim that the ideas they like are the truth. While we are accustomed to approving a decision which seems to be good, sophists would rather label a decision as 'good' only if they approve of it.

The image that we have of these people is certainly far from flattering. But let's not forget that everything we have heard about them was claimed by people who didn't appreciate them, starting with Plato, who considered sophists to be the impostors of philosophy.

We run the risk of not thinking ... critically enough while under Plato's influence, believing that sophists are the bad guys that the good philosophers must defeat, that the former are in the shadows of the Cave and the latter in the light.

---

8. 'Two friends decide to take an expensive fishing trip to Montana, but after a week of fishing, they only manage to catch one fish. So, on the way home one friend says to the other, "The way I figure it, that fish cost us $5.000." "Yeah", his friend replies, "Good thing we did not catch more"'. John M. Capps and Donald Capps, *You've Got to Be Kidding! How Jokes Can Help You Think* (Chichester, West Sussex, 2009).

This is not true and this resistance to caricature appeared very quickly.

For example, in his play *The Clouds*,[9] Aristophanes already mocked Socrates and even claimed that he was the first of the ... sophists!

Amongst the sophists' defenders, you'll also find Nietzsche. His project of 'reversing Platonism' with one blow should inevitably have brought him closer to sophists and in *Twilight of the Idols*,[10] he showed the interest and even the admiration he had for them.

The sophists have also filled several gaps in Greek civilization. They were asked to organize the structures of education into a variety of fields such as grammar, science and philosophy.

The sophists were, in a way, Enlightenment philosophers before their time. Their main theme was humankind and the laws that govern its actions, as opposed to laws that are unchanging or divine. But Socrates' way of condemning them to hell in his *Apology* seems to be irreversible and the word sophism will keep its negative connotation for a long time to come.

A fallacy is an argumentation which resembles valid reasoning despite being, often deliberately, rigged to distract or mislead the interlocutor. A fallacy is not just a thought but a weapon whose prime purpose is to dazzle and trap others or, if they suspect a scam, to trigger logical embarrassment. Subtly hiding the flaw makes it more difficult for the interlocutor to refute the argument.

As already mentioned at the beginning of this chapter, Aristotle was the first to study the nature and structure of fallacious arguments. He identified thirteen types which he illustrates through shining examples, such as:

> *5 is 2 and 3*
> *2 is an even number and 3 is an odd number*
> *Therefore, 5 is even and odd*

or

> *A man who has a fever is warm*
> *Therefore, a man who is warm has a fever*

Logic and argumentation

In Chapter 5 we saw that in duelling modes, logic and argumentation are distant cousins. Let's remind ourselves of their pair of family traits.

Propositions come together through inference, and claims come together to form arguments.

---

9.   Aristophanes, *The Clouds* (Athens).
10.   Friedrich Nietzsche and Reginald J. Hollingdale, *Twilight of the Idols and The Anti-Christ*, Penguin Classics, Repr. with a new chronology (London, 2003).

Three new definitions are necessary:

Premise

A proposition that provides support for an inference or an argument's conclusion.

Claim

A proposition that indicates the taking of a position in order to persuade or to influence people.

A claim somehow belongs to whomever asserts it. Claims can be put into two groups, which we will come back to later on:

- a descriptive claim: Jupiter is larger than Saturn
- a prescriptive claim: There should be a President of Europe

Argument

The literature on this topic is plentiful, but here are three possible good quality definitions:

- An inference used to persuade us, to influence our beliefs and our actions.
- A sequence of statements such that some of them (the premises) give reason to accept another one of them (the conclusion).
- A discussion in which reasons are advanced in favour of a claim.

8.3. On fallacies

A fallacy can be defined as an instance of faulty reasoning in a critical thinking context.

A fallacy:

- is often an invalid argument that can easily be mistaken for a valid one.
- can be very persuasive, sometimes more than sound reasoning.
- violates one or more of the principles that make an argument sound, such as good structure, consistency, clarity, order, relevance or completeness.
- But while all invalid arguments are fallacious, not all fallacies involve arguments.

In the following pages, we will mention over forty types of sophism, organized into two groups. Eight of them are depicted on the fresco.

We will start by discussing the fallacious arguments that still maintain some sort of relationship with the laws of logic (formal fallacies). These arguments are not valid because their formal structure is faulty. The chain of reasoning itself is defective.

We will then analyse types of sophism where logic is useless, such as those based on personal attacks or which digress from the subject. These arguments are not valid because of their content and context. Informal fallacies deal with every kind of reasoning mistake, other than formal ones.

Formal Fallacies

Some arguments are fallacious despite an undisputable logic!

It is acceptable to consume farm animals since they've been bred to be eaten.

This is what we call begging the question, or circular argument. The conclusion blends with the premise.

Despite being logically useless, tautology – a proposition which is always true – is nevertheless used as an argument.

It is not good to have too much freedom.

We agree with this quote, thankfully, since it would be impossible to disagree. Too much camembert is never good, too much football is never good and too much travel is never good. 'Too much of x is never good', is true, regardless of what x is, since the definition of too much means it is not good.

An approach to argumentation which is ... too logical can make us dizzy. Therefore, the proposition:

These two companies are incomparable

is a contradiction, meaning it's always false, because in order to make such a statement, both companies would have had to undergo a comparison. They are therefore comparable …

A reasoning can also be plagued by circularity:

> *People wishing to study logic must be intelligent people. If they weren't, they wouldn't want to think logically.*

●

Oratory tricks built on an excess of logic are not the most frequent. At the other extreme, some fallacious arguments are blatant violations of the laws of logic.

This leads us to *modus ponens* and *modus tollens*, the Remus and Romulus of logic.

These two laws of reasoning seem so obvious that we question why they have been discussed so much and for so long!

The *modus ponens* is an illustration of correct reasoning.

> If A, then B
> A
> Therefore, B

> *If I'm stuck in bed, I'll write a book*
> *I'm stuck in bed*
> *Therefore, I'm writing a book*

The *modus tollens* is another illustration of correct reasoning

> If A, then B
> Not B
> Therefore, not A

> *If I'm stuck in bed, I'll write a book*
> *I'm not writing a book*
> *Therefore, I'm not stuck in bed*

Modus ponens and *modus tollens* are two historical foundations of logic. And yet, the number of breaches of these laws is still as high! Both of the fallacious arguments that follow illustrate this really well. They are the product of deliberate confusion between a necessary condition and a sufficient condition. In other words, between implication (if A is true, B is also true) and equivalence (if either one is true, the other is also true).

Affirming the consequent involves affirming that the consequent is true in order to claim that the antecedent is also true.

If I'm stuck in bed, I'll write a book
I'm writing a book
Therefore, I'm stuck in bed

Denying the antecedent involves affirming that the antecedent is false in order to claim that the consequent is also false.

If I'm stuck in bed, I'll write a book
I am not stuck in bed
Therefore, I'm not writing a book

●

One of the sophists' most recurring practices is to ignore one of their hypotheses or one of their assertions.

In the case of a false dilemma, certain options are hidden.

A true dilemma is a situation which offers only two possible issues. During a referendum, voters usually only have one choice: yes or no. This reasoning forces them to choose between two options, and that choice inevitably leads to the rejection of the other. But these cases of dichotomy are not that frequent and a fallacious argument often involves presenting as simple a problem which in reality allows several answers. Indeed, if the voters face a true dilemma, the phrasing of the question itself usually hides other possible options.

If you're not with us, then you're against us.

Even Nietzsche uses the false dilemma when he states:

What doesn't kill me makes me stronger.[11]

False dilemmas often work in pair with another fallacy, which is called No true Scotsman. The canonical example goes something like this:

No Scotsman puts sugar in his tea
Well, my uncle is a Scotsman and he puts sugar in his tea
But no true Scotsman puts sugar in his tea

By denying that the uncle is a real Scotsman, you can keep your categories well separated, and maintain the false dilemma.

Another case of messing with categorization is sophism of the implicit, where you discuss all options presented, but hide one of the premises.

We must not add a course in philosophy because that would deprive us of time to teach useful things.

---

11.   See Nietzsche and Hollingdale (2003) cited above.

Indeed, it is assumed, without actually saying it, that philosophy does not teach us anything useful. We, of course, strongly disagree.

We'll end this first exploration of fallacious arguments with four frequent stratagems.

Deduction through analogy is not rigorous. It's subjective and inductive and can never serve to justify a deduction.

I am a successful entrepreneur. Vote for me and I'll be your successful mayor.

The leap in logic relies here mainly on assuming that a good entrepreneur and a good mayor have the same qualities, skills, etc. This in itself is debatable, but the general working of this fallacy, of assuming that two things work in the same way, or have the same characteristics, when in fact they do not or might not, can be very hard to spot.

A person who claims *Comparaison n'est pas raison*, translated as 'comparison is not reasoning' ... is therefore right!

And yet, how many argumentations are built on this mode?

In a relatively similar aspect, we can mention discredit through association.

In this fallacy, anything can be discarded without being evaluated, by irrelevantly associating it with a generally disliked entity (person, group, school of thought ...). An especially tricky part of this is that, especially in politics, it being a fallacy often hinges on whether the association actually is relevant or not.

Don't be obsessed with punctuality. Mussolini also wanted trains to be bang on time.

Our last example is called *post hoc ergo propter hoc*, translated literally as 'after that, so because of that'.

Imagine the shock of someone sneezing just before an accidental gas explosion nearby. That person could, for a second or two, imagine having been themself the cause of the blast! We have a tendency to establish a causal link where there is nothing more than a sequence in time. This is what some people call the achoo effect.

I joined the BCG in 2001 and revenue has since quadrupled.

Finally, a harder fallacy to spot is confusing correlation and causality.

In this case, two (or more) phenomena might be connected in some way, but not have any causal link between them. They might occur together by coincidence, or be both (or all) caused by something else.

Rats fled this ship minutes before it sank, therefore the rats sank this ship.

Informal Fallacies

Let's leave behind the stratagems for which the tools of logic are useful to detect traps, and move on to those that no longer have much purpose, that have even become paltry compared with the brutality or the violence of those who do not respect much, such as:

The ad hominem attack which consists in saying 'you are wrong because of what you are'.

> *You don't have kids, don't talk about education.*

The tu quoque counter which consists in saying 'you are wrong because of what you do'. We are criticizing the interlocutor for the discrepancy between their acts and principles, a gap between what they have said and the way in which they react.

> *You're against hunting, but you eat meat.*
> *And you are against animal exploitation, but you eat cheese.*

Debate champions also formulate questions as a sort of trap that we could name fallacious questions since the deceit is at the starting point of the debate.

> *Has the fake news you have started at least been useful?*

There are two questions rolled into one here. And by answering the most obvious one, we sometimes answer the other one without really noticing.

A similar technique is called a loaded question.

> *Are you in favour of this so-called tax reform which has already proven to be totally ineffective in Italy?*

Poisoning the well is a figure of speech where the public is given prior negative information about an opponent, which is either true or false. The goal is to discredit or ridicule what they will say next. Once again, evaluating whether the information is relevant or not can make the difference between a fair warning and a fallacy. A generally unreliable source might be perfectly right once in a while, and vice-versa: caution is advised in any case.

> *We shall now hear from a witness of the accident but I must warn you, this person is an incorrigible liar.*

●

Attacking someone is not the only fallacious argument used to digress from the subject. Another sophism that has the same objective is called the red herring.

This strange name is said to be derived from a common practice used in the past by prisoners on the run. They were said to have left smoked or even rotten herring behind them to distract the dogs out to hunt them down.

During a discussion, the purpose of this trick is to make you suddenly change topic, to set you on another path than initially planned.

> *The budget has exploded, we cannot afford to buy this building.*
> *But our website has more hits than ever!*

Craftsmanship is necessary to choose a red herring capable of fooling an interlocutor without them noticing. The following is needed:

- Contains some true information.
- Gives the impression of being directly related to the original subject.

When the argument has nothing to do with the original subject, it's described as a *non sequitur*, literally 'it does not follow'.

French President and general Charles de Gaulle once said during a debate:

> *How can you govern a country with 258 varieties of cheese?*

We're still looking for the argument over sixty years later …

A pretty close type of sophism is the argument against the origin. It involves avoiding the main subject but instead of attacking someone, the critique is focused on the genesis of the idea.

> *Kekule thought of the molecular structure of benzene while dreaming of a snake biting its own tail?*
> *What kind of science is that?*

Sophists like to exaggerate, caricature and twist the counter-arguments put to them and they have developed a broad spectrum of methods aimed at dismantling their opponents' comments.

The straw man fallacy deliberately caricatures or distorts an opponent's argument:

> *I'd like to take a few days off just to be fresh before starting on that new project.*
> *So, you think the best way to accomplish things is by not working at all?*

A sophisticated variation of the straw man has been called the slippery slope, which is an attempt to discredit a proposition by arguing that accepting it leads to a sequence of one or more undesirable events.

> *Never forgive anyone. If you forgive one person, then the others will expect the same. Pretty soon, people will be walking all over you.*

The two following sophisms can be considered to be systemic. They are indeed built on an incorrect relationship between the whole and the parts.

The sophism of composition involves attributing properties of one or several of its elements to a set.

> *Sodium and chlorine are toxic, therefore sodium chloride (salt) is toxic.*

A fallacious argument often has a corresponding symmetrical fallacy and that is the case here.

The sophism of division involves affirming that what is true for a set is necessarily true for each of its elements:

> Denmark is one of the richest countries in the world, there are therefore no problems linked to poverty in Denmark.

●

A lot of our decisions are based on decisions made by other people, sometimes even by putting our own convictions on the back burner. We follow those who we assume are an authority on the matter at hand.

Appeal to experts

Subjects are so complex nowadays that we often need help, we need to call on experts. But these experts can be in conflict or disagree.

Three cases are possible in which calling on an expert becomes fallacious:

- the mentioned area of expertise does not really exist, or isn't developed enough.
- the expert is unreliable because they have a vested interest in what they are talking about.
- the expert is discussing a subject outside their area of expertise.

Appeal to authority

> Do you not believe in alchemy? Even Newton researched it!

Appeal to majority (Bandwagon fallacy)

If there is no expert to act as an authority figure, our instinct can be to find out what the biggest number of people think. This practice is one of the preferred types of sophism in advertising.

> Venice is the most beautiful Italian city. It is visited by more tourists than any other city.

●

For the record, let's have a look at some additional frequent fallacies.

Appeal to tradition

This argument plays on the idea that the seniority of a practice reinforces its quality or its reason for existing.

> How can we claim that the monarchy should be abolished? It has played an essential role since this country was created.

Appeal to novelty

Contrary to the previous one, this argument involves claiming that an idea is correct or superior specifically because it's new!

Get a brand new computer, they're always better.

Hasty generalization

As its name states, this sophism involves wanting to draw conclusions about a set, but based on a very limited number of elements.

Acupuncture works. Both of my sisters stopped smoking after seeing an acupuncturist.

Vague generalization

A politician in Parliament can sense a strong resistance towards his new project on regulating meat trade and cries:

'But Ladies and Gentlemen, we need laws!'

Non-anticipation argument

Subtly different from the appeal to tradition, this fallacy assumes that the reason things have not changed before is because there was no reason to.

If tobacco was really as dangerous as you claim, how is it that it has not been banned for years?

Reversal of the burden of proof

This fallacious argument involves avoiding demonstrating a thesis by requiring that the opposing party proves the opposite claim instead.

Unless you can prove that aliens don't exist, I will believe that they do.

Using ignorance

This is a generalization of the previous case. This type of manoeuvre is frequent when proving the existence or non-existence of God, for example. Some believe that anything that proves his existence is false and deduce that he does not exist. Others, on the other hand, believe he exists because we cannot prove that he doesn't.

The moderation argument, sometimes called sophism of grey, suggests that a compromise position – whatever it may be – is the right one, simply because it's between two extremes.

'I ought to do something'

Suggests that doing something, even if it is pointless, is better than doing nothing at all.

Illusion of precision

Eighty-two per cent of people cannot tell the difference between butter and margarine.

Wishful thinking

The negotiations will be successful because if they aren't, we're doomed.

Panglossian reasoning

The structure of a melon shows that it is intended to be eaten as a healthy snack with your family.

We could continue listing fallacies for another twenty pages: there is an incredible number of them out there, and readers are invited to look them up if they are interested.

8.4. Using critique against critical thinking

When we talk about voting, arguments usually gravitate around who to vote for, and what they might do once elected. It is much rarer that we ask, for example, how the voting system should work.

On the one hand, by focusing on the content of the system, we fail to see the bigger picture. And on the other hand, focusing only on changing how the system works can be a good way to distract from actual programs and policies. So drawing attention to the voting system, or away from it, can be a good move to ... attract votes!

When we study only the content of arguments, we miss the central fact that speech is also an action in a specific context.

More concerning, by forgoing the study of context, we also miss other actions which come totally outside the sphere of argumentation but shape discourse in entirely different ways. In Chapter 5, we mentioned Martin Luther King's *I Have a Dream* speech, and while we could spend years analysing the merits of his argumentation, we should not forget that his rhetorical feats were cut short: he was assassinated, without a chance to argue back.

In the game of critical thinking, we've discussed the rules and their transgressions. But this game, of course, has other players, who might try to use the rules to their advantage: to use the tools of critique in order to prevent actual critical thinking. Here are a few examples of such tactics.

Tone policing

Tone policing consists of rejecting an argument based on its emotional content or form, rather than its message.

This tactic is common when the debate involves a power differential. For example, feminist arguments and anti-racist arguments are often attacked on their form, or on the basis that they show emotions, rather than on their real content. This allows for bypassing entire arguments without evaluating them.

> *We'll think about paying interns when they stop whining about it.*

Moving the goalposts

Moving the goalposts means changing the conditions under which you will accept evidence, or accept that you have been proven wrong, during the course of the debate.

We often see it when critiquing excessive use of police force, with debaters asking for more and more context before condemning what seems to be blatant abuse. The goalposts are often quickly and implicitly moved from 'could the police have avoided killing them?' to 'did they deserve it?'.

This tactic allows its user to keep rejecting arguments without confronting their core.

Raising the bar

A specific form of moving goalposts, where the bar for evidence is continually raised in order to accept arguments, no matter how self-evident.

We often see this when talking about breaking gendered segregation in organizations for example. Defendants of the inclusion of women will be asked to provide more and more sources, sometimes of higher and higher academic standing, to 'prove' that women deserve to be included in all parts of society.

Gish gallop

The Gish gallop – named after American creationist Duane Gish – consists of spewing a large number of claims at an opponent. It becomes almost impossible to address or refute them all in the time allotted for the discussion, as it takes much longer to refute false claims than it takes to make them.[12] The galloper can then point to the unaddressed claims as evidence that their opponent is ignoring relevant information.

Sealioning

Sealioning is a tactic by which one or several people solicit an opponent repeatedly, asking for more and more evidence or explanations of a previously addressed point, pretending not to understand. Especially common online, its goal is to exhaust the other party.

Motte-and-bailey fallacy

The motte-and-bailey fallacy takes its name from a type of fortified construction. In this fallacy, one party advances an argument which is hard to defend – the bailey – then retreats to a much safer argument or version of the same argument – the motte – when criticized. This allows for advancing very extreme but very indefensible ideas or arguments while minimizing possible backlash. It also often gives you the opportunity to accuse your opponent of making a straw man argument.

> *People are abusing unemployment benefits, we should stop paying for it.*
> *You mean we should not help unemployed people at all?*
> *I'm just saying we can't keep letting people cheat!*

These tactics target the context in which arguments take place, or try to take advantage of the conventions around them: the expectation to engage in debate, to provide quality evidence, to accurately represent your opponent's arguments, etc. They are important to keep in mind when examining a debate critically. Who gets to present their arguments? Who gets to reject debate? Under what circumstances? Is there a good reason for not including a speaker, or a viewpoint?

---

12. This is also known as Brandolini's law.

While we should always remain alert, we should not see conspiracy, bias and ill intentions everywhere. When wondering why TV journalists invite some experts and not others, one should of course think about possible biases, but also about how many experts they know who are willing and able to go on live TV. Critical thinking calls for constant vigilance, but also for knowing when to let go.

Even outside of deliberate tactics, we should ask ourselves how the context of debates shapes their form and content.

If you want to have a debate with school teachers, don't schedule it in the middle of a school day! If you want to know what Spanish customers think of your new product, your survey should be in Spanish!

8.5. The critical thinker's toolbox

On criteria

Except for maybe lawyers or politicians, we are neither debate nor speech professionals. Systematic suspicion or using irony are not second nature to us. What should we do when faced with biased slogans or advertising, personal attacks or paradoxical injunctions?

As mentioned at the beginning of the chapter, the answer can be summed up in one word. We must absolutely resort to 'critical' thinking.

For scientists, the word 'critical' means a state or moment beyond which a phenomenon changes in meaning or in nature. For fissile materials like uranium, critical mass is the threshold from which a nuclear chain reaction can be triggered.

For philosophers, on the other hand, a critical thought process involves a reasoned analysis of a concept or situation, capable of highlighting qualities and faults, and then making a value judgement.

For a scientist, the critical point is the moment when something important happens. For a philosopher, the critical point is the moment when we are thinking about important things.

'Critique' stems from the Greek word *krinein* meaning 'to discern' or 'to filter'. The same root brings us closer to the word *crisis* which in mediaeval Latin describes the most acute stage of an illness, when violent symptoms such as intense sweating, shaking or even bleeding are present. This is also the point where the patient may or may not begin to recover. A crisis is a pivotal, painful moment over the course of which everything will be determined, the 'now or never'.

The word 'crisis' also comes from the ancient Greek word *krisis* which means 'decision' or 'judgement'.

As we explained before, 'crisis' is linked to *kriterion*, which gave us the English 'criterion', a rule or principle for judging.

Kant used it in this sense and added it again to philosophers' agenda. His *Critique of Pure Reason*[13] is an invitation to pinpoint the strengths and weaknesses of our ability to think. In this monument of early modern philosophy, he tries to answer the question 'what can we know?'

So, in the end, what are we talking about? Let's define the critical thinker in terms of attitude, skill, abilities and requirements.

---

13.   See Kant (1929) cited above.

Attitude

An attitude is the state of mind vis-à-vis an object, an action, an individual or a group. It's a mental predisposition to act in one way or another. Above all, it describes an intention and is therefore not directly observable. Ideally, the critical thinker:

- is curious, transdisciplinary and open to the world and other cultures.
- is not influenced by the judgement of authority figures.
- is the opposite of indifferent: both tolerant and demanding.
- is aware of their own biases.
- can show impartiality.
- is able to question themself.

Skills

A skill is a profound and proven knowledge which confers the right to judge or make decisions on certain topics. The critical thinker:

- seeks causes of phenomena.
- takes the global situation into account.
- masters methods of investigation.
- can distinguish between facts and interpretations of facts.
- can discern the rational and the irrational.

Abilities

An ability is the possibility of success and the execution of skills when accomplishing a task. The critical thinker:

- senses when a piece of information is useful.
- explains the methods that they have used.
- clearly states the problem and their position.
- keeps the initial concern in mind.
- goes beyond superficial understanding.
- practices critique in a constructive manner.

Requirements

A requirement is a constraint that an activity must satisfy, or an imperative that the individual imposes on themself. The critical thinker:

- asks for agreement on the definitions and standards used.
- demands the systematic use of criteria.
- seeks other explanations.
- questions the veracity and reliability of facts and opinions.
- clarifies parameters and limits that must not be crossed.
- does not confuse 'I believe that' with 'I think that'.

To summarize, we could say that the critical thinker is looking for a place between two frequent non-critical profiles:

– On the one hand, there are those who combine slogans, stereotypes and commonplaces without giving it much thought. They rarely forge personal convictions and seek above all to build consensus. They often make decisions that are based on what others have decided.
– On the other hand, there are those who certainly build sophisticated reasonings, but use their intelligence specifically to defend their beliefs *a priori*. They are interested in other people's opinions only to the extent that they reinforce their own.

A sequence to respect

As we explained at the beginning of this book, successful critical thinking enables us to ensure that we have good reasons to believe or do that which people attempt to persuade us to. But how can we achieve it? The same goes for critical thinking as for creative thinking: there is a wealth of literature available on this topic, such that everyone should be able to find some of it to their taste, no matter how familiar they are with the subject. But no single piece of literature offers a foolproof theory or method. Only practice makes perfect. As an example, the three stages described below are useful when faced with written or spoken discourse.

Recognizing

– Is there an argument?
– Is this an argument? (as opposed to being a rhetorical technique)
– Is there a 'hence', 'therefore', 'thus', 'so', or anything leading to a conclusion?

This line of questioning is necessary because sometimes the answer to one or several of these questions is no! See the two following examples:

No conclusion
John went to the bookstore.
When he was there it started to rain.
John had no umbrella.

Conditional
If John loves new ideas,
Then he goes to the bookstore.

Analysing

- What is this argument about?
- What is the context?
- What is the issue?

We must analyse the argument in depth to get rid of anything extraneous and to reveal its logical structure.

- Identify the conclusion.
- Identify the premises.
- Eliminate irrelevancies: sentences such as 'everybody probably noticed'.
- Eliminate emotions (thankfully) and emphases.
- Remove synonyms and inconsistent terminology.
- Supply controversial premises that have been deliberately suppressed to give the impression of a stronger argument.
- Remove cross-references, such as 'they', and replace them with the words they refer to.

This is hard work, as the situation of 'combined claims' shows when you contrast these two sentences:

A. Cecilia is smart but boring.
B. Cecilia is boring but smart.

Each of these two sentences makes three claims:

1. Both A and B state that Cecilia is both smart and boring
2. There is a conflict between the two claims
   i. You want to spend time with someone who is smart but you don't want to spend time with someone who is boring.
   ii. It would sound odd to say 'Cecilia is smart but tall'.
3. Both A and B suggest that the claim after the 'but' puts the claim before it into question, and this third claim explains the difference between A and B.

Evaluating

- Is this argument valid?
- Should we be persuaded by this argument?

We must evaluate the quality of the logical structure with two more definitions:

- Inductive argument: 'a line of reasoning that produces only a probable conclusion. This is to say that, even if all the premises of the argument are true, the conclusion may still be false'.[14]
- The deductive argument: 'a line of reasoning in which the truth of the premises guarantees the truth of the conclusion. This is to say that, if all the premises in the argument are true, then the conclusion has to be true'.[15]

We also have to remember the principles of thought:

- A deductive argument is valid if its conclusion is a logical follow-up of its premises. It is otherwise said to be invalid.
- A deductive argument is sound if it is valid and if its premises are true.
- A deductive argument can be evaluated *a priori*.
- If a deductive argument is valid, it will remain valid regardless of what we might learn.

- An inductive argument is strong if, in the case its premises are true, then it is highly probable that its conclusion is also true.
- An inductive argument is cogent if it is strong and its premises are in accordance with the facts. It is otherwise said to be un-cogent.
- Inductive arguments can only be evaluated *a posteriori*.
- No inductive argument is valid. It can only go from strong to weak, or vice versa.

14.   Sharon M. Kaye, *Critical Thinking: A Beginner's Guide (Beginner's Guides)*(Oxford, UK, 2008).

15.   See Kaye (2008) cited above.

8.6. Being critical in a digital world

The attention pirates

In the 1950s, a psychologist from Harvard University named B. F. Skinner conducted research on the learning abilities of rodents. For the sake of his experiments, he invented the operant conditioning chamber, usually know as the 'Skinner box', and led to major discoveries on how these animals behave.

The principle is simple: a rat is placed in a cage with a lever which, once pulled, dispenses pellets of food. The first drop might be accidental if the rat knocks the lever. The rodent very quickly understands how it works and becomes used to bumping into the lever when hungry.

Skinner was a big believer in behavioural psychology which claims that only the observable can be scientifically studied. This gave Skinner more ammunition to support his conviction: a living being's behaviour can be understood by analysing its reactions to a variety of stimuli. But he also noticed that if the rat receives an identical pellet with every pull of the lever, it will only use it when it wants to eat. The animal feels in control of the situation, which puts its mind at ease.

Skinner then thought of varying the reward. The same procedure was used, with a lever dropping pellets. But this time, sometimes several pellets, or no pellet at all would be released. The result was surprising. Despite what was expected, the rat's inability to predict the consequence of pulling the lever didn't put it off. Quite the opposite: the rat got excited, pulling it more and more frequently, even when it wasn't hungry!

The variable reward makes the animal act compulsively, making it 'addicted' to the system and more obsessed with the lever than with the food.

Skinner's conclusion can be summed up as follows: when the rodent can predict an outcome, it develops a habit. When it cannot, it develops a dependency and stays hooked, trying to better understand the underlying logic.

The concept of a variable reward, or even a completely random reward, is the principle behind slot machines, of which the famous Jackpot is a good example. These machines, sometimes called 'one-armed bandits', work similarly to the Skinner box: one same motion – pulling a lever – has varying effects.

Social media developers drew inspiration from the efforts of the American psychologist. Some researchers in cognitive science believe that Facebook or LinkedIn are nothing more than digital Skinner boxes in which we, poor rats, are no longer behaving in a reasoned or controlled manner. Social media is indeed designed to reward us in a variable manner so that we shift from habit to dependency.

Owning a smartphone is like having a casino in our hands. When scrolling through social media, we never know what we might find. We could get several notifications, or we could get none. They can be a pleasure to read, or sometimes not. They might come from people we know, or sometimes not.

Similarly, two consecutive clicks on the same home button can give different information. This unpredictable side of one-armed networks and social bandits piques our interest and makes us click more and more, even when we are no longer hungry.

Social media developers are, in a way, calibration geniuses. They know that when a game is not engaging enough, it becomes boring and that, if it is too frustrating, we are put off. In both cases, we stop playing, which is the opposite of what these social casinos hope for: keeping the digital player hooked for as long as possible to make as much money as possible.

Technology and psychology

Our smartphone dependency has nothing to do with chance or coincidence. A successful app includes just as much technological know-how as it does psychological know-how. Professionals blend algorithms and neuroscience to create user addiction, and this variable reward is just one method among many others.

The architects of dependency know our weaknesses. They know that we, as human beings, are more cultural than rational, that we tend to prioritize finishing a task over knowing its significance, that we prefer using a tool that we were able to personalize, that we are attracted to revolving banners at the bottom of screens, and that we feast on simplified, caricatured or even divisive content. We are just as sensitive to cycles of gratification as we are to people criticizing us for not being available online. We use the acronym FOMO, or 'fear of missing out', which is the worry about not being up to date, of missing out on an event or an activity. Societal digital fracture and individual digital fragility go hand in hand.

A successful app satisfies a user's need before they're even aware that this need exists. Google is checked before we question a topic, YouTube is opened before we are bored, Facebook is used before we feel even slightly lonely.

None of this is truly surprising since, beyond the smartphone, colossal financial investments in software and infrastructure need to be monetized. Apps can only offer free services if they receive the most precious asset in return: your attention span. This rare commodity is fought over because the more connected we stay, the more data we produce, which is then sold to those who invest the most in targeted advertising. English speakers are correct when using the expression 'to pay attention'.

When you're using a screen, remember that a few hundred experts are being paid to make you lose control, to decide what is important for you, to push you to act without thinking too much. They want your attention, whether you like it or not.

With the internet, it is not the intention but the attention that matters. This is what has value, what needs to be instantly drawn in, caught firmly and held on to. While, for a user, the value of an app is based on what it can do, for the developer, it is based on the attention span that it generates. And some will do anything to make it grow.

The attention pirates behave like a utility company, eager to make you forget to turn off the lights. It does not matter if the attention is focused on truth or on lies, on the useful or the useless. They are only interested in what they can resell: data about the tastes, the habits, and the preferences of each user. Their strategy is built on three words: captivate, catch and capture.

Amazon's suggestion and recommendation algorithms are so lucrative because they generate purchases, but also because the user spends more time online. Unlike in a shopping centre, if a customer doesn't spend any money on Amazon, they are still making the company money.

Was it not the head of Netflix who once said that he was competing with ... sleep?[16]

Hopping and scrolling

For a while now, television has been a mediocre effort offered to politicians and advertising companies to grab attention. In 2004, the head of first French television channel TF1, Patrick Le Lay, described his business as follows: 'What we sell to Coca-Cola is available human brain time'.[17] Today, the internet and algorithms have been partially replaced by rotating banners, advertising clips before news broadcasts and 20m^2 physical adverts. We've gone from channel-hopping to mindless scrolling, randomness has disappeared ... and available brain time has skyrocketed!

Attention is made up of cognitive procedures that push us to select information, then channel it, and dig deeper. It then makes a selection, imposes a sequence, one objective at a time. It assumes that if we pull away from certain things, it is to focus on other ones more efficiently.

It is an active process. When we enter a train station at the last minute to catch a train, we only see useful information because our attention acts like a filter. This same filter will allow us to hold a conversation even while immersed in the bustle of a cocktail party.

But if we select what we want to see more clearly, we are also choosing what we do not want to see. When reading a text, we are incapable of checking for spelling mistakes and working on the style simultaneously.

Much like in the famous experiment, when we are paying attention to the basketball, we cannot see the gorilla.[18]

Intelligence can't be artificial

Mechanical objects have never been given the slightest sense of intention. A thermometer doesn't desire a constant temperature in a room, a filter doesn't want to stop bad smells. No, we're simply

16. *Netflix Q1 2017 Earnings Interview*, 2017, <https://www.youtube.com/watch?v=2Pm3ZmhnSRk> [accessed 30 May 2024].

17. 'Ce que nous vendons à Coca-Cola, c'est du temps de cerveau humain disponible'. Executive interim management, ed., *Les dirigeants face au changement: baromètre 2004* (Paris, 2004). The title can be translated as *French leaders and change: 2004 barometer.*

18. Daniel J. Simons and Christopher F. Chabris, 'Gorillas in Our Midst: Sustained Inattentional Blindness for Dynamic Events', *Perception*, 28/9 (1999), 1059–74.

content to see these objects correctly doing what they were designed to do. Our glasses help us to see but no one ever thanks them! No more than a pianist would ask an audience to clap for the piano.

With the arrival of computerized objects, it's as if another level had suddenly been reached. We've been thrust into an equal-to-equal relationship with machines, or, even worse, we've gone from being users to being used. You'll sometimes hear: 'the brain is a bit like a computer'. That's almost like saying: 'a plumber is a bit like a welding iron'.

Computers can increasingly imitate emotions, but they remain foremost a pile of metal and plastic fed by electricity. An algorithm can seem impressive in its capacity to simulate human behaviour, but that doesn't give it the slightest shred of humanity. At the digital ball, the robots are wearing masks.

So let's say it again, with even more vigour: you don't exchange anything more with a computer than you do with a toaster. The *raison d'être* of a digital device is to amplify intellectual gestures, sometimes in an impressive manner. But that changes absolutely nothing about its status as a technical object.

So we shouldn't be talking about artificial intelligence, we should instead be talking about artificial intelligences. And we should be using their names: Alexa, Watson, or ChatGPT.

A GPS doesn't tell you to turn left. No, a GPS synthesizes a set of data and converts it into a signal that imitates a human voice. A surveillance camera doesn't recognize a face. No, one day it was decided that cameras would be installed everywhere in order to know who is where, and to keep a trace of this.

A calculator doesn't calculate any more than a drill drills. Doing addition or drilling a hole is easier with a machine, obviously, but the approach remains that of someone who has an idea, a need, a project, a hobby, a reason, an obligation or a desire to do what they're doing: all things that a machine can't have.

Just like a drill doesn't know what a hole is, a calculator doesn't know what a result is. What appears on screen only fully makes sense when faced with the project of the human doing the calculation, because numbers never speak for themselves. They don't speak at all. Big data is mute. Any data analysis is done thanks to prisms, models, categories which are chosen *a priori* by a human being. Every organization of information has an underlying ideology.

A computer playing chess doesn't know what 'to play' means, or what 'chess' means. It doesn't know what a chessboard is, or why it's playing. It doesn't want to play or win, and can't be disappointed about losing. It doesn't have the slightest idea what 'learning' means, in fact it doesn't have any ideas at all.

A computer doesn't think and doesn't understand what it's doing. Because in order to really understand something, it is necessary to associate intellectual and sensory information. It is impossible to understand what fire is if you've never been burned, and it is impossible to understand sadness if you've never cried.

So let's stop crediting machines for the intelligence that we deploy when building them!

Neither a calculator nor a super-calculator have access to what is essential: a sense of action. Adding memory or power doesn't change anything about that. So it isn't correct to say that a machine is doing something, because acting implies the nature, the meaning, the context, the motivation, the words, the impact behind this action.

Intelligence can't be artificial because it isn't rational to be 100 per cent rational. If you want to plan an original holiday, don't try to choose the best holiday out of all the possible holidays, because there is an infinity of them. If you want to innovate next summer, you'll have to let go and give up going all the way to the end of the thought process. Otherwise, you'll never go on holiday.

Thinking against your brain

This process of letting go that is essential to the action is precisely what a computer is incapable of. It takes place in two stages:

First, creativity: a computer can't get out of its own program (as discussed in Chapter 7).

Second, responsibility: drugs are only authorized after years and years of testing by public agencies. Shouldn't there be a similar level of precaution with algorithms?

No algorithm can solve the great challenges of today's society, or your own, because we need to make decisions without getting to the bottom of the problem or having full knowledge of the facts.

Entire sections of the economy are in part beyond the reach of algorithms, like culture, hobbies and the whole of the fashion industry. No algorithm can understand common sense or context. More globally, there are no algorithms to fight poverty or the deterioration of the environment, to say what is right, fair, good or beautiful.

Many philosophers have shown that, even more so than doubt, it's refusal that is the sign of authentic thought. Without critical elaboration, there is no thinking, no opinion and no consent. According to French philosopher Alain, thinking is saying no, and nodding yes is like nodding off.[19] Thinking is fighting, it's contesting the order of established ideas, yet a machine can only obey. Bachelard maintained that we need to 'think against our brain'.[20] Yet an algorithm can't fight against itself.

Work-to-rule

People are afraid that machines are going to become so intelligent that they'll take control of our society. The real problem is that machines are stupid, and yet we've let them take control.

Politicians should be supervising the economy, and yet the opposite is happening. Billionaire entrepreneurs are supervising the politicians by deciding who can and who can't be on such and such social media platform. Some such instances might end up being happy accidents, but it remains worrying that companies hold such power. The casino of cryptocurrencies has developed outside of all

19. Alain, *Propos Sur Les Pouvoirs*, ed. by Francis Kaplan, Collection Folio. Essays (Paris, 1985). The title can be translated as *Remarks on the powers*.
20. 'Il faut penser contre le cerveau.' Gaston Bachelard, *La formation de l'esprit scientifique: contribution à une psychanalyse de la connaissance objective* (Paris, 1938). The title can be translated as *The formation of the scientific mind: contribution to a psychoanalysis of objective knowledge*.

legislation, and teenagers are now getting their news from TikTok without sufficient initiation into critical thinking.

Algorithms can't do everything: the essence of what is human is inaccessible to them. Life is dotted with important moments that escape all analytical reasoning. At the restaurant, an algorithm can calculate a supplement, but it can't give a tip, because a tip is a human gesture made in the moment, reasonable but not rational. The nuance between these two adjectives is important because it distinguishes us from machines.

To make what separates us even clearer, let's take a look at what we call 'work-to-rule'. This strange concept consists in paradoxically paralysing an organization by working perfectly well!

If work-to-rule is possible, it's because laws and other rules are never perfect, and will never be. Any procedure requires simplifications through arbitration and compromise, and always has, just as necessarily, a ridiculous side. In a way, it's absurd to not be allowed to vote the day before you turn eighteen.

Working well implies a distance from the rule, which is called discernment. Working well is only possible if you don't follow the rules to the letter. So an algorithm can't think well. It can proceed in the correct way, but it can't be subtle.

Algorithms are stubborn, narrow-minded, obtuse, zealous. Distance from the rule is a concept that is totally inaccessible to them. They are faithful to their programs, yet in many cases, it is being unfaithful that leads to talent, as illustrated by literary translators.

Artificial translation

According to Umberto Eco, perfect translation from one language to another is impossible. The Italian philosopher believed that even a good translation was saying 'almost the same thing' in another language.[21] As any translator knows, in order to be faithful to the spirit of the text, you have to be unfaithful to the words and sentences of that text. Paradoxically, this form of treason can only be beneficial for the translated work: it's the liberties taken by the translator that bring out the best in what they're translating.

An algorithm can't almost do what it's programmed to do. It can't think, it does what it is told, or more exactly, it does what it told itself to do. It does very well, and very fast, what it was built to do, because it requires no intuition, no perspicacity, no particular knowledge, no creativity, no critical mind.

Take human intelligence. Then take away its capacity to discern good from evil, sense of humour, doubt, intuition, conscience of what it's doing, intention, omissions, moods, aesthetic concerns, free will, the joy of finding and the sadness of failing, the capacity to listen to others, to let go, to overcome paradoxes or to find new analogies.

---

21. Umberto Eco, *Dire Quasi La Stessa Cosa: Esperienze Di Traduzione*, Studi Bompiani. Il Campo Semiotico, 1. ed (Milano, 2003). The title has been translated into English as *Mouse or Rat? Translation as negotiation* (London, 2004) by the author himself, but translates literally to *Saying almost the same thing: experiences of translation*.

If you take all of this away from human intelligence, there's not much left.

It's for this 'not much left' part that artificial intelligence is useful.

Nowadays it is often said that we can no longer live without the internet. That's forgetting that the opposite is even more true: the internet can't live without us. And while many tasks can now rely heavily on artificial intelligence, all AI, regardless of how powerful, will always remain dependent on humans at five key moments. These moments will always be necessarily human, essentially human, profoundly human.

1. Before turning on the machine

A computer has no will of its own, no intuition, no capacity to marvel, no access to context, no dreams. A computer therefore can't come up with any projects, it has no idea about what it could, would and should do. A computer has no ideas and no mind, so only a human being can turn a machine on with an idea in mind.

2. When the machine is turned on

The user needs to provide their tool with instructions, telling it what it should do. In the case of ChatGPT, this takes the shape of a prompt, so a well thought-out question that is capable of extracting the best from the machine. A computer can't take a step back from itself. The art of questioning, so dear to philosophers, regains its full importance today.

3. After the machine is turned on

The user is faced with a vast amount of information, of possible combinations, or new perspectives. This is the moment of choice that is only possible if there is a process of letting go, which the algorithm isn't capable of. Regarding most questions, no algorithm exists that could lead to certainty. It is therefore inevitable that a risk be taken in order to take action. No algorithm exists that is capable of telling me which title would be best for my book, or which accommodation would be best suited for someone.

4. After the machine is switched off

A computer has no values, no ethics, no discernment. A computer doesn't have a conscience, or emotions, or sense of humour. It isn't capable of critical thinking. It can't let things settle. It can't tell what is beautiful or what is good. A machine can't tell the difference between a new idea and a good idea, and we can't attribute any responsibility to a machine.

5. Before the machine is turned back on

A machine will always be too logical, and it can't be creative or critical. The I/D model that has been our companion throughout this book therefore leaves us with a lot of unanswered questions. On the other hand, artificial intelligence tries to give a single answer to every question. ChatGPT works like a ChatGPS, it takes you to your destination and not any further. This shouldn't come as a surprise. An artificial intelligence will never be capable of philosophizing because it is incapable of doubting. A philosopher never stops thinking. A machine will never be able to think.

ChatGPT can't write!

In November 2022, a free version of ChatGPT was released to the public by Californian company OpenAI. The release had such an effect that some even compared it to the first atomic bomb. But there is a huge difference. During the first two hours of the movie *Oppenheimer* (2023), we see men and women hesitating, arguing, exchanging, nuancing, hesitating again to then, in the end, decide and execute a plan that leads to the atomic explosion. The scenario of the ChatGPT movie is built the exact opposite way. From the very first images, boom, the ChatGPT bomb goes off, and only then do we start thinking and discussing ...

Cholera and chocolate

Flash back. Artificial intelligence has been a topic of conversation for a long time, but up until recently, researchers considered one hypothesis as given: there exists a logic of thought and of language. So if we provide a machine with all of the rules that underlie this logic, one day a machine will think and speak. This hypothesis has nowadays been abandoned because there are too many exceptions. Why do we say 'chocolate' and not 'cocolate' when we say 'colera' for 'cholera'?

Forty years of research have led to a dead end and the researchers have had to reset the system. But in the meantime, machines have become gigantic, almost limitless, and another path has opened up. When the volume of available information becomes almost unlimited, it becomes possible to get by without logic, and to replace it with a statistical approach.

ChatGPT sees a text as a series of words, and each of its sentences is seen as just one of the possible vocabulary combinations. The first role of ChatGPT is to predict which word will come next, based on the words that came before. The larger the sample of words, the more this probability calculation gives the illusion of reasoning. As most of these sample pages are in English, ChatGPT is the most impressive in the language of Shakespeare (at least at the time of writing this).

The words to write it

Boileau's alexandrine is well-known: 'What is well understood is clearly stated, and the words to say it come easily'.[22] But what about the words to write it? Boileau avoids the question but he's wrong to do so, because writing is the real test of clear and distinct ideas, to repeat Descartes' apt expression. It's only by writing an idea down that you grasp its full scope.

American philosopher Charles Sanders Peirce said that not only would he not be able to express himself without an inkpot, but he also wouldn't have any ideas without it.

When you think about something, you can usually manage to express it orally, but in order to know exactly what you're thinking, you need to write it down. And that's often when surprises occur. Sometimes even disappointment, as the discrepancy is revealed between what was written and what was said. So what should a philosopher's first responsibility be? To write, or furthermore, to rewrite?

---

22. 'Ce que l'on conçoit bien s'énonce clairement, et les mots pour le dire arrivent aisément.' Nicolas Boileau, *L'art Poétique* (Paris, 1674). The title has been translated as *Art of Poetry* in *Art of Poetry and Lutrin: Nicolas Boileau*, trans. by William Soame and John Ozell (Richmond, Surrey, 2008).

I believe so. An idea can only reach maturity and full strength once it's been translated into written words and sentences.

ChatGPT can draft a report, summarize a text and develop a concept. But only a human being can write, in the true sense of the word, and create concepts.

Writing is not describing. ChatGPT can indeed describe what a steam engine is. But when, in his novel *The Beast Within*,[23] Émile Zola depicts a steam engine, the reader is almost inconvenienced by the heat, the noise and the smoke coming from it. They almost feel the urge to wash their hands!

To write isn't to transcribe and even less to retranscribe. There's nothing more unpleasant than reading the text of a speech. How boring it is to read the minutes from a meeting! In French they are called *procès-verbal*, literally 'verbal proceedings', but we should call them 'oral proceedings'! The 'chat' in ChatGPT implies a somewhat informal oral exchange. 'WriteGPT' would be impossible.

To write is to always be on the lookout for the right word, the appropriate synonym, the most striking figure of speech.

To write is to implicate yourself, to explain yourself, to debate and to fight.

To write is to expose something, and most importantly to expose oneself. It is to offer something up, and also to suffer, as perfectly expressed in these alexandrines by Victor Hugo:

> 'Nor was I ignorant that the hand which wrought
>
> Deliverance for the word – delivered thought'.[24]

In my mind, from the very first line of this book, writing has meant writing to you, the reader.

---

23. Emile Zola, *La Bête Humaine* (Paris, 1890). Translated into English by Roger Whitehouse as *The Beast Within* (London, 2011).
24. 'Et je n'ignorais pas que la main courroucée qui délivre le mot, délivre la pensée'. English translation by Henry Carrington, 'Reply to an Act of Impeachment', in *Translations from the Poems of Victor Hugo*, by Victor Hugo (New York, 1885).

Living is no longer what it used to be ...

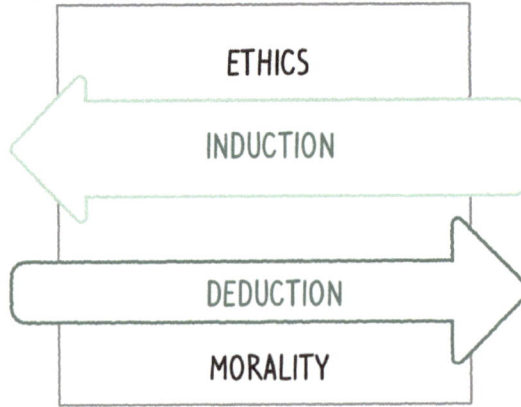

WITHIN US

BELIEF
CRITERIA
HUMAN RIGHTS
LAW
PRINCIPLES
PURPOSE
RULES
VALUE
ETC.

ETHICS

INDUCTION

DEDUCTION

MORALITY

IN FRONT OF US

EVENTS
POLITICS
CHAOS
INJUSTICE
GENETICS
ROBOTS
CLIMATE CHANGE
DILEMMA
OBSOLESCENCE
ETC.

In everyday life, norms are everywhere. Social norms, cultural norms, formal norms, mathematical norms, vector norms, democratic norms ... the word returns time and again.

But what actually is a norm?

A common way of defining things is by genus and specific difference. In this case, the result is quickly apparent: the norm is the genus and the species are the standards, the calibres, the templates, the protocols, the codes, the references, the canons, the milestones, the criteria and other formats.

In Latin, *norma* refers to a set square, something that is used to straighten things out. A set square is used to make sure that things are straight. *Et le droit ne peut se faire ni se dire sans ... règles.*[1] The literal and figurative meanings of the word norm have a tendency to get mixed up.

Everyone agrees that norms and standards are very useful. This is why a temple was dedicated to them in 1947: ISO, the International Organization for Standardization. Logically, this institution should have been called the IOS, but the high priests of standardization wanted to set an example and so chose initials that don't favour one language in particular. The story also goes that they chose this acronym to reflect the Greek word *isos*, which translates as 'equal'. A standard is necessarily the result of a consensus ...

Singing the same tune

When it comes to standards, part of the discussion will inevitably be technical. Numbers, abbreviations, calendars and procedures all have to be agreed upon. In 1955 for example, the members of ISO in charge of music followed their American Standards Association colleagues and recommended that the first A (la) above the middle C (do) on a piano should be tuned to a frequency of 440 Hz.

---

1. Translator's note: sorry reader, this doesn't translate into English. The author is French-speaking and had fun playing on words here in French: *droit* means straight but also the law and *règles* means rules but also ruler. So this would translate as 'the law can't be done or told without ... rules'.

The ISO is currently still a non-governmental organization, bringing together over 150 countries and made up of, unsurprisingly, as many state representatives as lobbyists. You only have to consider the number of different computer cables and incompatible software suites to see that ISO still has a few good years ahead of it.

But the technical debate hides another much more fundamental one. *Accorder un piano et accorder sa confiance*[2] are two very different approaches: the first is objective and the latter is subjective. When the word norm becomes synonymous with values, ideals, models or practices to be followed, we tip into a different world, moving from operating rules to life rules.

Descriptive or prescriptive

Philosophy can be organized into two different groups.

In the first, the aim of questions is to understand how things are, and in the second, the aim of questions is instead to establish how things should be. The first group is called descriptive philosophy and the second is called prescriptive philosophy.

Both groups are vast, varied and multidisciplinary.

In the case of descriptive philosophy, the role of the philosopher is to clarify. What is real? What is a language? What is true, what is false? What is the difference between mathematics and logic? It includes disciplines such as argumentation, but also epistemology, metaphysics and linguistics.

In prescriptive philosophy, the role of the philosopher is to guide. What is good, what is bad? What is right? What is beautiful? What is the difference between equal and fair? It includes disciplines such as ethics, morals, aesthetics and the theory of justice.

The barrier between these two worlds isn't watertight. Even technical norms are established according to the ethical convictions of their authors, and in return we position our behaviours in relation to the established standards.

'I can't complain'

Language sometimes adds to the confusion.

Let's take this statement as an example: 'I can't complain'. It can be understood in three different ways, the first two of which are descriptive:

- There are no administrative procedures that would allow me to lodge a complaint.
- I live in an organization or a country where I am not allowed to complain.

---

2.   Translator's note: take two, the repetition of *accorder* also doesn't translate into English. *Accorder un piano* means 'tuning a piano', and *accorder sa confiance* means 'granting your trust to someone'.

The third one is prescriptive:

– When I realize how lucky I am, it would be indecent to want even more.
The notion of norm can be found in both the descriptive and prescriptive groups, but the word 'normal' can be understood in two very different ways.

When the weatherman is comparing the freezing temperatures to seasonal norms, it's a mathematical reasoning. A memorized history is used as a basis for calculating the differences between an existing situation and what was observed in the past. The norm is then the objective average of temperatures recorded on the same dates in previous years, and any significant deviation is qualified as *ab-normal*. This is a judgement of fact, in which the norm is objective and technical.

Back to abnormal

When we hear that it isn't normal that people should sleep outside when it's very cold, then we're no longer in the realm of statistics. The word 'normal' becomes a synonym of what is fair, advisable, imperative even. We're now talking about a judgement of value, in which the norm is subjective and ethical.

The difference between these two points of view is significant. The usual traffic jams in Brussels at rush hour can be qualified both as normal (because they're a daily occurrence) and abnormal (because they shouldn't be).

The same can be said for the whole of society. Before the Covid-19 pandemic, many things weren't normal. Climate change, the social divide, the situation of migrants, the disintegration of Europe – nothing was normal about all of this, and we shouldn't have tried to get back to abnormal.

The 'art of thinking' that is discussed in this book is mostly descriptive. It examines questions of true and false, of what is rigorous and what isn't, in the construction of knowledge. But other vital questions deal with right and wrong, happiness, politics or even aesthetics, which are usually combined under the name of 'art of living'.

Thinking and living are obviously inseparable. According to Plato, the art of one can even merge with the art of the other!

We have decided not to explore this question in this book, but the I/D model can nevertheless be used to distinguish morality from ethics, which also need to be radically reassessed in a world that is changing so much.

Ethics comes from the Greek *ethos* meaning 'behaviour'. Morality comes from the Latin *mores* meaning … 'behaviour'! But the nuance between both words is greater than we think. The roots of *ethos* are to be found in a Greek setting. We embrace it freely, philosophically. Rome, on the other hand, is a place of law, of norm. We must comply with *mores*, legally or even militarily.

Morality is built on a set of rules established by the community. They allow each member to take action. Ethics is one of the disciplines of philosophy, the one that tries to grasp the origin, objectives, justification and founding principles of these moral laws. As a result, ethics comes before morality.

In a way, morality comes from above, or at least from the outside. It can be expressed as maxims, universal rules, in the same way that Kant theorized the categorical imperative, which is absolute. Ethics, however, grows inside each of us. It is also more situational, and tends to deal with defending specific values within a given context.

The hierarchy of human values is not absolute: it is only by realizing this and questioning this hierarchy that we are able to spot moral inadequacies.

The philosophical question about what is good can be broken down into two dimensions: morality and ethics. Morality exists thanks to ethics and vice versa. In the words used throughout this book, morality is deduced, ethics is induced. One cannot exist without the other, but as always, these two movements are not symmetrical: morality can be safely deduced, but ethics always involves taking risks.

Moral behaviour logically and simply stems from clear and accepted premises, and from rules that are applied and understood. Ethical behaviour, on the contrary, is constantly confronted with nuances, the unexpected, exceptions and often paradoxes. I am a happy grandfather and I pass on simple messages to my grandchildren such as 'you should be nice' or 'you must not lie'. But ... don't we sometimes tend to lie in order to be nice?

As Bob Dylan sang: 'to live outside the law you must be honest'![3]

In the life of organizations, the word 'value' is also everywhere. We want to create value and we are afraid of destroying value. We break down the value chain, we reflect on the countervalue, we speculate on technological values and we pay tax on added value. We want to communicate our values and make a decision based on a system of values. But when referring to value, what is it that we mean exactly?

At this point we need to go back in time. Value was once associated with life, with power, and with bravery. The Romans ended their letters with phrases such as *si vales, gaudeo* meaning 'if you are well, then I'm happy'. In the Middle Ages, the word appeared in the French language and a fearless knight would be called *valeureux*, meaning 'brave'.

---

3.   Bob Dylan, *Absolutely Sweet Marie* (1966).

The word value was then progressively used in very diverse fields. Mathematicians used the value of a function $f(x)$ that varies according to x, logicians used the term 'truth value' to describe the true or false options that could be attributed to a proposition.

But it was of course the economists who took control of the word by creating a very strong link between value and money. They were responsible for the dissolution of value in finance and this vision is dominant today: we talk of use value, exchange value, commercial value or even market value. In most conversations, the French word *valoir* essentially means 'to have a monetary value'.

The last semantic shift appeared in the eighteenth century when the word value was progressively used to refer to an esteemed trait, and the person conveying these qualities was called a worthy person, a person of value.

In this understanding, the value represents things that we give importance to, what we consider to be worthwhile. We can therefore define a value as 'an idea of what is desirable'.

Stress test

Using this last meaning, there are no absolute, objective, or universal values. Each one of them necessarily represents a choice, a bias, a prejudgement. A value also rarely works alone. They are presented as a system and it is together that they form a grid used to evaluate reality. Value and evaluation, the etymology is no coincidence here.

Values can be defended. They raise questions and they are what we want to pass on to our children. From the moment a business announces their values, it must embody them, letting them shape its everyday life.

Values can also be trying. Just as someone will suffer if their values are not respected, a business might accept to see its stock rate plummet as long as it is staying true to its values.

The debate surrounding business values is even more important than the one surrounding personal values, because business values are more devalued than ever before. They need clarifying, because confusion is at the heart of advertising. Businesses no longer seem to believe in the values they put forth, or to stick by them when the going gets tough.

Too many speeches use flawed reasoning, too many messages are hollow despite there being a need for thorough deliberation on the meaning of our actions. Spinoza believed that values must 'increase our power of being'. Start-up incubators have grasped this and present themselves as accelerators of potential.

When using our values, two extreme points of view should be avoided.

The first is ideology. A business is neither a church nor a temple. Its aim is not to preach values that must be lived by as absolute truths: this could only lead to intolerance.

The second is nihilism. If all values are relative and everything is subjective, why should we give values any importance? If it is impossible to decide which system of values is better than the other, what is the point?

Somewhere between ideology and nihilism, businesses need to take a stand. This process is important because values are ultimately ... invaluable!

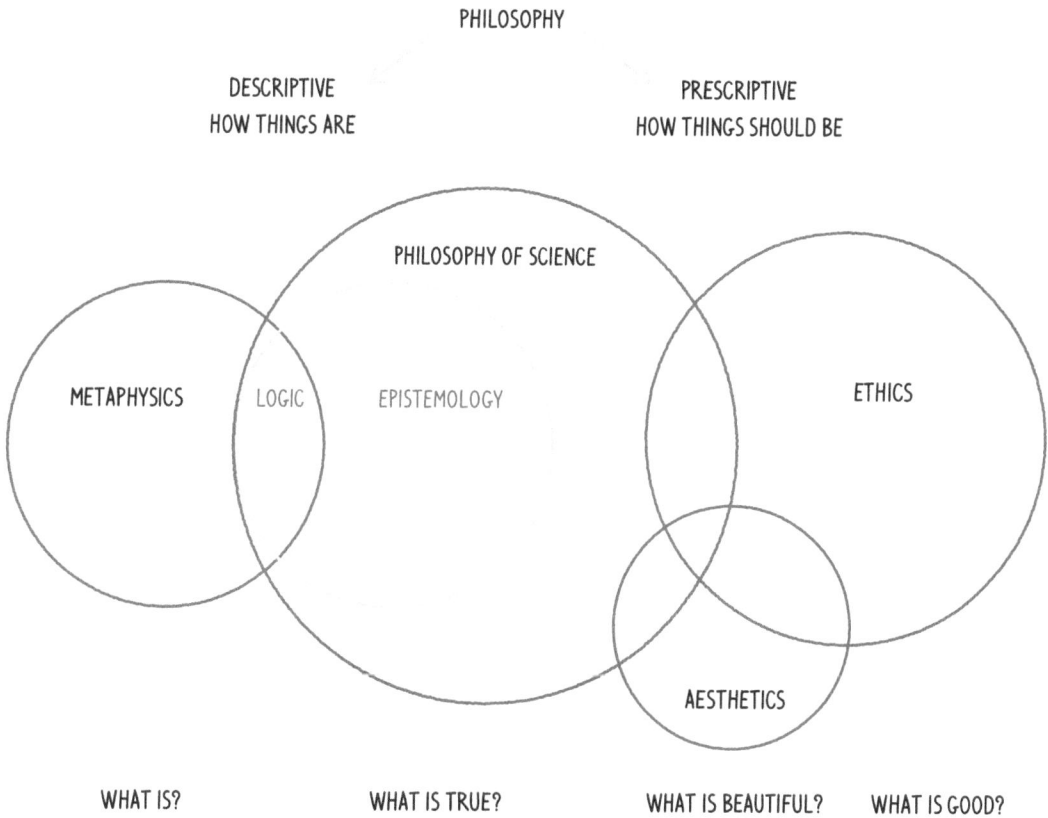

PHILOSOPHY

DESCRIPTIVE
HOW THINGS ARE

PRESCRIPTIVE
HOW THINGS SHOULD BE

PHILOSOPHY OF SCIENCE

METAPHYSICS

LOGIC

EPISTEMOLOGY

ETHICS

AESTHETICS

WHAT IS?   WHAT IS TRUE?   WHAT IS BEAUTIFUL?   WHAT IS GOOD?

Misfit

In June 1971, I graduated from the 'Université Catholique de Louvain', in Belgium, as an engineer. But as I shook the Dean's hand, he added: 'Congratulations, you have graduated but you're not a true engineer'. I was taken aback and didn't really understand his remark. It only made sense later on.

Like many others who graduated at the same time as I did, I got my first job in a bank. Back then we were working on IBM 360 machines and other large centralized computers. The bankers, who aren't the best technicians, were hiring engineers to defend their interests against the large IT companies.

I thoroughly enjoyed programming a variety of applications, but one day my boss suggested I should take a different direction in my career. According to him, I was neither a true computer scientist, nor a true project manager. So I was named head of the back office as Trading Room Manager. I was in charge of the accounting, despite not really being a numbers guy. I learned a huge amount, up until the moment my boss decided that I wasn't a true banker either.

Friend of the Earth

I've always had a second life, alongside my professional life, as an active citizen, fully aware and understanding of the perpetually changing world I live in. This is how, in 1976, I built the first domestic wind turbine in Belgium, took part in the creation of the 'Friends of the Earth' association and stood in the general election as a Green candidate. It probably won't come as a surprise that the experience was short-lived, as my opponents were very clear that I was neither a true politician, nor a true environmentalist.

I needed to find a way to express and defend my ideas, so I started writing. Some of my columns were published in Belgian newspapers *La Libre Belgique* and *Le Soir*. I loved writing these articles but was soon told that I would never be a true journalist. My first book, *Les Infoducs*,[1] was published in 1985. In it I envisaged the advent of the internet, but without claiming to be doing any real forecasting.

My life took another unexpected turn in 1989 when I was headhunted and became the CEO of the Brussels Stock Exchange. It didn't take long for the stock brokers, who were reluctant to change, to decide to get rid of me. You can guess their excuse for firing me by now, can't you? Yep, I wasn't a true CEO.

---

1. Cited above.

This was the perfect opportunity to fulfil an old dream, I cycled from Belgium to Santiago de Compostela. But in order to be a true pilgrim, you have to walk there.

Changing the paradigm

I then decided to turn my passion for creativity into a job, and to put the necessary resources into it. I published *Le Latéroscope*[2] and went back to university, to study philosophy this time. Even though, according to most of the professors, I was wasting my time as I would never be a true philosopher.

I was able to work part-time thanks to my new job as a consultant for a company called Paradigm. Don't worry, it was too late for me to be a true consultant. And anyway, when you provide a CEO with more questions than answers, there never seems to be much budget available.

In 2000, I co-founded a communication agency based on illustrations, Cartoonbase, momentarily forgetting that I wasn't a true entrepreneur or a true businessman. I also went knocking on the door of a major international consultancy firm, the Boston Consulting Group. They welcomed me with open arms, and two years later I was made partner. Even though, according to most of them, a true partner should be more concerned with numbers than letters ...

I've enjoyed an exceptionally good work environment and have so far published over twenty books, but without ever being considered as a true author. Booksellers still don't know which shelf they should put my book on ...

That's not quite a wrap

I'm no longer a BCG partner, but that doesn't mean I've become a true alumnus as I've been named a Fellow and remain active and useful to them. Nowadays I'm devoting more and more time to education. I'm an enthusiastic teacher but according to my students I'm not a true academic.

My life really is strange. I was born in Ghent but I'm not truly Flemish. I was baptized but I don't think I'm a true Catholic. I would like to be a true humanist, but who knows what humanism truly is? I live in the countryside but I'm not truly a country boy. And I'm not a true Belgian, because no such thing exists. I'm 76 years old and I'll never be a true pensioner because you can never be an ex-philosopher.

But at the end of the day, does it really matter? By always being outside of the box, you end up building your own. I'm a true grandfather, a true European, a true enthusiast and a true popularizer. And every day I'm increasingly aware that as a 'boomer' I'm truly privileged.

I was pondering all of this last summer, as I was cycling – slowly – up the Col du Galibier in the French Alps. I felt good. Funnily enough, this climb is also considered to be beyond categorization.

---

2.   Luc de Brabandere, *Le latéroscope : systèmes et créativité* (Bruxelles, 1989).

Postface

As we close this book, it is important to reflect on the future of thinking through the profound insights shared by Luc de Brabandere, Lina Benmehrez, and Jonas Leyder within its pages. Their work explores how tools, from the earliest inventions to modern information technology, have continuously expanded human capabilities and reshaped our thinking. With the advent of the internet and generative AI, thinking is no longer what it used to be. The time has come to rethink thinking itself.

At the BCG Henderson Institute, the think tank of Boston Consulting Group, where Luc de Brabandere was a Fellow, the future of thinking is paramount. We, alongside our clients, require new mental models to unlock creativity, and this book provides a guide on how leaders can navigate the evolving nature of reasoning in our age of big data and algorithms. Since everyone now has access to machines, it is essential that we ensure that critical thinking has a future.

Luc and his co-authors' philosophical approach offers readers a unique lens through which to view the intersection of technology and human thought. The discussion encourages us to reconsider our cognitive processes and the tools we use, highlighting the significant influence that they have on our ways of modeling and experimenting with the world. This work is not just a reflection on the past and present but also a call to engage thoughtfully with the future of cognition.

The authors' passion and deep understanding of the subject matter are evident throughout the book. This is Luc's third book written as a BCG Henderson Institute Fellow. Following *The Forgotten Half of Change*, where he emphasized the need to change both reality and the perception of reality, and *Thinking in New Boxes*, co-authored with Alan Iny, which proposed a new paradigm for business creativity, *The Art of Thinking in a Digital World* synthesizes his main insights from 40 years of helping leaders develop their strategies.

As you reflect, consider how the insights and questions posed by the authors can inform your own thinking and approach to technology. Let this be a starting point for further exploration in the ever-evolving landscape of human cognition and technological advancement.

Thank you for embarking on this journey with us, and may it inspire continued curiosity and critical thinking.

Dr. Nikolaus S. Lang, Global Leader BCG Henderson Institute

Bibliography

Ackoff, Russell Lincoln, *The Art of Problem Solving: Accompanied by Ackoff's Fables*, A Wiley-Interscience Publication (New York, 1978)

Alain, *Propos Sur Les Pouvoirs*, ed. by Francis Kaplan and Collection Folio. Essays (Paris, 1985)

Almossawi, Ali, and Alejandro Giraldo, *An Illustrated Book of Bad Arguments* (New York, NY, 2014)

Anderson, Chris, 'The End of Theory: The Data Deluge Makes the Scientific Method Obsolete', *Wired*, June 2008, <https://www.wired.com/2008/06/pb-theory/> [accessed 24 May 2024]

Aristophanes, *The Clouds* (Athens, 423 BC)

Bachelard, Gaston, *La formation de l'esprit scientifique: contribution à une psychanalyse de la connaissance objective* (Paris, 1938)

Bacon, Francis, *Meditationes Sacrae*, 1597

——, *Novum Organum Scientiarum*, 1620

——, *Novum Organum Scientiarum*, ed. by James Spedding, Robert Leslie Ellis, and Douglas Denon Heath, trans. by James Spedding and unknown (London, 1858)

Baggini, Julian, *A Short History of Truth: Consolations for a Post-truth World*, Paperback edition (London, 2018)

Baggini, Julian, and Peter S. Fosl, *The Philosopher's Toolkit: A Compendium of Philosophical Concepts and Methods* (Malden, MA, 2003)

Barker, Joel Arthur, *Paradigms: The Business of Discovering the Future*, 1st edn (New York, 1992)

Barrau, Aurélien, *De la vérité dans les sciences*, Nouvelle édn (Malakoff, 2019)

Bee Gees, *Words* (London, 1968)

Bentham, Jeremy, *The Book of Fallacies from Unfinished Papers by Jeremy Bentham* (London, 1824)

Bergson, Henri, *Le Rire: Essai Sur La Signification Du Comique* (Paris, 1900)

——, *L'Évolution Créatrice* (Paris, 1907)

Bergson, Henri, and Arthur Mitchell, *Creative Evolution* (New York, 1911)

Bergstrom, Carl T., and Jevin D. West, *Calling Bullshit: The Art of Skepticism in a Data-Driven World*, 1st edn (New York, 2020)

Berlinski, David, *The Advent of the Algorithm: The Idea That Rules the World* (New York, 2000)

Boileau, Nicolas, *L'Art Poétique* (Paris, 1674)

Boileau Despréaux, Nicolas, *Art of Poetry and Lutrin: Nicolas Boileau*, trans. by William Soame and John Ozell (Richmond, Surrey, 2008)

Bowell, Tracy, and Gary Kemp, *Critical Thinking: A Concise Guide*, 4th edn (London, 2015)

Brabandère, Luc de, 'Face à Internet, l'indispensable pensée critique', *La Libre*, 30 May 2024, <https://www.lalibre.be/debats/opinions/2019/11/21/face-a-internet-lindispensable-pensee-criti que-JEEK3TLZURBK3FDOQMM3KRJALA/> [accessed 30 May 2024]

——, *The Forgotten Half of Change: Achieving Greater Creativity through Changes in Perception* (Chicago, 2005)

Brabandere, Luc de, and Alan Iny, *Thinking in New Boxes: A New Paradigm for Business Creativity* (New York, 2013)

Brabandere, Luc de, and Anne Mikolajczak, *Les Infoducs: Un Nouveau Mot, Un Nouveau Monde: L'informatique Au Macroscope: Essai* (Paris, 1985)

Brel, Jacques, Corti, Jean, and Jouannest, Gérard, *Les Vieux* (Paris, 1963)

Camus, Albert, 'Sur une philosophie de l'expression', *Poésie* 44 (1944)

Capps, John M., and Donald Capps, *You've Got to Be Kidding! How Jokes Can Help You Think* (Chichester, West Sussex, 2009)

Carr, Nicholas, *The Shallows: What the Internet Is Doing to Our Brains* (New York, 2011)

Carrington, Henry, trans., 'Reply to an Act of Impeachment', in *Translations from the Poems of Victor Hugo*, ed. by Victor Hugo (New York, 1885)

Cave, Peter, *How to Think Like a Philosopher: Scholars, Dreamers and Sages Who Can Teach Us How to Live* (London, 2023)

Chauve, Alain, *Logique & Verité : Le différend entre Russell et Wittgenstein*, Philosophie en cours (Paris, 2018)

Chomsky, Noam, *Syntactic Structures* (The Hague, 1957)

Chrisman, Matthew, Duncan Pritchard, Jane Suilin Lavelle, Michela Massimi, Alasdair Richmond, and Dave Ward, *Philosophy for Everyone* (Hoboken, 2013)

Christian, Brian, and Tom Griffiths, *Algorithms to Live by: The Computer Science of Human Decisions*, 1st US edn (New York, 2016)

Cullum, Leo, *The New Yorker*, September 2001

Davies, E. B., *Why Beliefs Matter: Reflections on the Nature of Science* (Oxford, 2010)

De Ketelaere, Geertrui Mieke, *Mens versus machine: artificiële intelligentie ontrafeld*, ed. by Tom Cassauwers (Kalmthout, 2020)

Descartes, René, 'Règles Pour La Direction de l'esprit', in *Oeuvres de Descartes*, trans. by Victor Cousin, Levrault (Paris, 1826)

——, *Regulae Ad Directionem Ingenii*, 1701

Diderot, Denis, and Jean Le Rond D'Alembert, *Encyclopédie, ou Dictionnaire raisonné des sciences, des arts et des métiers* (Paris, 1751)

Dieguez, S., *Total Bullshit ! Au Coeur de La Post-Vérité*, 1re édn (Paris, 2018)

Dylan, Bob, *Absolutely Sweet Marie* (1966)

Eco, Umberto, *Dire Quasi La Stessa Cosa: Esperienze Di Traduzione*, Studi Bompiani. Il Campo Semiotico, 1st edn (Milan, 2003)

——, *Mouse or Rat? Translation as Negotiation*, Phoenix Literature (London, 2004)

——, *Reconnaître le faux: dire le faux, mentir, falsifier*, trans. by Myriem Bouzaher (Paris, 2022)

Eco, Umberto, and Thomas A. Sebeok, eds, *The Sign of Three: Dupin, Holmes, Peirce*, Advances in Semiotics (Bloomington, 1983)

Edwards, A. W. F., *Cogwheels of the Mind: The Story of Venn Diagrams* (Baltimore, 2004)

Engel, Pascal, Richard Rorty, and Patrick Savidan, *À quoi bon la vérité* (Paris, 2005)

Evans, Dylan, *Emotion: A Very Short Introduction*, Very Short Introductions, 81 (Oxford, 2003)

Evans, James R., and James Robert Evans, *Creative Thinking in the Decision and Management Sciences* (Cincinnati, OH, 1991)

Executive interim management, ed., *Les dirigeants face au changement: baromètre 2004* (Paris, 2004)

Foresman, Galen A., *The Critical Thinking Toolkit* (Chichester, West Sussex, 2017)

Frankfurt, Harry G., *On Bullshit* (Princeton, NJ, 2005)

Gide, André, *L'évolution Du Théâtre* (Brussels, 1904)

——, *Nouveaux Prétextes* (Paris, 1911)

Gilhooly, K. J., *Thinking: Directed, Undirected, and Creative* (London, 1982)

Goleman, Daniel, *Emotional Intelligence* (New York, 1995)

Hanscomb, Stuart, *Critical Thinking: The Basics*, The Basics (London, 2017)

Heinrichs, Jay, *Thank You for Arguing: What Aristotle, Lincoln, and Homer Simpson Can Teach Us about the Art of Persuasion*, 1st edn (New York, 2007)

Hersch, Jeanne, *L' étonnement philosophique: une histoire de la philosophie* (Paris, 1981)

Hinton, Perry R., *Stereotypes, Cognition, and Culture*, Psychology Focus (Hove, East Sussex, 2000)

Horace, *Epistularum Liber Primus (First Book of Letters)*, 20AD

Hublet, Laurent, and Béatrice Delvaux, *Bruxelles mondiale: de Paul Otlet à nos jours* (Waterloo, 2023)

Hugo, Victor, *Translations from the Poems of Victor Hugo*, trans. by Henry Carrington (New York, 1885)

—, *William Shakespeare* (Brussels, 1864)

Hume, David, 'An Enquiry Concerning Human Understanding', in *Essays and Treatises on Several Subjects* (London, 1777)

James, William, 'Attention', in *The Principles of Psychology*, American Science Series – Advanced Course, 2 vols (New York, 1890), I

Jankélévitch, Vladimir, and Béatrice Berlowitz, *Quelque Part Dans l'inachevé* (Paris, 1978)

Jean, Aurélie, *Les algorithmes font-ils la loi ?* (Paris, 2021)

Jones, Morgan D., *The Thinker's Toolkit: Fourteen Skills Techniques for Problem Solving*, Rev. and updated (New York, 1998)

Kafka, Franz, *Die Zürauer Aphorismen*, 1931

Kahneman, Daniel, *Thinking, Fast and Slow*, 1st edn (New York, 2011)

Kant, Immanuel, *Critique of Pure Reason*, trans. by Norman Kemp Smith (London, 1929)

—, *Groundwork of the Metaphysics of Morals* (Riga, 1785)

Kant, Immanuel, and Lewis White Beck, *An Answer to the Question: 'What Is Enlightenment?'* (Indianapolis, 1963)

Kaye, Sharon M., *Critical Thinking: A Beginner's Guide (Beginner's Guides)* (Oxford, UK, 2008)

Kepler, Johannes, *Astronomia Nova* (Heidelberg, 1609)

Kierkegaard, Søren, *Journalen* (Copenhagen, 1997)

Klein, Étienne, *Le goût du vrai*, Tracts, n° 17 (Paris, 2020)

——, 2022, <twitter.com/EtienneKlein/status/1573960821629222912> [accessed 29 May 2024]

Knaap, Guido van der, *Van Aristoteles Tot Algoritme: Filosofie van Kunstmatige Intelligentie* (Amsterdam, 2022)

Koestler, Arthur, *The Act of Creation* (London, 1964)

——, *The Sleepwalkers: A History of Man's Changing Vision of the Universe* (London, 1959)

Korzybski, Alfred, *Science and Sanity: An Introduction to Non-Aristotelian Systems and General Semantics* (Lakeville, CT, 1933)

Krivine, Hubert, Guillaume Lecointre, and Jacques Treiner, *On nous aurait menti ? De la rumeur aux fake news* (Louvain-la-Neuve, 2022)

Kuhn, Thomas S., *The Structure of Scientific Revolutions*, 3rd edn (Chicago, IL, 1996)

Lampedusa, Giuseppe Tomasi di, *Il Gattopardo* (Milan, 1958)

——, *The Leopard*, trans. by Archibald Colquhoun (London, 1963)

Lanier, Jaron, *You Are Not a Gadget: A Manifesto* (London, 2011)

Lecointre, Guillaume, *Savoirs, opinions, croyances: une réponse laïque et didactique aux contestations de la science en classe*, Guide de l'enseignement (Paris, 2018)

Lee, Edward A., *Plato and the Nerd: The Creative Partnership of Humans and Technology* (Cambridge, MA, 2017)

Leibniz, Gottfried Wilhelm, 'Second Explanation of the New System', January 1696

Locke, John, *An Essay Concerning Human Understanding* (London, 1689)

Loewenstein, George, 'The Psychology of Curiosity: A Review and Reinterpretation', *Psychological Bulletin*, 116/1 (1994), 75–98

Lynch, Michael Patrick, *The Internet of Us: Knowing More and Understanding Less in the Age of Big Data* (New York, 2017)

Macchiavelli, Niccolò, *Il Principe* (1532)

——, *The Prince*, trans. by William Kenaz Marriott (London, 1908)

Magritte, René, *La Trahison Des Images*, 1929

Mankoff, Robert, 'September 11th: Ten Years, with Robert Mankoff', *The New Yorker*, 6 September 2011, <https://www.newyorker.com/news/news-desk/september-11th-ten-years-with-robert-mankoff> [accessed 29 May 2024]

Martin, Robert M., *For the Sake of Argument: How to Do Philosophy* (Peterborough, ON, 2017)

Maslow, Abraham H., *Psychology of Science* (New York, 1966)

Mayer-Schönberger, Viktor, *Delete: The Virtue of Forgetting in the Digital Age* (Princeton, NJ, 2011)

McGrayne, Sharon Bertsch, *The Theory That Would Not Die: How Bayes' Rule Cracked the Enigma Code, Hunted Down Russian Submarines, & Emerged Triumphant from Two Centuries of Controversy* (New Haven, 2011)

McInerny, Dennis Q., *Being Logical: A Guide to Good Thinking*, Random House Trade Paperbacks, Trade paperback edn (New York, 2005)

McLuhan, Marshall, *The Gutenberg Galaxy: The Making of Typographic Man* (Toronto, 1962)

——, *Understanding Media: The Extensions of Man* (London, 1964)

Messerli, Franz H., 'Chocolate Consumption, Cognitive Function, and Nobel Laureates', *New England Journal of Medicine*, 367/16 (2012), 1562–4

Milgram, Maurice, *Les paradoxes n'existent pas, mais sont quand même très utiles* (Paris, 2019)

Nahin, Paul J., *The Logician and the Engineer: How George Boole and Claude Shannon Created the Information Age* (Princeton, 2017)

Netflix Q1 2017 Earnings Interview, 2017, <https://www.youtube.com/watch?v=2Pm3ZmhnSRk> [accessed 30 May 2024]

Nietzsche, Friedrich, and Reginald J. Hollingdale, *Twilight of the Idols and the Anti-Christ*, Penguin Classics, Repr. with a new chronology (London, 2003)

Nilsson, Nils J., *Understanding Beliefs*, The MIT Press Essential Knowledge Series (Cambridge, MA, 2014)

Noucher, Matthieu, Sylvain Genevois, and Xemartin Laborde, *Le Blanc des Cartes : Quand le vide s'éclaire* (Paris, 2024)

O'Connor, Joseph, and Ian McDermott, *The Art of Systems Thinking: Essential Skills for Creativity and Problem Solving* (London, 1997)

Osborn, Alex Faickney, *How to 'Think Up'* (London, 1942)

O'Toole, Garson, 'Humor Can Be Dissected, as a Frog Can, But the Thing Dies in the Process – Quote Investigator®', *Quote Investigator®*, 2014, <https://quoteinvestigator.com/2014/10/14/frog/> [accessed 29 May 2024]

Papin, Denis, *Traité de plusieurs nouvelles machines et inventions extraordinaires sur différents sujets* (Paris, 1698)

Pascal, Blaise, *Expériences Nouvelles Touchant Le Vide*, 1647

——, *Pensées* (Port-Royal des Champs, 1670)

——, 'The Art of Persuasion', in *Blaise Pascal*, ed. by Charles William Eliot, trans. by Orlando Williams Wight (New York, 1910)

——, 'Thoughts', in *Blaise Pascal*, ed. by Charles William Eliot, trans. by William Finlayson Trotter (New York, 1910)

Peirce, Charles Sanders, 'Deduction, Induction, and Hypothesis', *Popular Science Monthly*, 13 (1878), <https://en.wikisource.org/wiki/Popular_Science_Monthly/Volume_13/August_1878/Illustrations_of_the_Logic_of_Science_VI> [accessed 31 May 2024]

Perelman, Chaïm, and Lucie Olbrechts-Tyteca, *Traité de l'argumentation, la nouvelle rhétorique* (Paris, 1958)

Pinker, Roy, *Fake News & Viralité Avant Internet: Les Lapins Du Père-Lachaise et Autres Légendes Médiatiques* (Paris, 2020)

Pirie, Madsen, *How to Win Every Argument: The Use and Abuse of Logic* (London, 2006)

Rabelais, François, *Gargantua* (Lyon, 1535)

——, *The Works of Rabelais, Books I and II*, trans. by Thomas Urquhart, 1653

Regalado, Antonio, 'Who Coined "Cloud Computing"?', *MIT Technology Review*, 31 October 2011, <https://www.technologyreview.com/2011/10/31/257406/who-coined-cloud-computing/> [accessed 29 May 2024]

Renard, Jules, and Claude Barousse, *Journal: 1887–1910*, Babel, 152 (Arles, 1995)

Rushkoff, Douglas, *Program or Be Programmed: Ten Commands for a Digital Age*, 1. print (New York, 2010)

Russell, Bertrand, 'On Denoting', *Mind*, 14/56 (1905), 479–93

——, 'On the Notion of Cause', in *Mysticism and Logic and Other Essays* (London, 1917), <https://en.wik
isource.org/wiki/Mysticism_and_Logic_and_Other_Essays> [accessed 29 May 2024]

Russell, Bertrand, and Norbert Whitehead, *Principia Mathematica*, 1st edn, 3 vols (Cambridge, 1910)

Rutherford, Albert, *Models for Critical Thinking: A Fundamental Guide to Effective Decision Making, Deep Analysis, Intelligent Reasoning, and Independent Thinking* (Berlin, 2018)

Searle, John R., 'What Is Language? Some Preliminary Remarks', *Etica & Politica/Ethics & Politics*, XI/1 (2009), 173–202

Shenefelt, Michael, and Heidi White, *If A, Then B: How the World Discovered Logic* (New York, 2013)

Simons, Daniel J., and Christopher F. Chabris, 'Gorillas in Our Midst: Sustained Inattentional Blindness for Dynamic Events', *Perception*, 28/9 (1999), 1059–74

Sinnott-Armstrong, Walter, *Think Again: How to Reason and Argue* (New York, NY, 2018)

Sturmark, Christer, *The Flame of Reason: Clear Thinking for the Twenty-First Century*, trans. by Douglas Hofstadter (London, 2023)

Swatridge, Colin, *The Oxford Guide to Effective Argument and Critical Thinking*, 1st edn (Oxford, UK, 2014)

Taleb, Nassim Nicholas, *The Black Swan: The Impact of the Highly Improbable* (London, 2007)

Thaler, Richard H., and Cass R. Sunstein, *Nudge: Improving Decisions about Health, Wealth, and Happiness* (New Haven, CT, 2008)

Thorne, Paul, *Organizing Genius: The Pursuit of Corporate Creativity*, Developmental Management (Oxford, UK, 1992)

Thouless, Robert H., *Straight and Crooked Thinking*, revised and enlarged edn (London, 1953)

Tversky, Amos, and Daniel Kahneman, 'Judgment under Uncertainty: Heuristics and Biases: Biases in Judgments Reveal Some Heuristics of Thinking under Uncertainty', *Science*, 185/4157 (1974), 1124–31

Venn, J., 'On the Diagrammatic and Mechanical Representation of Propositions and Reasonings', *The London, Edinburgh, and Dublin Philosophical Magazine and Journal of Science*, 10/59 (1880), 1–18

Viguet, Jérôme, 21 November 2019, <https://www.lalibre.be/debats/opinions/2019/11/21/face-a-internet-lindispensable-pensee-critique-JEEK3TLZURBK3FDOQMM3KRJALA/> [accessed 30 May 2024]

Vince, 12 January 2023, <https://www.lalibre.be/debats/opinions/2023/01/12/jai-teste-chatgpt-SCGXZAPDXJCIBLRKY6VN7HHECI/> [accessed 30 May 2024]

Vlerick, Michael, *Kritisch & wetenschappelijk denken: een korte introductie* (Tilburg, 2023)

Weinberg, Gerald M., *An Introduction to General Systems Thinking*, Wiley Series on Systems Engineering and Analysis (New York, 1975)

White, Elwyn Brooks, and Katharine Sergeant White, *The Saturday Review of Literature*, October 1941

Wiener, Norbert, Doug Hill, and Sanjoy K. Mitter, *Cybernetics: Or Control and Communication in the Animal and the Machine*, Reissue of the 1961 2nd edn (Cambridge, MA, 2019)

Wittgenstein, Ludwig, *Philosophical Investigations*, trans. by Gertrude Elizabeth Margaret Anscombe (1953)

——, *Tractatus Logico-Philosophicus*, trans. by Charles Kay Ogden (London, 1922)

Zola, Emile, *La Bête Humaine* (Paris, 1890)

——, *The Beast Within*, trans. by Roger Whitehouse (London, 2011)

Index

Printed by
CPI books GmbH, Leck